The Vintage Rolex Field Guide

A SURVIVAL MANUAL FOR THE ADVENTURE THAT IS VINTAGE ROLEX

A practical mini-encyclopedia for enthusiasts, collectors, hunters and spotters of vintage Rolex wristwatches. This easy-to-use book of critical facts, data, and specifications, catalogs essential details and variations of the most desired and collectible examples of pre-owned Rolex watches.

Practical to cartry, fun to read, and easy to use, it demystifies the secret coded language of the collector community and helps the reader find, purchase and wear high-quality examples of the most beautiful pre-owned Rolex.

The Vintage Rolex Field Guide

Dedication

To all those with interests and passions. And N & B, who I hope will one day want to wear these hunks of metal I leave them. Thanks and gratitude to Carla, a constant inspiration and role model. I love you more than you know.

Credits & acknowledgements

Photography: Watch Geek YouTube, Jan Johnson (watchblog.dk), Benn.ch, Jocke, Orchi Pilar, Grenville Lawrence, Dominic Byrne, Melvin Hollenberg, Flickr The Commons, Wikimedia Commons, Imperial War Museum, The Internet Archive CC, Unsplash Creative Commons, Pixabay CC, Vecteezy, John Torcasio.

Copyright

All rights reserved. No part of this book may be reproduced, stored in a retrieval system, or transmitted in any form without the permission of the Author and publisher. Every effort has been made in the preparation of this guide to ensure the accuracy of the information presented. However, the data in this book is sold without warranty, either express or implied. Neither the author, agents, and distributors will be held liable for any damages caused or alleged to be caused directly or indirectly by this book.

Legal Note

This guide is an unauthorized work compiled without help from Rolex, associated companies or serving employees. It is an independent initiative with no legal, economic or personal ties to the famous luxury watchmaker. It is not sponsored by, associated with and affiliated with Rolex S.A., Rolex USA or any respective subsidiaries or affiliates.

The following are trademarks of the Rolex Watch Company Limited, Geneva, Switzerland: Rolex, the coronet logo, Oyster, Oysterquartz, Sea-Dweller, Explorer, Submariner, Tridor, Jubilee, Milgauss, Air-King, Cellini, Tudor, Tudor Prince, Tudor Princess, Tudor Day-Date, Mini-Sub, Lady-Sub, Tudor Monarch, and the Tudor shield logo. The author acknowledges the intellectual property rights of the company and its subsidiary companies and distributors.

Preface

This guide is for collectors of pre-owned and vintage Rolex watches. It is a quick-reference field guide intended to be concise, factual and data-oriented. It summarizes the product lines and references while highlighting the essential nuances important to watch collectors. Many of these subtle details are of little interest to the casual modern Rolex customer, but crucial to the vintage Rolex buyer.

This guide aims to fill a gap between the glossy coffee-table book and the watchmaker's technical reference. It summarizes the insider knowledge and experience of several collectors, streamlining the essential education needed to purchase a vintage Rolex. This guide is not a biography of Hans Wilsdorf or a historical account of his companies, but a focused look at the watches themselves from a collector's viewpoint. If you want the facts and data necessary to make a good purchase, then this is an essential buyer's survival guide.

This book came about as a summary of the notes and data I mined and researched over many years. As much as I would like to claim it is entirely without error, I cannot do so. I have made serious effort to verify and validate the data with service manuals, catalogs, and sales materials. However, much of the information also comes from secondary sources, such as auction catalogs and online watchmaker forums.

This collective knowledge is summarized here to share with others. I hope to equip the reader with the intellectual firepower to take on the unsavory characters that lurk in the shadows of the vintage watch market.

Data & Validation

Considerable effort was made to verify the completeness and accuracy of the data in this guide. Verification and validation involved modern crowd-sourcing techniques and quality control practices.

Validating reference descriptions involved Amazon Mechanical Turk (MTurk) Human Intelligence Tests (HIT). Mturk is a platform to coordinate individuals performing internet searches. Their task was to confirm specifications and descriptions of Rolex reference numbers.

The human researchers resolved inconclusive searches based on the predominance of results. Application of judgment (by a non-expert, lay-person) can produce imperfect results, much like the imperfect use of reference number conventions by Rolex themselves.

In particular, rare and obscure references were subject to this human discernment. While the number is few, inconsistency errors are likely to be present.

The HIT results were subject to quality control (QC) verification through a separate process. Individuals contracted through Fiverrr.com performed random sampling validation of the Amazon results.

The Vintage Rolex Field Guide

QC verification involved performing the same internet search approach as the Amazon HIT teams. Approximately 150 references were randomly selected for verification (roughly 1 in 10 of the HIT results). The detected error rate was negligible.

The quality of the data compiled here is acceptable for most collectors. However, and some data is incomplete. If you have data and a reference you know to be correct but missing, please feel free to send it to me. I am happy to accept corrections and additions and would love to hear from any readers of this guide.

morningtundra@gmail.com

revised: IV 2020

TABLE OF CONTENTS

WHAT'S INSIDE

INTRODUCTION 1
    Antique Rolex. 3
    Vintage Rolex 5
    Modern Classic Rolex 7
    Contemporary Rolex. 8
    The Oyster Case & Crown 9
    The Perpetual Movement. 10

AUTHENTIC, ORIGINAL & CORRECT 11
    Authenticity 12
    Originality 12
    Correctness. 13
    Transitions 14

ACQUISITION 15

BY THE NUMBERS 21
    Case Serial Number Timeline. . . . 25

CONDITION. 27
    Cases 28
    Hallmarks 34
    Assessing Dials. 37
    Hands 46
    Winding Crowns. 49
    Crystals 50

ANTIQUE & POCKET WATCHES 51
    Pocket & Folio Ref. Summary. . . . 53
    Rolex Prince 53
    Prince & Princess Ref. Summary . 56
    Other Antique Wristlet Refs 57
    Antique Moon Phase & Chronos. 63
    Dato-Compax Ref. Summary. . . . 65
    Antique Chronos Ref. Summary . 68

PROFESSIONAL TOOLS. 73
    Oyster Perpetual Submariner . . . 71
    Submariner Ref. Summary. 88
    Oyster Perpetual Sea-Dweller . . . 92
    Sea Dweller Ref. Summary. 101
    Oyster Perpetual Yacht-Master . .102
    Yacht-Master Ref. Summary. 104
    Oyster Perpetual Explorer 105
    Explorer Ref. Summary. 107
    Explorer II Ref. Summary 107
    Oyster Perpetual Explorer II. 108
    Oyster Perpetual Milgauss 113
    Milgauss Ref. Summary 115
    Cosmograph Daytona. 116
    Oyster Perpetual Air-King. 122
    Air King Ref. Summary 125
    Oyster Perpetual GMT-Master. . .126
    GMT Master Ref. Summary 131

CLASSICS & CROSSOVERS 135

- Oyster Perpetual 141
- Oysterdate Ref. Summary 152
- Oyster Perpetual Datejust 156
- Oyster Perpetual Day-Date 167
- Rolex Bubbleback 174

FORMAL DRESS 185

- King Midas 187
- Cellini Prince................. 189

BRACELETS 195

- End Links & Spring Bars 199
- Bracelet Codes & Models 204

MOVEMENTS................... 217

- Movement Timeline 226
- Movement Ref. Summary.......227

ACCESSORIES 235

EPIGRAPH 243

INTRODUCTION

"The writer who breeds more words than he needs is making a chore for the reader who reads."
- Dr. Seuss

Rolex have been making watches in a variety of styles for over a century. Styles and product lines have come and gone with prevailing tastes and fashions. Groups of similarly styled watches belong to a *Collection*. Collections themselves have come and gone too.

Each watch within a Collection has a reference number. Hardened watch enthusiasts (serious nerds) will refer to a particular watch model by its reference (ref.) number. The same unhelpful practice is common when talking about internal mechanics.

Known as the *movement*, watch engines come in a variety of configurations. Each has variants called a *caliber* (cal.) which is also identified by a unique number. A caliber may have a particular function like a stopwatch (or chronograph), a calendar, or a second time zone. These additional functions are known as *complications*.

This cryptic shorthand and jargon can be an infuriating barrier to entry for newcomers. These same enthusiasts are also fond of nicknames, many of these are childishly silly (and include comic heros and movie stars).

The peculiar habits of the vintage Rolex community are as strange as their members and it takes patience to understand them and their watches. In doing so, acquiring their madness is inevitable. Symptoms include compulsive obsessiveness and disconnection from reality; while acute symptoms are known to include bankruptcy and divorce.

If you are still interested in acquiring a vintage Rolex watch in spite of these peculiarities, this guide will serve as a Rosetta Stone – a universal translator for the coded language of this strange obsession.

This uncertainty leaves much mystery and controversy surrounding specially-issued watches. Particularly over examples produced for VIPs and royalty. Or the short production runs for commercial clients like Comex and Pan American Airways (Pan Am). There are also special versions for armed forces and prototypes that never made it to market, which can be especially challenging to validate.

There are over 1,400 unique references addressed in this guide. The official number and production volume remains a secret and Rolex has never disclosed official records on the matter.

What knowledge exists comes from owners, collectors, enthusiasts, archivists, and scholars. Their data comes from old dealer catalogs, advertisements, and watchmakers service manuals.

Combined with direct observation, scholars can infer a great deal about undisclosed or unacknowledged details.

The information vacuum leaves space for controversy and speculation. These gaps in public knowledge have been the subject of considerable academic and research effort in recent years.

Most information today comes from inference and extrapolation from surviving catalogs and technical service documents. While they are detailed they contain errors in translation and regional differences.

References and production volume varied by era as the fortunes of Rolex ebbed and flowed. Manufacturing processes and management practices had to respond to social and economic influences. These included the two World Wars, depressions, technological disruption and rapid changes in tastes and fashions. These events make each period distinct and challenging for collectors and buyers.

Collectors group the watches from these periods into three general groups - Antique, Vintage and Modern Classic. Then into sub-genres, such as Bubbleback, Military, Arabic or Transitional. The definition of each term remains controversial and subjective, despite their everyday use. This is a continual source of confusion for inexperienced buyers.

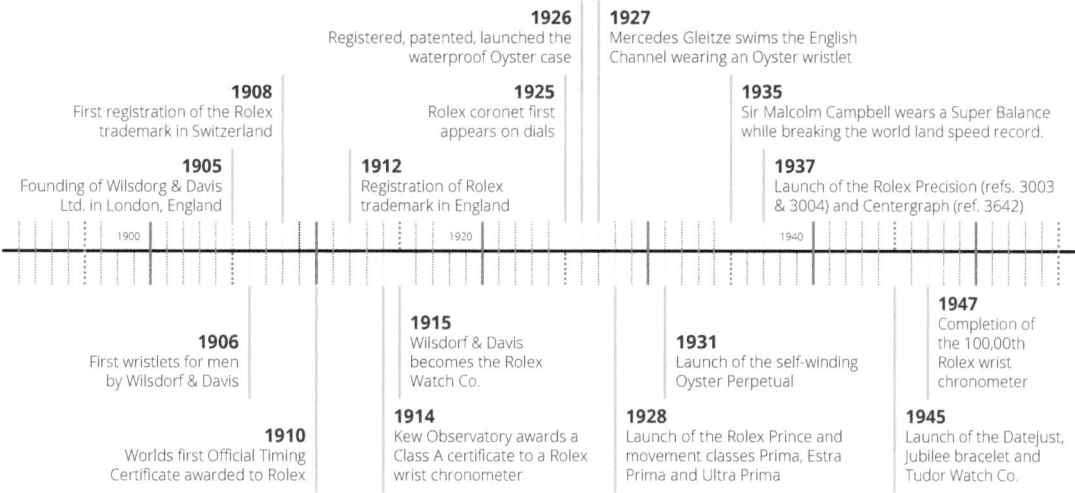

Antique Rolex

Antique watches are considered to be those produced until the late 1940s and are smaller than we've become accustomed to in the 21st century.

Pre-war and war-era examples are rare, fragile and seldom all original. Though beautiful to look at, they are fragile and can be impractical for daily use. Styles include pocket, trench and dress watches for both men and women.

During this era, Rolex experimented with brands and names, targeting different regions and markets throughout the British Commonwealth and colonies. There is considerable interest in antique Rolex and these experimental sub-brands.

These are a specialized domain with repairs and servicing becoming more challenging as time goes on.

Surviving antique Rolex watches are amazing feats of early 20th-century design. They are particularly remarkable considering their historical context.

The early 20th century was a difficult period in which to prosper as an entrepreneur. German businesspeople in particular, would have found this a haostile and unreceptive marketplace.

Antique Rolex appeals to fewer collectors because of characteristics like size and durability. In spite of this, they are historically significant in any condition and examples in good to excellent condition are highly sought after, commanding strong prices.

Alternate Rolex sub brands

Admiralty	1914-1923	Jeweler co-branded pocket watch with half hunter movement.
Aqua	1927-1959	Early water proof Oysters and marketed alongside the Submarine.
Buick	1940s	Thought to be used in the Canadian market only.
Eaton ¼ Century Club	1930s-1950s	Eaton's department store employee service award.
Genex	1920-1933	Registered in 1922 and sold to A. Schild in 1933.
Hans Wilsdorf Geneva	1935-1940	Rarely seen and only on Oyster cases.
Hofex	1920s	A movement brand only.
Ingersol	1920s	Complex history as the brand changed ownership several times.
James Walker Ltd, London	1920s	Distinguished English retailer who also sold Rolex and Marconi.
Lonex	1915-1920	An unsuccessful pocket watch brand.
Marconi	1909-1920	A precursor to Tudor.
Neptune	1930s	Early Oysters and assumed to be Canadian market only.
Oyster	1930 - 1940	Used in Commonwealth countries (Canada, Singapore, India).
Panerai	1930's	Rolex supplied movements, dials and cases for Panerai.
Rolco	1927-1930	Appear through Commonwealth countries.
Rolwatco	1922-1926	Evidence suggest a Ladies brand. Usually 9k gold cases.
Sky-Rocket	1930s	Canadian market.
Solar Aqua		Made for Eaton's Department Stores and Lund & Blockley
Tudor	1926t	Formally adopted in 1946, deprecating all other brands listed here (exceptions being Solar Aqua and ¼ Century Club).
Turtle	1930s-1942	Made for the Zell Brothers, a retailer in Portland, Oregon. May also include Turtle Timer, Turtle Deluxe, Turtle Perpetual, Turtle Lipton, and Turtle Royal
Unicorn	1919-1933	A common brand that appears to supercede Marconi. Marketed along side Rolco. A. Schild bought the brand in 1933.
Viceroy	1925-1935	Trench watch brand.
Victory	1945	Commemorative brand celebrating the WW2 Allied Victory. Sold in Commonwealth countries.
Wilson & Sharp Edinburgh	1920s	A distinguished Scottish retailer and jeweler.
Wintex	1920s	A movement brand only.

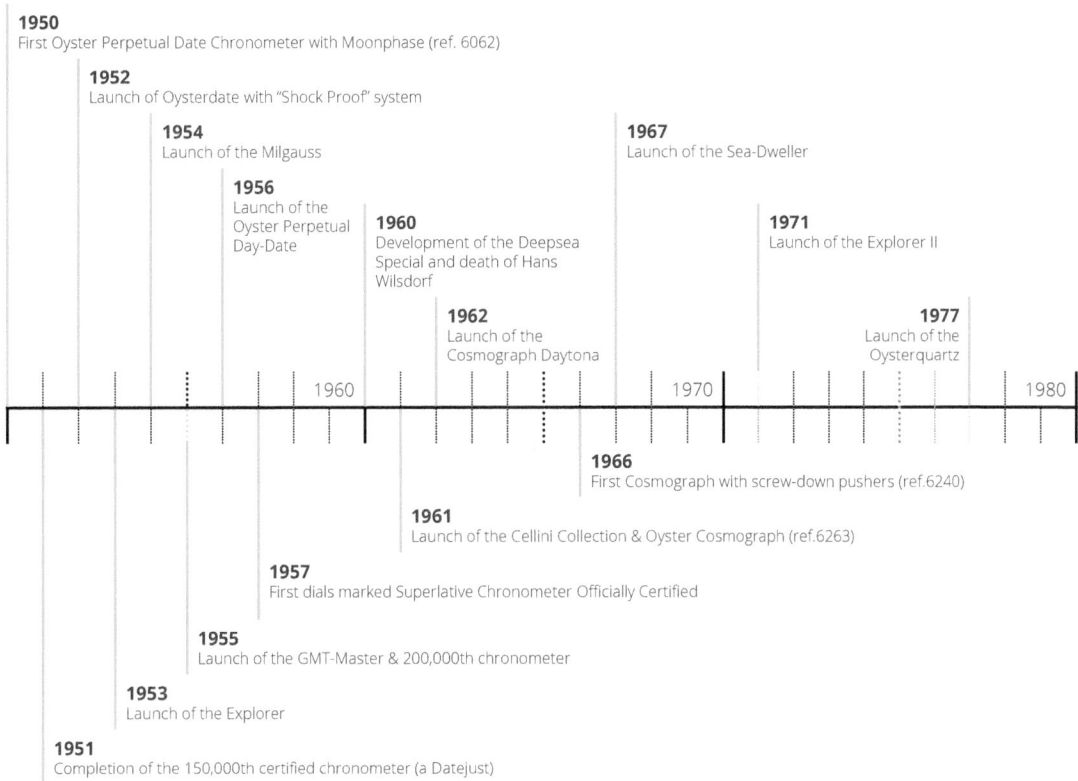

Vintage Rolex

Watches made from the early 1950s through the 1970s fall into the vintage era.

This period was a particularly prolific time for Rolex. They found commercial success in their new sporting and professional watches. It was also a calm period in world history, allowing Rolex to grow into new markets with new products.

In the absence of war, great men and women were free to pursue remarkable human achievements. The 1950s and 60s were an exciting time for these fantastic firsts. Freedom to travel and relative prosperity fueled these pursuits and records were broken all around the world.

Precision timekeeping was crucial in pursuits like mountaineering, aviation, exploration, space travel, and saturation diving. A wristwatch was a life-critical instrument, and Rolex was on a mission to make the best.

Collectors consider this the Golden Age as references are robust and wearable. Many are historically significant and survive in excellent condition.

The market for vintage Rolex is large and liquid, and prices have been on a steady upward trajectory for several years; attracting new collectors, investors, and speculators. Watches designed as tools for challenging outdoor pursuits have lead this price surge. The most popular, and practical are those made in stainless steel.

Rapidly rising prices have attracted the attention of investors and speculators. However, young buyers should be reminded that vintage watches are not an investment asset class. Unlike investment assets, they have high upkeep costs, and are prone to damage and theft. With volatile prices, they generally perform poorly as a long term store of wealth.

Buyers, enthusiasts and collectors moving into this class of watch should examine their motives carefully.

Later in this guide we'll examine individual examples and the particular buying-challenges with each model. These problems range from outright counterfeiting to poor restorations. Finding original examples in acceptable condition is not easy.

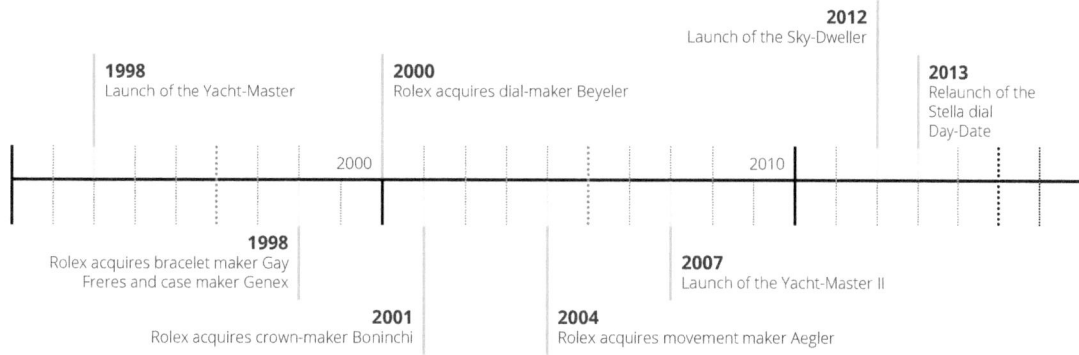

Modern Classic Rolex

Modern Classic watches are those from the 1980s to the turn of the century. The term is unofficial and coined by collectors and shouldn't be confused with the Rolex Classic Collection or classically styled models.

This genre of watches are generally evolutions of iconic vintage designs. Rolex service centers can still work on them thanks to their contemporary movements and parts availability. Serviceability makes them accessible and practical for new collectors.

This class of modern classic watches has won the hearts of new, younger collectors. These less experienced enthusiasts often lack the experience, the means and the knowledge to dive straight into more technical vintage examples.

The market for Modern Classics is the fastest growing. It is liquid and still offers reasonable price and value today.

This era was a period of aggressive business acquisitions by the Rolex CEO, Patrick Heiniger. His goal to achieve vertical integration of the supply chain was mostly successful. The rate at which he was able to acquire and integrate subcontractors, suppliers, and partners is a masterful leadership and management achievement.

The result is a more consistent product with fewer defects and anomalies. These vintage-era characteristics are much less common in Modern Classic watches thanks to streamlined production and improved quality controls.

Oyster Perpetual Classic	Oysper Perpetual Professional	Cellini
Oyster Perpetual	Cosmograph Daytona	Cellini Time
Datejust	Sea-Dweller	Cellini Date
Day-Date	Submariner	Cellini Dual Time
Pearlmaster	GMT-Master II	Cellini Moonphase
Sky-Dweller	Explorer	
	Explorer II	
	Milgauss	
	Yacht-Master	
	Yacht-Master II	

Contemporary Rolex

Historical significance is an attractive characteristic of antique, vintage and classic Rolex watches. Amazing human achievement enabled by precision timekeeping only adds to the general aura and nostalgia.

Calculating flight time, oxygen, daylight, and other life-critical functions burnish their reputations even further. Horological history has come to recognize them as essential tools, and their modern descendants proudly claim them as part of their genealogy.

Rolex continues to capitalize on their history, marketing it heavily. Many buyers of contemporary Rolex believe they're buying a piece of history. While beautiful, these are mass produced, modern luxury jewelery, and an homage to their vintage ancestors.

The current family tree of products gets much of their value from these old watches and their nostalgic heritage. Each current Collection has examples of these ancestors. Distinct model reference numbers are used to uniquely identify each of them.

Reference numbering conventions have evolved unevenly over the years. Even in stable periods of production, there are strange inconsistencies. These anomalies make collecting challenging and uniquely entertaining. This is not the case for contemporary Rolex, which have become uniformly pefect, thanks to sophisticated modern manufacturing methods.

The focus of this guide is pre-owned antique and vintage Rolex watches. However, context and completeness require the inclusion of some contemporary references from the current Collections. You'll encounter examples later in this guide, in an attempt to better paint an overall picture and setting for the collectible antique, vintage, and classic examples.

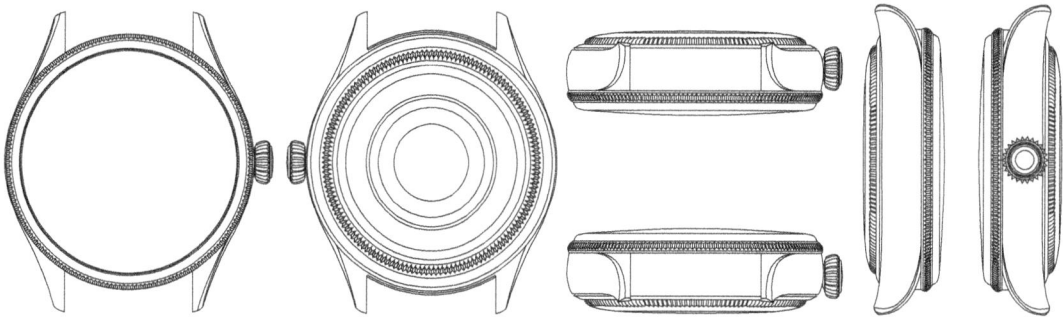

The Oyster Case & Crown

The name Oyster is most commonly associated with the iconic waterproof case. Few know that it was also used to brand a collection of early watches in 1926. Later sections of this guide examine this first Rolex Oyster collection.

Waterproof watch cases were in use well before Rolex introduced the Oyster. Dennison (a British watch case maker) secured a UK patent in 1872, and Ezra Fitch (the co-founder of the modern lifestyle brand Abercrombie & Fitch) was awarded a US patent in 1879 and 1881. These patents and designs were combined and used in the Alcide Droz & Fils Impermeable, a waterproof pocket watch made in 1883.

In 1917 two Royal Navy submarine commanders commissioned the Submarine Commanders Watch. It was a watertight wristwatch with a screw-on case back and bezel both with compressible gaskets. It also had a waterproof compressible seal in the stem tube to avoid water ingress from the crown. While the configuration is now familiar to Rolex, it was not a commercial success in its day.

In October 1925 Paul Perregaux and Georges Perret registered Swiss patent No. 114948 for a crown that could be screwed onto the case to create a waterproof seal. It was this patent that Hans Wilsdorf acquired the rights to and subsequently extended and improved.

Less than a year later in 1926 Wilsdorf registered patent No. 120,848 and paired the design with his Oyster case.

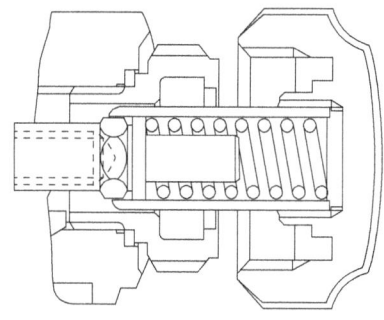

Patent drawing : Sectional view of the Triplock waterproof crown.

The Perpetual Movement

The story of the Oyster case is intimately related to the invention of the automatic self-winding Perpetual movement.

In times past, it was common for owners to forget to screw down the crown and hermetically seal the case. Forgetfulness would result in terminal damage to the inner workings of their watch. Rolex concluded that the solution was to eliminate the need to unscrew the crown and wind the watch in the first place. This lead to the aggressive pursuit of an automatic self-winding movement.

Rolex first used the term *Perpetual* with their early self-winding bumper movements in 1931. A bumper movement uses a spring-loaded weight that oscillates back and forth (or up and down), as opposed to a rotary weight.

The rotary design was by no means an industry first as that credit goes to John Harwood of the Isle of Man in 1923. He was unable to commercialize his invention or exercise the patent, leaving the field open to players like Rolex.

By 1931 Rolex had laid the foundations for success by acquiring the necessary patents and making their own small and incremental design improvements. These lead to the 360-degree winding rotor retrofitted to a conventional manual movement, enclosed in a water and dust proof case.

The height and thickness of the resulting package were heftier than competing products, many of which had more technically sophisticated, designs.

This oversized hack of a product should not have been a market-beating success. However, with marketing prowess and an uncanny ability to influence customer perception, Rolex came to dominate the industry with these small innovations.

Rolex offered something robust and substantial on the wrist that didn't need winding (but could take one) and was impervious to the elements. It wasn't *haute horology*, but it was a practical and effective compromise, packaged cleverly and launched quickly.

And so nearly a century later the words OYSTER and PERPETUAL adorn almost every Rolex dial that leaves the factory.

AUTHENTIC, ORIGINAL & CORRECT

"And those who were seen dancing were thought to be insane by those who could not hear the music."
- Friedrich Nietzsche

The vintage Rolex watch community is diverse, and the range of views they hold is broad and often contradictory.

There exists (particularly on the internet) an unhealthy and exaggerated obsession with originality, authenticity, and correctness. While these things matter, newcomers should maintain some perspective, look for context and remember their priorities.

For most of us, we're seeking 1) an authentic Rolex, 2) in a cosmetically attractive condition and 3) in good running order. While this guide won't help you to identify a fake, it will reduce your odds of being conned while you try to meet these criteria and stay within budget.

Fake or replica watches are assembled with the intent to deceive. Refinishing and restoration are sometimes done in the same spirit, to pass the piece off as entirely original. While counterfeiting is illegal, undisclosed restorations are not, and buyers should be looking for signs of undisclosed enhancement or modification.

Counterfeit dials can be extremely difficult to identify, even for supposed experts. Advances in technology, materials, and decades of practice has produced extremely convincing fakes. Many are printed on genuine Rolex dial plates from donor watches. Counterfeiters are well informed, higly trained, generously resourced and have fooled experts the world over. So if you fall for one of these, don't be too hard on yourself; it happens to even the most dilligent and well informed buyers.

Authenticity

Many authoritative sources can authenticate a vintage Rolex. The best places to go are authorized Rolex Service Centers (RSCs) and acknowledged independent vintage Rolex specialists.

It comes as a surprise to many that Authorized dealers (ADs) and general Rolex retailers are not skilled at authenticating antique and vintage Rolex watches.

Authenticity describes whether a watch contains any non-Rolex, counterfeit or aftermarket parts. Authenticity is a question of degree and can range from outright counterfeit at one end of the spectrum, to a genuine Rolex with a few after-market parts at the other. The term should be used carefully with the understanding that it is not always clear-cut.

Authentication requires opening the caseback and examining the mechanical movement. An experienced watchmaker should perform this in person with the appropriate tools. If not possible, other options exist.

Begin by taking well lit and focused photos from all angles. Remove the strap or bracelet and get pictures of the engravings between the lugs. If possible open the caseback and get pictures of the markings and the movement too.

Rolex Service Center Prague, Czech Republic

Then submit these photos to online watch forums. Experienced collectors and enthusiasts will share their often brutally honest opinions. A range of views can help a collector decide the degree of authenticity and relative risk.

Originality

When talking about *originality*, we are assuming everything is authentic. The question of originality concerns the presence of service or donor parts. While these parts may be genuine, they are installed after leaving the factory.

Originality matters most to a small subset of elite collectors. These folks are interested in the top end of the market for rare, high-value examples; particularly those in unused, mint and otherwise unmodified condition.

These watches will have spent decades locked away in a safe, and remain in New Old Stock (NOS) condition. NOS is a brand new, unsold watch from old inventory.

The overwhelming majority of vintage watches available to average enthusiasts are not NOS. They have been used and worn, acquiring a charm and character unique to each piece. For these watches, the issue of originality matters much less than other factors like condition, correctness, and authenticity.

The term *all original*, means a watch contains only the parts it left the factory with. This label implies it has never been opened or serviced. These are museum grade examples and not something you'd want to wear.

Modern restoration and refinishing services can return a watch to almost any condition desired, including NOS. This work is the equivalent of turning back a car's odometer. With refinishing practically impossible to detect, many claims of being all original are usually either misguided or dishonest.

Correctness

Correctness describes whether all the authentic Rolex parts are the right ones for the reference and belong together. This is referred to as *period correctness*.

It's common to find caseback reference numbers that don't match the mid-case reference. Many casebacks are interchangeable and can get unintentionally mixed up while on a watchmaker's bench. Sometimes parts aren't available, and the watchmaker has to use whatever fits.

It is also common to see a bezel insert that is not appropriate for the age of the watch or not originally offered on a particular reference. An incorrect bezel is common on GMT Master watches, where owners have changed colored bezel inserts out of personal preference.

You might also see a watch paired with a bracelet that was never an official option. While switched-out Rolex parts shouldn't be a deal-breaker for a watch you like, recognizing them can help understand the value of the piece and negotiate a fair price.

Transitions

Swiss watchmakers, in general, have a frugal and cost-conscious culture. Parts and components were often designed to be shared and reused across model lines and references.

It is common to see a caseback with a reference number crossed out, and a new later one applied. This correction is of no concern if the serial number dates the watch to a known transitional time frame. You can also expect to see old dials and movements paired with newer cases (e.g. Submariner ref. 168000), or new movements deployed into outgoing references (e.g. GMT-Master ref. 16710 with cal. 3135).

Introduction of a new reference often involves using up surplus inventory and many watch manufacturers engage in this practice.

These curious watches with their anomalous configurations are known as Transitionals. Transitionals are those models that include features and parts of previous or future references. Collectors are divided over whether they are more or less desirable or collectible.

While they are made in relatively small volumes and are often rare, they don't command any price premium over non-transitional models.

Transitional Submariner ref. 168000

Inexperienced collectors will often brush these off as fake, or Franken watches assembled from surplus or leftover parts. Informed collectors will recognize them as an opportunity.

All mature Rolex product lines have acknowledged transitional examples, but few have distinct reference numbers like the Submariner ref.168000.

They are not always easy to identify, and legitimate transitional models can be challenging to assess for originality. However, you will find data in later chapters, that will help evaluate the authenticity and correctness of transitional references.

ACQUISITION

"Money can't buy you happiness but it does bring you a more pleasant form of misery."
- Spike Milligan

If you're interested in vintage Rolex, you will eventually ask, "How much are they?"

Things get technical quickly and much depends on whether the intent is to buy or sell and if the counter-parties are businesses or individuals. Either way, valuations, and opinions vary widely.

Prospective buyers should consider very carefully the difference between price and value, and what each means to them personally.

They should begin by examining their own motives. Are they looking to mark an occasion with a piece of jewelry, or find a long-term store of wealth? Are they planning to build a long-term collection, or find a gift for someone special? Is this their first Rolex or their last, or something in between? These questions shape how we think of value and price.

Neglecting introspection and merely riding the wave of shopper's enthusiasm will result in unexpected surprises and disappointments.

If a *price* is the money necessary to acquire a watch, then the *value* is the desirability of that watch in terms of its exchangeability. While they are related, they should not be confused with one another.

For example, a stainless steel Submariner ref. 1680/1 will command a lower price than its solid gold counterpart, the ref. 1680/8.

However the stainless steel version is considered more valuable, due to higher demand and the ease with which it can be resold.

The value, in this case, is based on market size and liquidity. While the solid gold 1680/8 is beautiful and desirable, fewer collectors can afford them, and they can take much longer to resell.

Prevailing tastes and attitudes towards a heavy, solid gold Rolex also vary widely by region. The overall market for the 1680/8 is smaller and less liquid than the stainless steel counterpart.

For a prospective *buyer*, value involves peace of mind, communication, service, and convenience. Value to a *seller* includes transaction speed, low fees, and commissions, repeat or volume business, and reputational gain.

For both buyer and seller, there are risks to be calculated. They must each take into account what they know about the watch itself and about each other. This requires patient research and delving into historical sales data. While many will tell you to just *buy the seller* (meaning a seller's reputation) this is only one factor in quite a complicated equation.

Sources of price data include auction house sales, eBay, Chrono24 and watch forum listings. Sources of value data include reputation from feedback, endorsements, and recommendations. These might be found on Yelp and BBB ratings for business sellers. Professional membership and accreditation like AWCI and NAWCC are seller credentials that can also be verified. AWCI (American Watchmakers-Clockmakers Institute) exists to set service standards and educate the horological community. NAWCC (National Association of Watch & Clock Collectors) exists to educate and promote ethical practices. General market conditions can be assessed by conversing with dealers and collectors at meetups and online forums.

Even with careful research, the risk will never be zero. If a watch is well bought, there still remains long-term risks inherent to vintage watch ownership. While vintage Rolex prices hold up better than competing brands, this is no guarantee of sustained long term price appreciation. You must factor in the rising cost of servicing and the declining availability of parts, plus economic conditions and current tastes. It is definitely possible to lose money on a well-bought vintage Rolex, and there are no-rock solid guarantees of any type in vintage Rolex ownership.

Markets

The location of a watch you want to buy can complicate your price and value calculation. If the piece is crossing national borders, either on your wrist or via a courier service, there are costs and risks to consider.

It's helpful to recognize that regional markets (e.g. EU, Americas, Asia, Far East) have seasonal and local tastes and customs which vary widely. For example, prices and exchange rates tend to surge during holiday and bonus seasons. This boom runs from around Thanksgiving in November through Chinese New Year in February.

Trends vary too; steel sports references like Submariners, GMTs and Explorers are more popular in North America and Europe. Asian and Eastern markets often favor smaller cases forged from precious metals, in part due to the cultural significance of gold, the way darker skin tones look with different-colored metals and that slender wrists are more common. Having said this, Asian collectors are among the most informed, aggressive and ambitious; particularly at the elite and top end of the market.

For the price-sensitive collector in the middle and lower end of the market, sales taxes, import duty, shipping and payment processing fees can provide further price variables. For example, the UK VAT (Value Added Sales Tax) at 17.5% is required to be included in dealers asking price. In the US, sales tax is applied separately to the asking price.

The UK import duty on a vintage watch is not the same as US import duty on that same watch. Local shipping rates and courier insurance also vary, with shipping from the UK to the US via UK Royal Mail being less expensive than shipping from the US to the UK via USPS. This is important if you're returning a watch you're unsatisfied with.

All these fees can be significant and unexpected additions to the total cost of buying a watch.

Recourse and protections for a watch purchased from overseas are, in practice, close to none. Shipper's insurance is tricky to claim against if your purchase is lost or damaged in transit. All the major courier companies specify the maximum they will pay out on an insurance claim in their Terms and Conditions (the small print). Buying additional insurance is seldom worth it.

While eBay and PayPal offer some buyer protection, exercising these rights is challenging and will require you submit comprehensive documentation and communication records. Credit card protections on overseas internet purchases are also challenging to use, and procedures and coverage vary depending on the card issuing company.

Even if a site or seller claims lots of happy international clients and global endorsements, you should know there is a risk. You should have a plan in case things go wrong, and be ready for the associated expenses, paperwork, time and effort.

WHERE TO PURCHASE

The balance of risk is always higher for a buyer. The best purchases are achieved by maximizing trust and transacting in person with someone you know personally. This is known euphemistically as the *friends & family trade*.

The next best type of purchase is with a gray dealer with whom you have transacted before and developed trust and rapport, preferably in person. Gray dealers are independent, unofficial and unaffiliated with Rolex. They acquire their inventory from Rolex Authorized Dealers through trade channels like watch fairs and at discounted trade prices. They are typically known for selling new watches, but often have access to, or hold vintage pieces in inventory.

Many gray dealers use online forums as sales channels and invest heavily in their online reputation. The value of a gray dealer is access to their wider network and diverse inventory. Concierge services can also be especially valuable. This service involves seeking out a watch, in a specific condition and price, for a retainer or engagement fee.

The next best is a vintage retailer such as the popular online stores. Popular and reputable sites include HQMilton and BobsWatches. Buyers rely heavily on their descriptions, photos, reputation and return policies. Expect to be low-balled on pieces you are trying to sell and charged what they think the market will bear on inventory being offered. The spread can be wide depending on the model (typically 8% to 10%).

The last is the Rolex Authorized Dealer. Few are interested in selling pre-owned or vintage pieces, preferring to unload this inventory through trade channels to the pre-owned dealer network. These outlets may occasionally (and unofficially) have pre-owned watches they've taken in part exchange on new purchases. They generally have very little expertise in the highly technical vintage market.

Research & Due Diligence Tips

An excellent way to determine the prevailing price of a specific vintage watch is to trawl the internet collecting prices from wherever they can be found. This can include watches currently offered for sale as well as sold items. Seasoned collectors tend to enjoy this education and research while less experienced buyers can find it frustratingly tedious and confusing. In other words, the learning curve is steep but eventually gets easier.

As you collect this price data, try to account for the presence and condition of a bracelet, boxes, papers, hang tags, booklets, and other accessories. It would also be sensible to limit the time period to say, the last 12 months, or even less for really desirable references. This will enable you to calculate an average price for average condition in the current market - a useful benchmark. eBay has a particularly useful search filter that allows you to list sold items and their final selling price.

The next step is to seek a third party opinion on the condition, originality, and desirability of a particular watch. You should *not* ask, "What is this watch worth?" but instead ask, "How do you rate the condition of this watch?"

Opinions on condition will help you place it above or below the average benchmark you calculated earlier. Expect opinions to be harsh and widely varied but remember, you are seeking a balance of views, or what most observers think.

It is also worth consulting others about local market conditions and local interest in a particular reference. If considering an international transaction, seek out the experience of others, particularly those with logistics and duty expertise.

If you don't move in watch collector circles, make use of the two popular online watch forums for Rolex collectors. These are considered authoritative and are frequented by seasoned collectors as well as watchmakers specializing in vintage references.

While the members' opinion and expertise are invaluable, the forum format can make research frustrating and tedious.

- The Rolex Forums (www.rolexforums.com)

- Vintage Rolex Forums (vintagerolexforums.com)

Perspective

Confirming any pre-owned Rolex as definitely authentic, all original and entirely correct, is virtually impossible without the aid of advanced forensic lab equipment (like radio mass spectrometers), and lots of verified historical data.

A buyer must accept that a level of risk is ever present and that even elite collectors struggle to reach certainty. You need to get comfortable with this idea if you want to avoid analysis paralysis or buyers remorse.

The overwhelming majority of vintage watches have experienced maintenance servicing during their lifetime. With Rolex service parts dwindling or gone, after-market and even hand made parts are often used to keep old watches running. Genuine Rolex service parts are acceptable but less desirable than original parts, and prices for serviced watches reflect this preference. If a watch with service parts is priced lower than one with original parts, consider this...

There is a thriving global market for watch components that have been *parted-out*. This term means a watch is broken down, and its parts sold individually.

If a vintage watch has some of these donor parts installed rather than identifiable service parts, is it still original? Would you care? Would anyone be able to prove parts come from another Rolex watch? Do you personally prefer newer components that are genuine service replacements or older looking, well worn, donor parts? Knowing there might be mismatched donor or service components, would you pay a premium for a well-used watch that claims to be all original?

Like vintage cars, collectors accept that non-original parts are required to keep an old car running and valuable. Aftermarket parts might include tires, filters, hoses and even paint. Comparable consumable parts for a vintage watch would be barrel springs, crystals, crowns, tubes, gaskets, bracelets, clasps and a host of moving parts. A vintage watch may no longer be all original, but it can still be beautiful, functional and highly desirable.

There are many legitimate, minute variations within references. These include crown size, crown markings, dial text, hour markers, bezels, inserts, and hands to name a few.

These variations extend to customizations like co-branded dials with favored jewelers and retail partners (such as Serpico y Laino, Joyer a Riviera, and Tiffany). There are further variations in Rolex service parts which have also evolved over the years. All these variables complicate any assessment of authenticity, originality or correctness. Buyers are encouraged to embrace the ambiguity and mystery as part of the unique character of each vintage watch. These signs of a well owned vintage Rolex should be welcomed, not shunned.

A class of watch known as *marriage watches* also exists. These are Rolex pocket watch movements re-cased in wrist watch cases. While not original, they are legitimate and can be beautiful and artistically executed. New collectors are advised to stay away from marriage watches, as they're a very specialized and niche domain.

BY THE NUMBERS

"The only insult I've ever received in my adult life was when someone asked me, "Do you have a hobby?" A HOBBY?! DO I LOOK LIKE A FUCKING DABBLER?!"
- John Waters

Vintage Rolex model reference numbers are engraved rather than stamped on the Oyster case between the lugs on the 12 o'clock side. Serial numbers are on the 6 o'clock side.

This practice is limited to Oyster cases. Non-Oyster cases such as Cellini and antique Rolex like early Bubblebacks have their reference and serial numbers engraved on the inside of their case backs.

On Oyster cases, there is considerable variation in the exact positioning and font of these engravings. They were written using a mechanical Pantograph, and the text is not as consistent and uniform as that of computerized laser etching.

Furthermore, some previous RSCs would re-engrave numbers if they were worn off or becoming too hard to read. Thankfully this practice has ended.

Identifying authentic and original engravings requires experience and practice, and even then is debatable.

Engravings can be obscured by dirt and corrosion or worn away by poorly fitted end links (often the result of incorrectly sized spring bars). In these cases, a jewelers loupe is required to read them.

Collectors should be on the lookout for signs of re-engraving, over-engraving or other attempts to tamper with these markings. Any corruption of these engravings will seriously devalue a vintage Rolex.

The conventions used for these reference numbers are inconsistent. While generalizations are possible, many exceptions exist.

Some models are dual-referenced meaning the same case reference number can be assigned to two different models. For example, some vintage Air-Kings carry the same case reference number as vintage Explorers.

A reference number can usually be split into three parts indicating the model line, the bezel style, and the case material. For example a GMT with ref. 16710 would be 167 denoting a GMT Master II, 1 indicating a steel bezel ring (not the aluminum bezel insert) and 0 indicating a Stainless Steel case.

Case Material Key (Reference Suffix)

Occasionally you'll see old reference numbers with a suffix separated by a slash ("/").

For example, a ref. 1675/8 with the /8 denoting an 18k solid gold case. The use of the slash is not consistent and typically associated with four-digit references. By the time Modern Classics emerged with five digit reference numbers, the slash had fallen out of use. So our example would become a ref. 16758.

The following table will help translate that last digit and can be used to validate warranty papers and confirm they match the accompanying watch. They can also be used to check the crown is correct for the case.

Suffix	Case Material
0	Stainless Steel
1	Yellow Gold Filled
2	White Gold Filled
22	Stainless Steel & Platinum
3	Stainless Steel & Yellow Gold
4	Stainless Steel & 18k White Gold
5	Gold Shell or Everose (Rose Gold)
6	Platinum
7	14k Yellow Gold
8	18k Yellow Gold
9	18k White Gold

Model Collection (Reference Prefix)

A reference number prefix can be used to validate which Collection a watch (or that particular Oyster case) belongs to. This is relevant because Oyster cases come in standardized sizes and can be reused across models.

If you're looking for an original watch, the case prefix should reflect the model on the dial. For example, if you are looking at a vintage Submariner with a reference number of 167x, then you are looking at a Franken watch that has been assembled from a parts bin.

Model	Prefix
Submariner No Date	55, 140
Submariner Date	16, 166, 168
Sea-Dweller	16, 166
GMT Master	16, 65, 167
GMT Master II	167, 1167
Day-Date	65, 66, 18, 180, 182, 183
Datejust	16, 162
Daytona (Manual)	62
Daytona Cosmograph	165, 1165
Explorer II	165
Oyster Perpetual	10, 140, 142
Air King	55, 140
Date	15, 150
Oysterquartz Datejust	170
Oysterquartz Day-Date	190
Yacht-Master	166, 686, 696
Datejust (Mid Size)	68, 682
Oyster Perpetual (Ladies Size)	67, 671, 672
Date (Ladies Size)	65, 69, 691, 692
Datejust (Ladies Size)	65, 69, 691, 692
Oysterdate (Mid Size)	65

Case Serial Numbers

Each Rolex watch leaves the factory with a unique serial number that can be used to approximate the production date. However, the numbering format can be inconsistent, and there are exceptions, with some antique watches having no serial number at all.

Rolex reset serial numbers in 1954 after they reached 999,999 making it possible for a watch made in the 1960s to have the same serial number as one from the 1950s. To help distinguish between the duplicates Rolex engraved case backs with date codes, making it easier to differentiate between a pre-1954 and a post-1954 serial. However, it's conceivable that case backs could get mixed up on a watchmakers bench.

When serials reached 9,999,999 by mid-1987, Rolex began using a character prefix followed by six digits. Curiously, they did not start with the letter A. Instead, they started with R, followed by L, then E, followed by other non-sequential characters.

The most significant change in serial number conventions came at the end of 2010 when Rolex adopted random serial numbers, making it impossible to determine a year of production. The prevailing theory is that Rolex did not want to disclose annual production volume to competitors or customers, while others speculate it was an anti-counterfeiting measure.

A watch's serial number can be found on its warranty papers as well as on the watch itself. Watches made before 2007 will have the serial number engraved on the case in between the lugs at 6 o'clock. Seeing the number requires removing the bracelet, and depending on the case's condition, a jeweler's loupe may be needed to read it.

In late 2006, Rolex began laser etching the serial number on the rehaut (the perpendicular ring around the outer edge of the dial). In 2008, Rolex phased out the case engraving of serial numbers and began relying exclusively on the rehaut etching.

The serial number on the case is unrelated to the serial number on the movement. The mechanical movements were manufactured under different processes, and in some cases by different companies (e.g. Aigler, Valjoux). Production and assembly records which match case serials with movement serials remain a closely guarded secret. These records are available only to Rolex employees at Rolex Service Centers. There is an ongoing debate about how complete and accurate they are for vintage watches.

Case Serial Number Timeline

2010s		2000s		1990s		1980s		1970s	
2019	Random	2009	V	1999	A,000,001	1989	L,980,000	1979	5,737,030
2018	Random	2008	M OR V	1998	U,932,144	1988	R,598,200	1978	5,000,000
2017	Random	2007	M OR Z	1997	U,000,001	1987	R,000,001	1977	5,008,000
2016	Random	2006	D OR Z	1996	T,000,001	1987	9,400,000	1976	4,115,299
2015	Random	2005	D	1995	W,000,001	1986	8,900,000	1975	3,862,196
2014	Random	2005	F	1994	S,860,880	1985	8,614,000	1974	3,567,927
2013	Random	2004	F	1993	S,000,001	1984	8,070,022	1973	3,200,268
2012	Random	2003	F	1992	C,000,001	1983	7,400,000	1972	2,890,459
2011	Random	2002	Y	1991	N,000,001	1982	7,100,000	1971	2,589,295
2010	G	2001	K OR Y	1991	X,000,001	1981	6,520,870	1970	2,241,882
		2000	K,000,001	1990	E,000,001	1980	6,434,000		
		2000	P,000,001						

1960s		1950s		1940s		1920s		1920s	
1969	1,900,000	1959	399,453	1949		1939	71,224	1929	
1968	1,752,000	1958	328,000	1948	628,840	1938	43,739	1928	23,969
1967	1,538,435	1957	224,000	1947	529,163	1937	40,920	1927	20,190
1966	1,200,000	1956	133,061	1946	367,946	1936	36,856	1926	1
1965	1,100,000	1955	97,000	1945	302,459	1935	34,336		
1964	1,008,889	1954	23,000	1944	269,561	1934	30,823		
1963	824,000	1953	855,726	1943	230,878	1933	29,562		
1962	744,000	1952	726,639	1942	143,509	1932	29,132		
1961	643,153	1951	709,249	1941	106,047	1931			
1960	516,000	1950		1940	99,775	1930	23,186		

CONDITION

"The only thing I know is that I know nothing"
- Socrates

The condition of a watch is the primary driver of price, and both vary widely. When assessing the state of a vintage Rolex, you're looking for consistent, all-over, even aging and wear. If it appears uneven, with some parts looking new and others looking tattered, this is a red flag and price should be much softer. Uneven wear and inconsistent aging suggest unoriginal components.

Patina is a sign of aging and extends to the inside of the watch too. You should be looking for other indicators such as corrosion and pitting. Particularly around the opening where the case back screws down onto the mid case. Obviously, this applies only to stainless steel as gold will tarnish but not corrode.

If the case and internal mechanical parts look pristine with no apparent signs of age, you'd expect the dial and hands to be in similarly good condition and vice versa. Similar rules of thumb apply to bracelets, clasps and even boxes and packaging.

If you inspect the movement, pay close attention to the state of screw heads. You're looking for consistency (all similar color and type). You do not want to see burring. This is minor damage resulting from removing and reinstalling screws with an incorrect or poorly maintained screwdriver. You might also see empty screw holes with a missing screw. Hopefully, it's just been lost and isn't rattling around in the movement waiting to cause expensive damage. Even the most expert and careful watchmakers are prone to occasional mishaps.

None of the things described in this section should be deal breakers preventing you from buying a watch you like. They are, however, useful indicators of value and price. If a watch has issues in ALL the areas mentioned in this section, it will be priced at the low end of the range, hard to resell and expensive to restore.

Cases

Rating the condition of a vintage watch case is subjective, and there is no standardized scale. Over the years different case makers have supplied Rolex. These have included C.R.Spillman (sometimes spelled Charles-Rene Spielman) and Genex which Rolex acquired in 1998. Cases from both suppliers were sent to be finished and polished by a company called Joi Poli which Rolex also bought the same year.

Vintage watches experience disassembly and cleaning several times during their lifetime. Such servicing nearly always includes case polishing. A polished case suggests a watch has been well cared for by a conscientious owner.

Collectors consider polished cases undesirable, and this is reflected in prevailing prices. For newcomers, this is counter-intuitive and confusing. There exists an unrealistic and idealistic pursuit of original mint condition vintage watches. While such examples exist, they are seldom seen in the wild and change hands with high price premiums.

It is essential to understand that polishing a watch case is a skilled craft. An unskilled watchmaker can ruin a watch in seconds. These poorly polished examples should be avoided. However, they shouldn't be mistaken for watches that have been repeatedly, but skillfully polished. Recognizing and distinguishing between the two takes practice.

Elite collectors are willing to pay auction house premiums for top condition cases. These

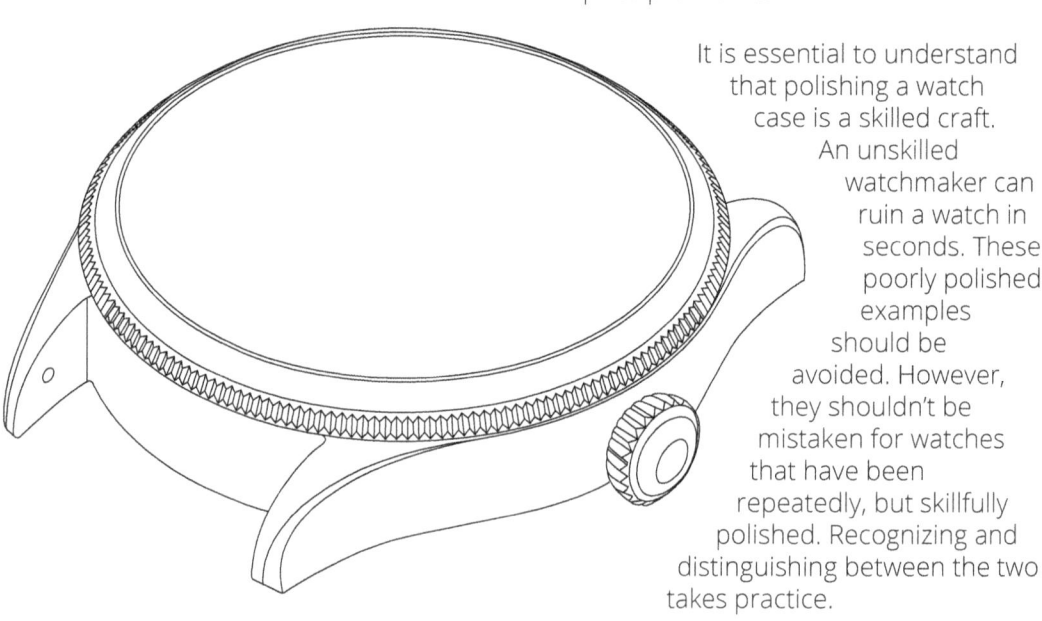

Patent D733,582S drawing of the original Oyster case.

are investment grade watches that will never experience a sweaty wrist. Novice collectors hear the mantra that, the *condition is everything*, and conclude that only mint condition and unpolished is desirable or collectible. This is misguided.

An average to a well-polished case should not put you off a watch you like. However, a poorly or over-polished case can be expensive to restore, and will impact any future claims of originality and authenticity. The line between average and poor can be wide and is in the subjective eye of the beholder.

The unhealthy obsession for like-new cases with their crisp chamfers and satin finish has fueled the demand for refinishing services (known as case milling, or lapping). These have become increasingly popular and available at a lower and lower cost.

The craftsmen (and women) offering these services are skilled industrial engineers, proficient in computer-aided design and computerized lathes and milling machines. It is a highly professional undertaking which can precisely mill (re-cut) a case back to its original form, complete with correct satin or even exotic finishes.

By combining milling techniques with modern advances in laser welding (reapplying metal), a heavily distressed or over-polished case can be made to look brand new and indistinguishable from New Old Stock (old inventory, never sold, but changing hands amongst dealers as new).

The vintage Rolex market is now so heavily polluted with refinished cases that collectors should be highly skeptical of barn finds and claims of being all original, unpolished or NOS. Without documented provenance, these claims should not command a price premium.

Social media (Instagram in particular), is full of vintage watches with perfect refinished cases paired with ghost bezels and deeply patinated dials. A ghost bezel is heavily weathered and faded. If you like the look, there are plenty to choose from but be warned; the taste for these strange looking watches could pass as quickly as it emerged. These watches could be destined to become tomorrow's parts donors.

Casebacks

Casebacks are interchangeable between oyster cases of the same size irrespective of the reference. For example, a caseback from a 40mm GMT-Master will fit a 40mm Explorer, and it will not effect waterproofing. So it's not uncommon to see mismatched cases and casebacks.

Oyster casebacks usually do not feature any markings on the outside (the Sea-Dweller and some Tudors being exceptions). Rolex left them intentionally blank to allow owners to personalize them with engravings. These can be removed by skimming or polishing the caseback but success depends on the depth of the engraving and the skill of the watchmaker. An engraved or personalized watch can be charming but difficult to resell, unless it plays a role in the provenance of the watch (such as belonging to a celebrity).

Clear or display casebacks were only used on one reference, the modern (but discontinued) Cellini Prince. Any examples you encounter with clear casebacks will be aftermarket additions or pocket watch conversions (marriage watches).

The inside of a caseback will feature various stamped markings. These vary by reference and have evolved over the years. Typically you can expect to see the Rolex makers mark, a model reference number and in some cases a date of production and in others a serial or issue number. The adjacent illustration will help you determine if the case back is period correct for the Oyster case.

CONDITION

ROLEX 7 WORLS'S RECORDS GOLD MEDAL GENEVA - SUISSE ✠ 114948	OYSTER WATCH Co GENEVA SWISS GRANT BRITAIN PATENTS 260554/1925 274.708 274.789 SWISS PATENTS + 114.940 + 120.848 + 120.851 + 122.110 FRENCH PATENTS 630.179 630.180 U.S.A PATENT 1.661.232 GERMAN PATENT 443.386	ROLEX 20 WORLD'S RECORDS GREAT BRITAIN PATENTS 260554/1925 274.789 SWISS PATENTS +114.948 +120.851	OYSTER WATCH Co GENEVA-SWISS GRANT BRITAIN PATENTS SWISS PATENTS FRENCH PATENTS U.S.A PATENTS GERMAN PATENTS
1926	**1928**	**1929**	**1932 - 1945**
OYSTER WATCH Co GENEVA SWISS GRANT BRITAIN PATENTS 260554 1925 274780 274780 SWISS PATENTS 114948 120848 120851 122110 U.S.A PATENT 1661232 D.R.P 471002	BREVETEE Rolex S.A. GENEVE - SUISSE 31 VICTORIES HAUTEPRECISION	Oyster Watch Co GENEVA - SWISS PATENTED IN ALL COUNTRIES	(crown logo) GENEVA R SWISS ROLEX PATENTED
1934 - 1945	**1938 - 1945**	**1941 - 1945**	**1945-1949**
(crown logo) GENEVA R SWISS ROLEX PATENTED	ROLEX GENEVA SWISS PATENTED	MONTRES ROLEX S.A. GENEVA SWISS	(crown logo) GENEVA SWISS MONTRES ROLEX S.A.
1949-1954	**1952-1953**	**1953-1954**	**1953-1955**
MONTRES ROLEX SA GENEVA SWITZERLAND PATENTED	MONTRES ROLEX SA GENEVA SWITZERLAND	MONTRES ROLEX SA GENEVA SWITZERLAND	ROLEX GENEVA SWITZERLAND
1955-1982	**1982-1985** Patented removed	**1982-2005**	**2005-Today**

Caseback interior stamp markings.

Lugs

The primary way to evaluate case condition is to look side-on at the position and shape of the lug holes.

The spring bar holes should appear crisp and centered vertically. If they appear off-center (disproportionately close to the top edge), the case has been aggressively polished and only laser welding can add this lost material back.

Lug holes should also appear round (not an ellipse or conical) and consistent on all sides. If they are splayed, off-center or uneven then you're looking at a bad polish.

The visual appearance of lugs wants to be consistent, meaning the width and curvature. While the top and bottom lugs won't be perfectly symmetrical, they should appear even in length and width.

Not all case lugs had a chamfered or bevelled edge. The presence and degree of chamfer varied by model and even within a reference. The edges and corners of lugs should be sharp and crisp, with a clear contrast between the satin and polished surfaces. Curved and rounded lug edges are the clearest indication of past polishing.

Finish

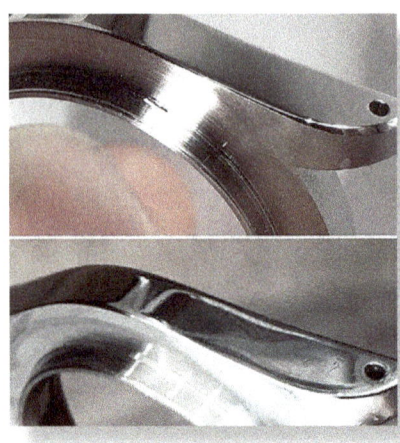

Another essential indicator is the case finish; especially satin and polished surfaces. While they are subtle, Rolex went to great lengths to apply them. Buyers should be looking for signs of the different finishes as they may well have been worn or polished away. If they are still visible, are they correct for the reference?

Most vintage Rolex Oyster cases have a satin finish on the top surface of the case and a high polish on the sides. A few references have this combination reversed with satin sides and polished top surfaces.

On some references such as the Datejust, the sides of the case are slightly bowed (convex) while others like some of the Oysterdate references (e.g. ref. 6518) had square, straight sides.

You should determine which is correct for the reference you're looking at and note whether these cues are still visible.

On some precious metal Datejust and Day-Date models, you can expect to find exotic finishes such as Bark or Morellis (e.g. ref. 1806). These conceal signs of wear and can be difficult to restore if damaged. While an acquired taste, they are rare, coveted and collectible.

Corrosion

The stainless steel used in Oyster cases is an alloy recipe made from iron ore, chromium, nickel, molybdenum, and a few other trace elements. These trace elements give the iron ore its stainless, corrosion-resisting properties. Metallurgists call this alloy 300 Series Austenitic Stainless Steel.

316 stainless steel is considered standard marine grade stainless steel. Despite the name, it is not resistant to warm seawater corrosion (specifically, chloride, fluoride, iodide, and bromide). 304L and 316L (316L is the low carbon version of 316) are derived from this 300 Series and are used in many pre-1987 vintage Oyster cases. Later Oyster cases use 904L steel with subtly different properties.

The common misconception is that 904L is harder and more scratch-resistance. The fact is, 316L has a higher Rockwell Hardness Rating (HR B 95) than 904L (HR B 79), and 316L is also more scratch resistant and tougher to mill than 904L. 316L is said to hold a better polish too. 904L does, however, have better salt and acid resistance.

In the mid-1980s Rolex adopted 904L as a solution to pitting and crevice corrosion. This is a common problem on Oyster mid cases of sport and tool watches. It was first used on the transitional Submariner Date ref. 168000.

Urine attacks all austenitic stainless steel, so don't pee on your watches (!) and rinse them thoroughly after swimming to remove any chlorine. Bromide is just as harmful so keep vintage watches out of the hot-tub and away from the saltwater spa.

It's said that stainless steel needs to breathe and that regular cleaning with fresh water is necessary. When two pieces of stainless steel touch one another (such as a case back and mid-case), cleaning and breathing is inhibited. Despite the trace elements that provide the stainless properties, corrosion will begin. Waterproof gaskets can accelerate this by trapping and retaining salts and oxidants, which, with time will trigger a galvanic reaction.

Like seawater, human sweat is highly acidic and rich in halides. Osmosis and capillary action will draw these corrosive elements into the case. With repeated exposure and evaporation the concentration of halides and oxidants accumulates and concentrates, giving rise to a reaction that compromises and penetrates the stainless protection offered by the trace elements.

This process is a chain reaction that is almost impossible to halt once started. It is observable as pitting and can only be prevented by grinding out the pit and filling the hole with laser welding. Even this drastic intervention is controversial, as it may not entirely halt the corrosion and may only serve to weaken the geometric lattice structure of the surrounding steel (through heat expansion and cooling contraction).

Pitting is bad news; it will shorten the life and destroy the value of a vintage watch. It is a slow and progressive chronic condition, and while some collectors enjoy the Wabi-Sabi aesthetic, others consider it cancer.

While corrosion shouldn't prevent you from enjoying the life left in a beautiful vintage watch, you should know that it will negatively affect longevity, collectability, and value.

Hallmarks

Hallmarks can be complicated and intimidating, but for antique and vintage Rolex we're really only concerned with 6 different hallmarks and fewer if you exclude silver-cased antiques. After 1995 things get even more straightforward.

If you're in the market for a Rolex in precious metal, hallmarks matter. If a watch is offered and priced as 18K gold, the hallmarks are your best way to validate the claim and ensure the entire watch, case, case back, bracelet and clasp are all 18K.

Hallmarks should be present on all Rolex made of precious metals. They appear on mid-cases (underside of lugs), case backs, bracelets, and clasp blades.

The absence of hallmarks indicates gold cap, gold fill or gold plate. Mismatched hallmarks suggest a Franken watch assembled from various parts.

Hallmarks are defined by an official Swiss government assay office and applied under license by the manufacturer (Rolex).

There are seven assay offices in Switzerland and Rolex uses the Geneva office exclusively.

The symbol for the Geneva Assay Office is a capital G, which will form part of a larger hallmark.

Barry was of a breed (Bernhard) which was later called the St. Bernard. He worked as a mountain rescue dog in Switzerland and Italy for the Great St Bernard Hospice. He has been described as the most famous St. Bernard and credited with saving more than 40 lives during his lifetime. His German name is Menschenretter, meaning *people rescuer*.

Antique and vintage Rolex watches (pre-1995) have a hallmark symbol for each different purity of gold and platinum (9K, 14K, 18K). However, there is no distinction between different colors of gold (white, rose, yellow).

A Swiss government hallmark is exceptionally detailed, which makes it very difficult to copy. It must be consistent and flawless with each stamping. The assay office controls the quality and if not perfect, the item will be scrapped and can not be sold.

The crispness and detail of a hallmark are essential in establishing authenticity.

Solid 18K (750) gold watches will have the Helvetia Bust (ladies head) with a capital G below her neck. 14K (583) Gold will have the squirrel with a capital G at the top. Platinum would have the Ibex with the G between the antlers.

Hallmark symbol styles evolved and in 1933 a morning star (Morgenstern) was introduced for 9K (375) gold watches.

Current law (post-1995) has reduced the number of hallmarks to a single mark, the head of a St. Bernard dog. This official hallmark is used for all precious metals in all qualities.

The Office of Precious Metal Control refers to this St. Bernard dog as Barry. It appears near the Maker's Responsibility Mark and their indication of purity. Barry the St. Bernard Hallmark has an X marking the position of the capital G for the Geneva assay office.

Antique hallmarks, circa 1933

Vintage hallmarks, pre-1995

* only for watch-cases

Rolex watches imported into other countries are subject to local assay office inspection and may carry additional hallmarks to the Swiss ones. For example, watches imported for sale in France and England would have additional, but different hallmarks. National hallmarks are numerous and out of vthe scope of this guide.

Barry (top)and the makers mark (bottom) on the underside of the lugs on an 18K Submariner

Vintage ref. 9708 Case Back in 18K gold with Helvetia hallmark (upper left).

Assessing Dials

This is the most critical, confusing and technical part of evaluating a vintage watch. A dial can account for 50 to 100 percent of the value premium between watches of the same reference. The dials condition, originality, distinctive marks, original components and the degree of re-touching can be the difference between priceless and worthless

Rolex has used several suppliers for dials. These include Beyeler, Singer, Stern, Lemrich, and Metelem. Each stamped their name on the reverse side of the dial. Some of these marks are only visible under powerful magnification.

Small distinctions such as a retailers co-signature, a military mark or manufacturing defects can produce large price differentials. It is essential to look out for underhanded and dishonest practices concerning these descriptions and marks.

If you are pursuing high-value references, it is important to consult authoritative published sources. A specialist, technical volume exists for almost every vintage reference. Most will credit vetted sources of photographs and information, including acknowledgments to significant collectors, factory archivists, and museum staff. Recognized authoritative publishers include amongst others, Guido Mondani, Pucci Papaleo Editore, James Dowling, andv John Goldberger.

Dial Print

Manufacturing technology during the mid-20th century was not perfect, and printed dial text can vary significantly from the start to the end of the model run. Collectors can expect minor and subtle differences in font, color, and texture of printed text.

Except for some late Modern Classics, dial production was outsourced. Different batches of dials had minor variations in fonts, print quality, color consistency, finish, and texture.

Gilt dial text (bronze color) was achieved by a process of reverse osmosis, revealing the brass base plate below the paint. While finished with a clear coat of lacquer, the brass can still darken with age. These are very desirable and were made until the late 1970s. These gilt dials are also the subject of very sophisticated counterfeiters with very high-quality fakes in now wide circulation.

The top row of dial text (e.g. Rolex, Oyster Perpetual) often has a pinched or etched appearance that differs from the bottom row of text (e.g. Officially Certified Chronometer or the depth rating). The bottom row, or specification text, was commonly printed later in a separate production process. This allowed generic dials to be branded first, then customized for different models and movement grades. It also means there may be inconsistent fonts on the same dial.

The Rolex coronet on dials has also evolved and shows many variations. Some are reference specific while others are period-oriented. The details described in this guide attempt to capture the catalog configurations, as illustrated in marketing materials at the time of launch. It is known that dial print evolved throughout the product's life cycle, deviating from the original first batches of watches.

All the possible variations from catalog configurations cannot be listed in this guide due to their sheer number and a lack of an authoritative way to verify their correctness.

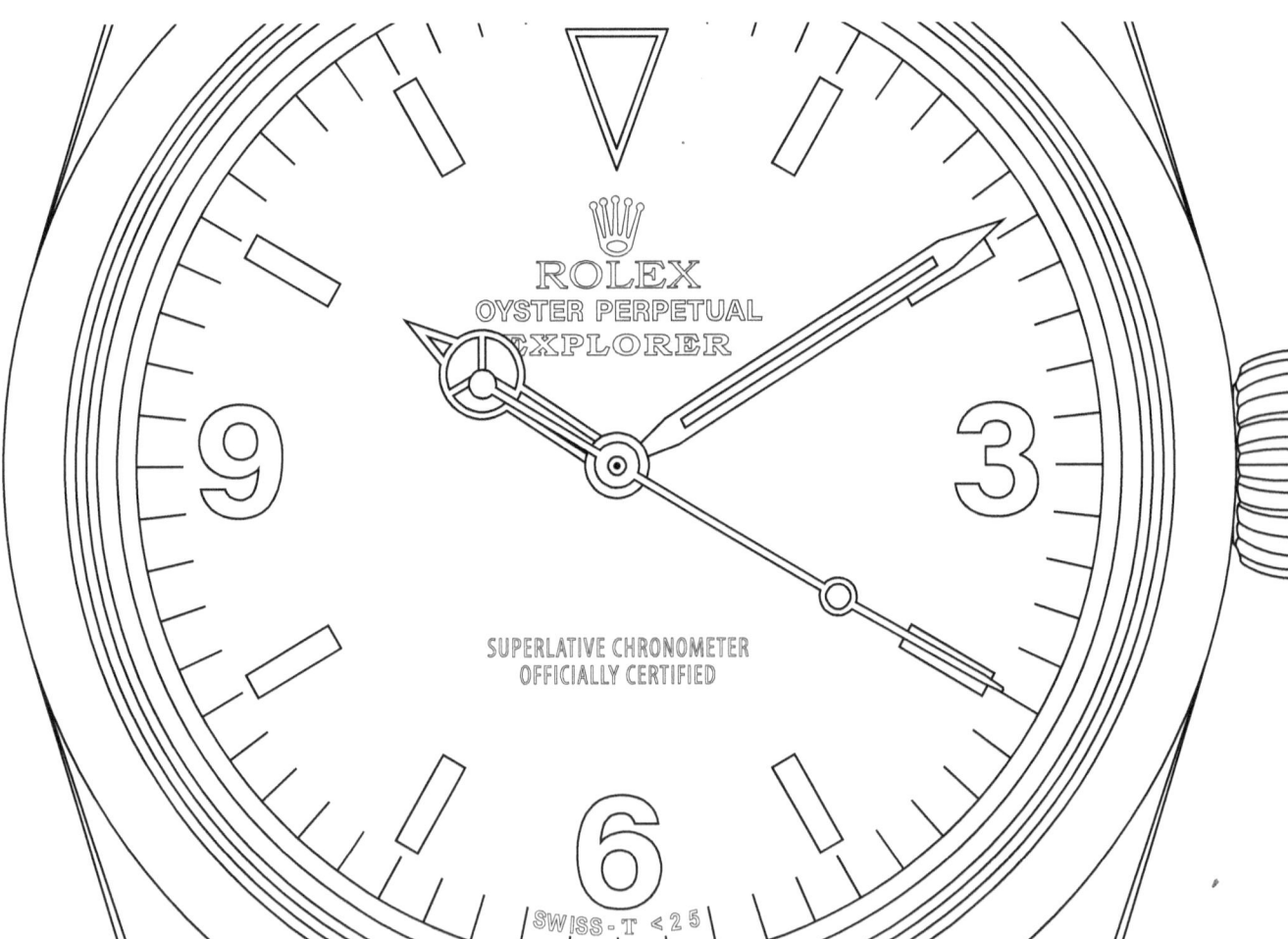

Fig. Bubblebacks and Explorers 6610 and 1016

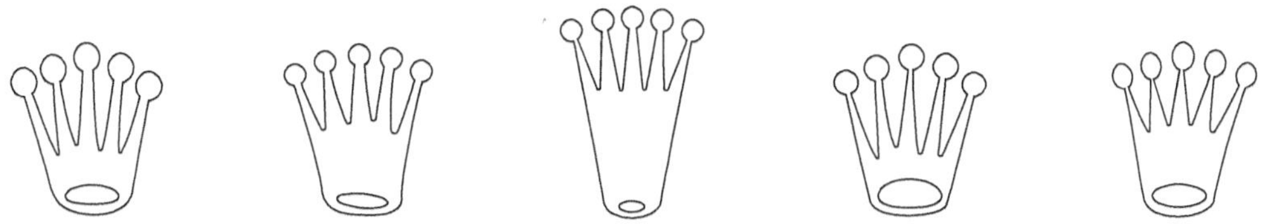

Fig. Submariners 6205, 6200, 6538, 5510 and GMT-Master 6542

Fig. Submariner 5512 (non-COSC), 5512, 5513 Gilt, 5513 White, 5513 Bart Simpson

Fig. Submariners 1680: MK1 Red, MK1 White, MK2 Red, MK4 Red, MK5 & MK6

Fig. Sea-Dweller 1665: DRSD MK2, White MK1, MK2 Rail Dial, White MK4, Single Red Service

Dial Luminous

There are five distinct types of dial lume used throughout Rolex history, each with unique characteristics (radium, tritium, luminova, super luminova, and Chromalight).

It is common for collectors to use a Geiger counter to assess radioactivity and infer the originality and authenticity of antique and vintage lume. This is in response to the increasingly high quality of counterfeit dials using degraded radium and tritium lume material.

The first generation of lume was radium, used in the 1920s to 1940s. This was highly radioactive and still poses a health risk today if accidentally ingested (i.e. by inhaling radium dust). As the dangers became apparent in the late 1930s, watchmakers attempted to reduce both the amount of radium applied to dials and the radioactivity by diluting the formulation.

When exposed to moisture and humidity, radium lume will age to a dirty green color, resembling mold. With time, radium will burn dials and corrode crystals. This cracking effect on acrylic crystals is called crazing.

The second generation of less dangerous radium was introduced in the 1940s and used in particular, on the earliest Submariners, Explorers, and Turn-O-Graphs from 1953 to 1956.

Tritium emerged in the early 1960s. The luminous material isn't pure tritium but a phosphorus compound which uses tritium as the energy source that causes it to glow green. The tritium has a half-life of 12 years (meaning zero glow after 12 years).

Radium burn on a vintage Bubbleback dial ref. 2940, circa 1940s. Note the green hour markers.

Aged tritium on a vintage Turn O Graph dial, circa 1950s. Note the cream colored hour markers

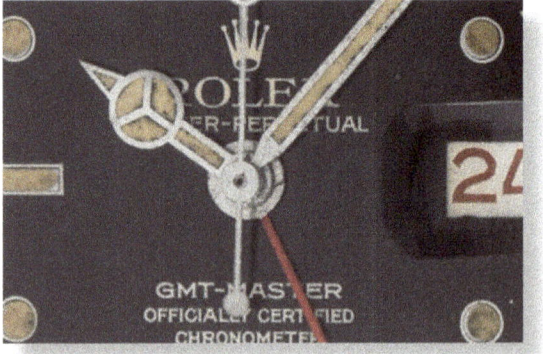

Moisture damaged tritium dial of a GMT Master ref. 1675 circa 1960s. Note the moldy appearance.

Type	Dial Marking	Lume Material	Period
1	SWISS	Early Radium	1920s - 1930s
2	SWISS	Later Radium	1940s - 1963
3	T Swiss T	Early Tritium	1963 - 1999
4	T Swiss T<25	Early Tritium	1964 - 1967
5	T Swiss - T<25	Later Tritium	1967 - 1997
6	σ T-Swiss-T σ	Later Tritium	1970 - 1979
7	- T SWISS T -	Later Tritium	1970s - 1998
8	SWISS	Luminova	1998 - 2000
9	SWISS MADE	Superluminova	2000 - 2008
10	SWISS MADE	Chromalight	2009 - Present

Depleted tritium (actually, the phosphorus in the tritium compound) will respond to UV light by holding a glow for a few seconds. Several tritium recipes and application techniques were tried over the years affecting the duration of the glow.

Before 1965, tritium was applied by hand, resulting in a raised puffy appearance. After 1965 it was pad printed resulting in a flatter, smooth appearance. From 1983 to 1997, tritium lume was edged with white gold surrounds. These are concave hour markers designed to hold the lume material in place. They prevent spreading, smudging, leaching and chipping.

Early hand-applied tritium responds under UV light today. Matte dials of the mid-1960s to 1970s had either the hand-applied raised puffy appearance or the smooth pad-printed appearance. The pad-printed style no longer responds to UV light stimulus.

By the late 1970s, lume had a look somewhere in between - a uniform domed appearance. This lume doesn't respond to UV light but glows faintly in a dark room. By the 1980s the appearance had changed again, with a smooth glossy look. While it doesn't respond to UV light, it will still glow in dark conditions.

Exposure to moisture and humidity will cause tritium to turn unevenly black, and is considered unattractive and undesirable. Without moisture, it will age (patina) evenly to various shades of brown.

Luminova and its derivatives (Superluminova and Chromalight) are considered thoroughly modern, and will still glow green and blue, respectively in the present day.

Sigma Dials

The characters of the type 6 dial are the lowercase Greek letter sigma, giving the dials the name, sigma dials. The sigma symbols were intended to indicate that the hands and indexes on a watch were made of solid gold. The dash marks shown as type seven indicate steel indexes and hands.

The sigma character was in use throughout the 1970s. Gold prices tripled during the early 1970s, and the sigma dial was an attempt to emphasize the intrinsic value of the watch. The quartz crisis (arrival of very accurate, inexpensive quartz watches from the Far East) was underway, and several Swiss watchmakers adopted the convention in an attempt to highlight their luxe credentials.

Arabic Script Dials

A class of dial exists that features Eastern Arabic script numerals. These are not to be confused with the Arabic numerals we have become used to seeing (1, 2, 3, and so on). These Arabic script dials feature symbols descended from the ancient Hindu-Arabic numeral system and are commonly referred to as, Arabic Script. Today these are used through the Arab world and in particular the Gulf States.

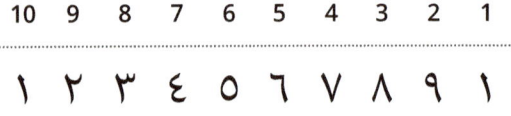

Rolex first offered dials with Arabic script in 1956 in the Day-Date refs. 6510, and 6511. In 1957, Rolex added refs. 6611, 6612 and 6613 featuring fluted and diamond bezels.

Rolex pioneered watches with Arabic script dials with matching Arabic script calendar functions. Rolex was an early entrant into the prospering Gulf market during the 1960s and these localized dials proved popular.

The introduction of Arabic script was gradual, starting with the day of the week being spelled out in Arabic.

Later references have Arabic script on the roulette date wheel too. Most of these Arabic dials appear in white gold or platinum, as Islam prohibits men from wearing yellow gold.

In 1961 Rolex introduced refs. 1802, 1803, 1804. The ref. 1804 acquired the nickname *Scheherazade*, after a female storyteller in the classic Persian collection of tales, *One Thousand and One Nights*. Platinum with a diamond bezel, it proved very popular, remaining in production for 20 years.

Ref. 1803 in pink gold was available with a unique tapisserie guilloche dial and acquired the nicknamed *Aladdin's Rose.* Phillips sold a well-documented example in 2015 which was made in 1974 and first sold in Damascus, Syria.

Throughout their production, these dials maintained consistent typography (font style and size) on the dials, day and date wheels. They were eventually retired in the early 1980s but the Arabic script day and date wheels remained available as an option which could be swapped-in by a authorized dealer.

CONDITION

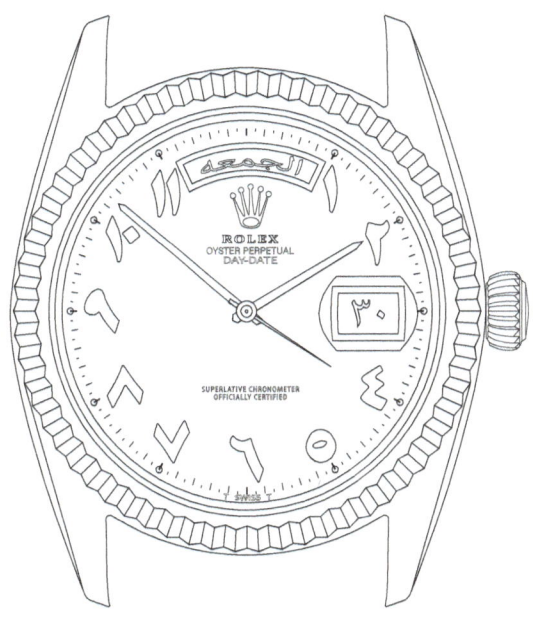

Later versions were ordered by Khimji Ramdas, an Authorized Dealer in Oman. These Rolex OEM examples have unique engravings on the inside of the caseback, which feature the case serial number and the name of the Jeweler.

Crests for other Gulf nations were applied by local dealers, rather than by Rolex at their factory.

Although less desirable, they are collectable as are other special logo-dials. Logo-dials feature all manner of corporate brands and were often awarded as long service or special recognition gifts.

In 2016 Rolex reintroduced a platinum Day-Date 40 with a dial featuring full Arabic script. The ref. M228206-0025 has a pale blue dial and contrasting dark blue hands and Arabic script. Curiously, the typography appears to be the same as the original versions. Distribution is limited to ADs in Kuwait, Qatar, Saudi Arabia, and the territories of the United Arab Emirates.

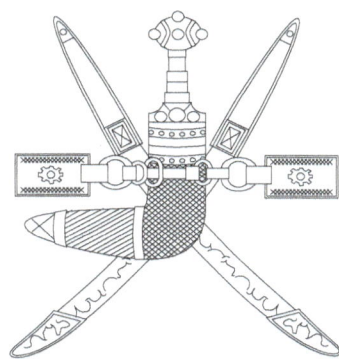

National emblem of the Sultanate of Oman, typically printed in red on the lower half of a dial.

ARAB CREST DIALS

A subgenre of Arab dials features crests (emblems & insignia) of various Gulf States. These are usually printed onto the surface of the dial but modern decals are often seen too.

The very first examples are thought to be special orders from the Sultan of Oman, Qaboos Al-Said. These were first ordered through Aspreys of Bond Street in London.

Submariner bearing the crest of the United Arab Emirates (UAE) for armed forces.

43

Dial Refinishing

Until about the 1980s, it was common practice during an independent service to refresh a dial with new paint or lacquer. Official Rolex Service Centers now replace them entirely at the owners epense.

The practice of refreshing dials often extended to reluming hands and dial furniture (hour and minute markers). This was done by hand with results ranging from awful to convincing.

Refinished Oysterdate ref. 6518 (Mid Size)

Like a refinished case, a refinished or relumed dial is viewed as undesirable. These are no longer considered original, despite often being quite attractive.

Advances in technology can now produce results so convincing as to be indistinguishable from the original, complete with faux aging.

The process of refinishing begins with stripping a dial down to the bare metal plate. The dial is soaked in a solvent to remove all traces of paint and lacquer. Dial furniture, such as applied indexes and the coronet, should also be removed during this process, though this step is sometimes skipped for fear of damaging parts during removal and reattachment.

The clean base plate is then repainted and reprinted. Ideally, this will be done before reapplying dial furniture. If not, you may see paint run up on the sides of the applied hour markers. This is a telling indication of a refinish.

Artfully refinished dials can be beautiful. This 65-year-old example was faithfully returned to what it would have looked like when sold in 1953. There was no attempt to make it look faux-vintage. Paint appears to run onto the hour indexes, as they were not removed due to a risk of damage to the dial plate and the markers.

Refinishing is sometimes confused with *redialing*. A redial is replacing a dial entirely with say, a service dial, or a naturally more attractive one from a donor watch.

A vintage refinish is considered more acceptable than a modern relume, but both are viewed negatively by collectors and will detract from the price and value.

The same rule of thumb applies to authentic Rolex service dials - less desirable but acceptable.

A modern refinish that attempts to recreate faux-patina is highly frowned upon.

Collectors are typically on the lookout for dials that have been refinished or otherwise restored. They should also be on the lookout for dials that have been artificially distressed.

A dial can be literally baked in an oven to increase or enhance the appearance of patina. Many Daytona ref. 16520 *Patrizzi dials* have been subjected to this controversial practice. Only serious expert collectors should dabble in this reference.

Dial Materials

Many collectors are surprised by the sheer variety of materials used to make dials. Modern collections are more conservative with the use of exotic materials. Mother of pearl and meteorite dials are still in use on the high-end, precious metal product lines like the Pearlmaster, Daytona, and Day-Date.

The exotic dial materials listed below are known to be correct for vintage Rolex and appeared predominantly on Datejust, Day-Date, and Cellini models.

Collectors should be wary of brightly colored dials as most are aftermarket refinishes or outright counterfeits.

Blue Coral	Rose Jasper
Pink Coral	Malachite
Yellow Coral	Meteorite
Ferrite	Nacre (MOP)
Lapis Lazuli	Obsidian
Sodalite	Onyx
Tigers Eye	Opal
Sugilite	Rubellite
Agate	Fossil
Ammonite	Grossular
Aventurine	Howlite (Marble)
Azurite	Green Jade
Bloodstone	Lavender Jade
Cacholong	Green Jadeite
Carnelian	Blue Jadeite
Chrysoprase	Green Jasper

Hands

Over the years, Rolex has used several watch hand styles from various suppliers (including Universal, Fiedler, and Virex). Knowing the appropriate style for a period and collection goes a long way towards determining authenticity and originality.

Newcomers often overlook the condition and correctness of hands when assesing a vintage Rolex. They may also dismiss a correct watch with unusual or rare hands. A few important rules of thumb to consider:

- The style of hands should complement the dial indices and coronet. For example, large, rectangular, baton style hour markers typical of the 1980s should have similarly-styled large baton hands. Diamond or arrow-shaped hour markers characteristic of the 1950s would be paired with dauphine or alpha-style hands.

- The color and material of hands should match the dial furniture, case, and bezel. You would not expect to see gold colored hands on an otherwise silver colored watch (whether it be white gold, patinum or stainless steel).

- The state of corrosion should reflect that of the dial. Solid gold hands may tarnish but will not corrode. Unlike the base metal beneath gold plate. A solid gold watch would not have electroplated hands.

Not all hands were lumed; even hands of similar style. For example, Alpha hands may or may not contain a lume strip, but they should still match the dial. If they have no lume, there should be no lume dots, strips or fills on the dial.

Radium and tritium lume on hands will corrode and patina. It is uncommon for this to be an exact match to the patina color of lume on the hour markers. Lume for the dial and hands would have been applied at different stages of production and would have come from different batches of material. It is the exception rather than the rule that they age perfectly evenly.

Dress watches like Cellini generally were not lumed, but there are a few exceptions.

Hands are made from a material that reflects the dial hour markers, which themselves complement the rest of the case and bezel. Hands may be electroplated, solid gold or steel. They can be finished in brightly-colored paint or heat treated to become blued steel (seen on early seconds hands).

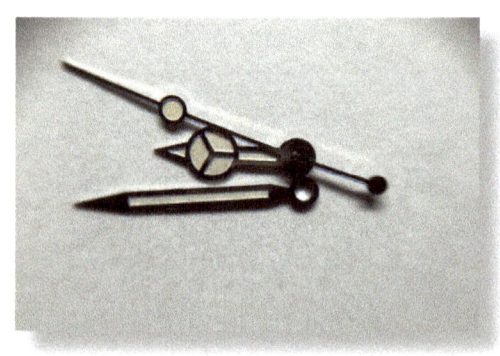

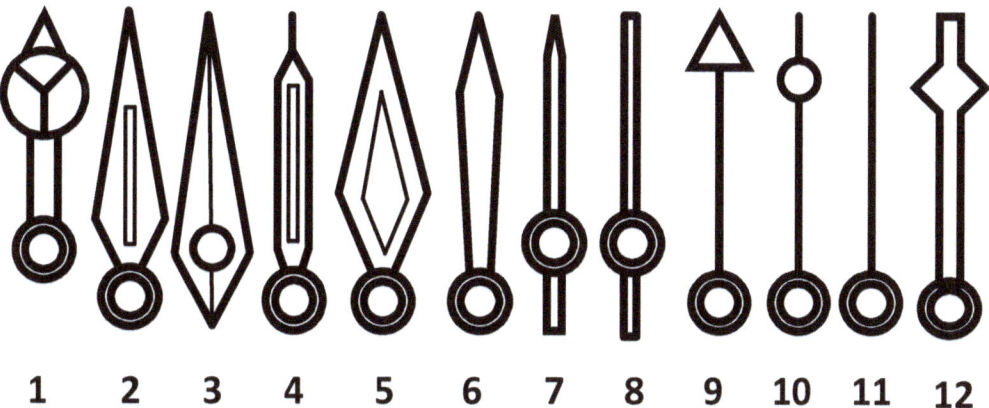

1. The formal name for *Cathedral* or Mercedes style hands is Squelette. They appeared on Rolex professional tool watches and were designed to hold more lume material. They are used only as hour hands. Early versions are flat with later versions being slightly curved.

2. Alpha hands have a broad base and narrow stem to attach to the mounting post at the center of the dial. The style is used for both hour and minute hands and they often have a tritium lume strip. This style is typical of the 1940s to mid-1960s and seen on Bubblebacks, Datejust, Oysterdate, the later Oyster Date, and Oyster Perpetual.

3. Dauphine hands are often confused with Alpha-style hands. They are used for both hours and minutes and are very traditional-looking, triangular shaped and faceted. They usually appear on Bubblebacks, Oyster Dates and Datejusts.

4. Syringe hands occasionally appear on antique Rolex pocket watches and early Bubblebacks. They are uncommon and usually have lost any radium lume material they may have held.

5. Plongeur Hands are high visibility hour hands for diving watches. They are broad and diamond-shaped appearing on military issue Submariners only. The accompanying minute hand may be a Pencil or Batten style.

6. Sword hands resemble a sword blade. They taper from the center mounting post and get progressively broader before narrowing to a sword tip. They may feature a lume panel of radium and are seen on Bubblebacks from the 1930s and 1940s.

7. Pencil hands are a cross between the Batten style and the Sword style. They have a straight body and narrow distinctly at the tip resembling a pencil. They were used widely in the 1960s and 1970s.

8. Broad Batten hands are formally called *Parformes*. They are straight, elongated and somewhat minimalist. They may or may not feature a lume strip and were used commonly on dress watches.

9. Arrow hands have a triangular arrow pointer on the end of a straight hand and are used for 24-hour GMT functions only. Variations can be seen in the size and color of the triangular tip. The Explorer II 1655 has a unique and unusual variation on this and described later in this guide.

10. Lollipop hands are used for second hands. They are used on professional tool watches only. The lollipop is filled with tritium or luminova for later watches. The Milgauss has a unique lightning bolt seconds hand not depicted here.

11. Narrow Batten hands are second hands which are typically seen on classic and dress watches from Bubblebacks to modern Datejusts. These are paired with Broad Batten hands.

12. Snowflake hands are only used on Tudor Submariners and feature a unique square on the end of the hour hand only.

Twinlock in Steel or Two-Tone, Gold and Platinum

Triplock in Steel or Two-Tone, Gold and Platinum

Winding Crowns

Rolex has patented several crown designs. Most were supplied by Boninchi SA which was eventually acquired by Rolex in 2001.

A wider variety of styles were used in the antique genre than during the vintage and classic genres. Later watches use one of only two crown styles. It is common to see aftermarket crowns or incorrect crowns on vintage Rolex watches. This obviously affects correctness and value.

The *basic crown* style is used on Cellini and dress watches. This is a simple pull-out style, typically with a raised coronet on the exterior surface. An onion-style is often seen on the antique models with cushion cases.

A screw-down crown is used on Oyster cases, with one exception. The non-screw-down Super Oyster crown was advertised as water resistant and was used on early Oyster references (such as the Oyster Precision and Oysterdate) in the 1950s. These are increasingly rare, and many were replaced during servicing. Early screw-down crowns may feature a Swiss cross and the word Brevet, meaning Patented.

There are two varieties of screw-down crown: *Twinlock* and *Triplock*.

The Twinlock is recognized by either no marking beneath the coronet or a single line (bar). These are used on classic crossover watches like the Datejust and Oyster Date, etc. Early versions may feature the word *Brevet* (meaning Patented) and a Swiss cross.

The Triplock has three small raised dots below the coronet. These crowns are used on Professional models like the Daytona, Submariner, Sea-Dweller, GMT-Master, etc. The size and position of the dots indicate the material of the Oyster case they should be paired with. So a platinum case should not be paired with a steel crown.

Crystals

Rolex crystals are either acrylic or synthetic sapphire. Acrylic crystals without the Cyclops date magnifier are called *Tropic* crystals.

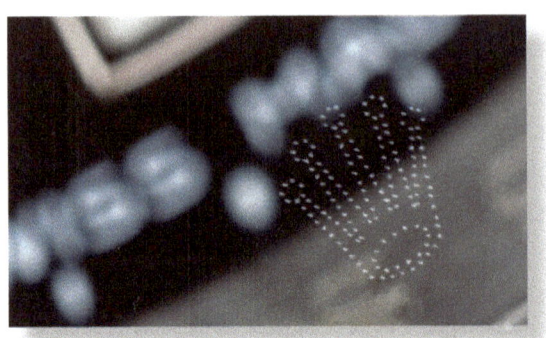

Tropic crystals are available in three shapes - domed, flat, and a high profile Top Hat (thick). These appear most commonly on the Professional watches.

Crystals are consumable components, intended to be replaced at service intervals. An original crystal is somewhat meaningless and doesn't command any collector premium (except for pieces claiming to be NOS).

Acrylic crystals can be polished, unlike sapphire. Collectors use a variety of techniques and materials to buff out scratches and scuffs. Two of the most popular things used as polish are toothpaste and Polywatch.

Sapphire crystals on modern classic models may feature a laser etched coronet (LEC) at the 6 o'clock position. This is an anti-counterfeiting measure and will require a loupe or excellent eyesight and lighting to see. LECs were introduced in 2001 and had spread throughout Rolex's range by 2003, with the notable exception of the Milgauss Anniversary GV Edition. This unique green-tinted crystal (Glace Verte) does not have a LEC.

6 ANTIQUE & POCKET WATCHES

"I'm very proud of my gold pocket watch. My grandfather, on his deathbed, sold me this watch."
- Woody Allen

During the earliest years, Rolex experimented with brand names liberally and interchangeably. Names like Prince and Imperial were mixed and matched across watches and pocket watches. Many of these early watches do not have case reference numbers or movement serial numbers.

The First World War (1914 to 1918) saw Rolex introduce trench watches. These were the first attempt by Rolex at a robust, tool-like, wrist-worn timepiece. They retained many design elements of the pocket watches they were sold alongside, including hinged case covers.

Similarities included brittle but highly visible enamel dials often with the 12 printed in red. This helped the wearer adjust to having their timepiece on their wrist, where the up position may appear oriented counterclockwise 90 degrees.

In the chaotic, low light of trench warfare, these small usability details were crucial.

Today's market for Rolex trench watches is strong, but the condition of the enamel dials is highly variable. Seldom worn by collectors, the top condition examples are highly prized at auction and carefully stored away as investments and heirlooms.

Other curious watches include stopwatches, pendant watches, and portfolio watches. Many of the folding-style timepieces were made in the 1930s and 1940s and come to be called purse watches.

very exclusive luxury pocket and pendant watches, but they were soon eclipsed by the success of their wrist watches.

We associate Rolex pocket watches with the war-era antique period, but Rolex continued making contemporary pendant pocket watches into the 1980s. These precious metal curiosities are not especially collectible but undoubtedly rare and usual. They command only a modest price premium over their base metal and gemstone value.

Pocket watches were the first products from Rolex and dominated sales until the start of WWII. Catalogs from the 1930s show open-face, semi- and full hunter style pocket watch cases. They were made in a variety of materials from rolled gold and silver to solid 18K gold. In 1932 Rolex launched the Rolex Prince Imperial pocket watch in 18K gold. It turned out to be one of the most accurate watches made by Rolex and was sold alongside the Prince wristwatch. Rolex continued to make some

Antique Rolex pocket watches are more typical of the 1910s and 1920s, and appear in solid yellow or rose gold. A typical example would be the 44mm ref. 1528 with a pop-open case back. By the 1930s Rolex had retreated from this line of business focusing on wristlets for both men and women.

Pocket & Folio Reference Summary

Name	Ref.	Cal.	Case	Description
Prince Imperial	1645	Chronometer	YG	Pocketwatch
Cellini	3717		YGWG	Round, pocketwatch
Cellini	3727		YGWG	Rectangular, pocketwatch
Cellini	3729		YGWG	Oval, pocketwatch
Cellini	3790		WG	Round, pocketwatch
Cellini	3791		WG	Rectangular, pocketwatch
Cellini	3799		WG	Oval, pocketwatch
Sporting Prince	1561	Extra Prima	SS	Purse Watch
Prince Imperial	1585		SS	Travel Watch
Sporting Prince	1599		YG	Purse Watch
Sporting Prince	1599		YG	Purse Watch

Rolex Prince

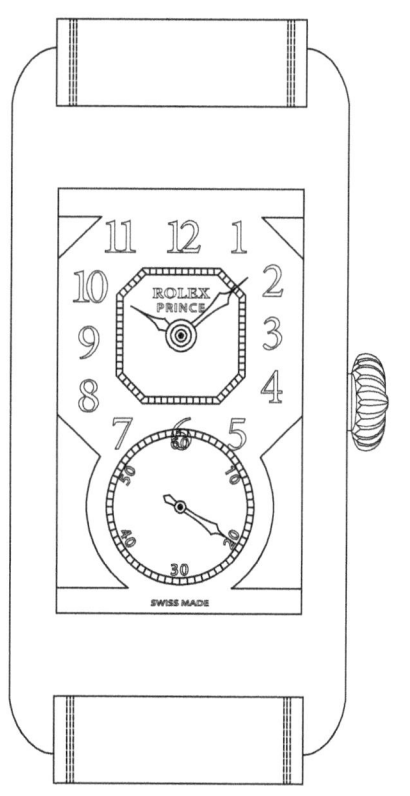

When launched in 1928, The Prince received rave reviews declaring it avant-garde and a la mode. Customers loved it. The rectangular case had a large top dial for the hours and the minutes and a lower subdial for the seconds. Both the dial text and case embellishments were distinctly art deco. Designed as a luxury dress watch, it was an immediate hit, and the Prince and its derivatives remained in production for nearly three decades.

The Rolex Prince models were the first Rolex watches made in large quantities to achieve Chronometer Certification. It is now recognized as the commercial breakthrough that put Rolex on the map.

The subdial with its jumping seconds' indicator became popular with doctors as a convenient aid in measuring a patient's pulse rate. The style subsequently came to be known as The Doctor's Watch.

The Prince was offered in two case style - a more rectangular Classic style (ref. 1343) and a more round design known as Brancard style (ref. 971).

Several materials were used to manufacture Princes including yellow gold, sterling silver, rose gold, platinum, two-tone combinations and later, steel. Soon after introduction, the manual-wound movement was replaced by an automatic one.

In 1935, Rolex launched the Railway Prince (ref. 1527). The design was inspired by locomotives and today acts as a reminder of the luxury of European rail travel in the 1930s.

The Railway Prince introduced a unique Jumping Hours complication; a genuinely new and futuristic design. The upper dial had only a minute hand and the hours could be read as numbers (1-12) through a window at the 12 o'clock position. Years later this provided the inspiration for the Rolex Datejust.

Of the Rolex Prince series, the last was the Super Precision Aerodynamic. This had one big dial for the hour, minute and second hands.

Sometime during the late 1940s production of the Rolex Prince came to an end and the line was quietly retired.

Rolex Princesse & Rolex Queen

In 1930, Rolex launched the Rolex Princesse, a Ladies version of the Prince line.

These were simple two-handed affairs offered in rectangular cases that were similar to but smaller than the Prince.

The Princesse was followed in 1932 by the Rolex Queen collection (refs. 503, 504 and 505).

These three different rectangular case designs were offered in 9k, 18k or stainless steel. The market for these is small, attracting little collector interest.

Unlike the larger Prince models, they are largely neglected, and examples can be found in surprisingly original and unrestored condition.

Today, the Princess brand is a Tudor asset.

Special Edition Prince

Several special editions of the Rolex Prince were made over the decades. The first was in 1935 when Rolex offered a special limited-edition Rolex Jubilee Prince. This short run of (a claimed) 500 units celebrated the Silver Jubilee of King George V.

The Sporting Prince was another limited edition to test the market. It was an unusual pocket watch designed to be used during athletic activities. The movement had a spring mechanism with which the dial could pop up from the case.

A well-known special edition Prince was the Quarter Century Club. These were made for a Canadian retailer to be gifted to employees who had achieved 25 years of service.

These watches had the 12 letters of 1/4 Century Club printed around the dial instead of the hour or minute markers.

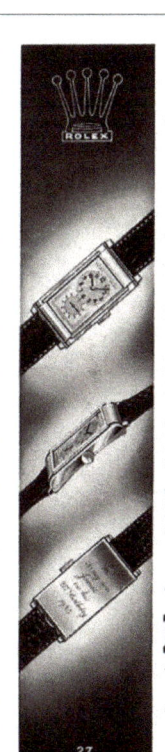

Prince & Princess Reference Summary

Name	Ref.	Cal.	Size	Case	Description
Chameleon	5003		Ladies	YG	Round
Elegant	2948		Full Size	YG	Round
Elegant	3004		Full Size	SS	Round
Elegant	3081		Full Size	SSYG	Round
Elegant	3167		Full Size	YG	Round
Orchid	9809		Ladies	WG	Round
Prince Brancard	971		Full Size		Rectangular
Prince Brancard	1490		Full Size		Rectangular
Prince Brancard	1491		Full Size		Rectangular
Prince Brandard	5068		Full Size		Rectangular
Prince Classic	1541		Full Size		Rectangular
Prince Imperial	1645	Chronometer	Full Size	YG	Pocketwatch
Prince Imperial	1585		Full Size	SS	Travel Watch
Prince Railway	1527		Full Size		Rectangular
Prince Railway	4376		Full Size		Rectangular
Prince Railway	1862	Extra Prima		SS	Rectangular
Princess	1772		Ladies	YG	Rectangular
Princess	2405		Ladies	SSYG	Rectangular
Princess	5877		Ladies	YG	Rectangular
Princess Egyptienne	1466		Ladies	WG	Rectangular
Queen	503		Ladies		
Queen	504		Ladies		
Queen	505		Ladies		
Sporting Prince	1561	Extra Prima	Full Size	SS	Purse Watch
Sporting Prince	1599		Full Size	YG	Purse Watch
Sporting Prince	1599		Full Size	YG	Purse Watch
The Golden King	9522	Precision	Full Size	YG	Round
The Golden King	9919	Precision	Full Size	YG	Round

Other Antique Wristlet References

Ref.	Cal. Grade	Size	Case	Description
5003		Ladies	YG	Round
2940		Full-Size	SS	Round
2948		Full-Size	YG	Round
3004		Full-Size	SS	Round
3081		Full-Size	SSYG	Round
3167		Full-Size	YG	Round
9809		Ladies	WG	Round
2565	Ultra Prima	Boys-Size	SS	Round
2007		Boys-Size	YG	Cushion
4325		Full Size	YG	Round
4364		Full Size	YG	Round
8029	Precision	Full-Size	SS	Round
9829	Precision	Full-Size	SS	Round
9022		Full-Size	SS	Round
9083		Full-Size	SS	Round
9106		Full-Size	YG	Round
2361	Chronometer	Ladies	YG	Rectangular
4645	Perpetual	Ladies	YG	Square
4374	Precision	Ladies	YG	Round
4496	Precision	Ladies	RG	Round
4595	Precision	Ladies	RG	Rectangular
8731	Precision	Ladies	WG	Round
8788	Precision	Ladies	YG	Round
8790	Precision	Ladies	RG	Square
8126	Super Precision	Ladies	RG	Rectangular
64		Ladies	WG	Rectangular
406		Ladies	RG	Tonneau
1383		Ladies	YG	Rectangular
1394		Ladies	Silver	Cushion
1401		Ladies	WG	Square
1966		Ladies	SS	Tonneau
2164		Ladies	WG	Round
2175		Ladies	YG	Square

Ref.	Cal. Grade	Size	Case	Description
2611		Ladies	YG	Round
2694		Ladies	RG	Rectangular
3073		Ladies	YG	Square
3118		Ladies	YG	Octagonal
3251		Ladies	YG	Round
3562		Ladies	SS	Square
3771		Ladies	YG	Rectangular
3911		Ladies	RG	Square
4184		Ladies	SSYG	Rectangular
4211		Ladies	YG	Square
4289		Ladies	YG	Rectangular
4291		Ladies	YG	Square
4294		Ladies	YG	Square
4334		Ladies	RG	Hunter
4381		Ladies	YG	Square
4391		Ladies	YG	Square
4401		Ladies	YG	Square
4405		Ladies	YG	Square
4454		Ladies	YG	Square
4457		Ladies	YG	Round
4473		Ladies	YG	Rectangular
4484		Ladies	YG	Hunter
4487		Ladies	YG	Round
4491		Ladies	RG	Round
4492		Ladies	YG	Round
4493		Ladies	YG	Square
4494		Ladies	YG	Square
4495		Ladies	YG	Square
4556		Ladies	SS	Round
4615		Ladies	RG	
4725		Ladies	YG	Round
4830		Ladies	SS	Rec
5088		Ladies	SS	Rectangular
8320		Ladies	RG	Square

Ref.	Cal. Grade	Size	Case	Description
8522		Ladies	RG	Square
8784		Ladies	RG	
9242		Ladies	RG	Square
9250		Ladies	RG	Rectangular
9638		Ladies	RG	Square
8858		Ladies	YG	Round
4663	Perpetual	Mid-Size	RG	Square
2524		Mid-Size	SS	Round
3078		Mid-Size	SS	Round
4579		Mid-Size	RG	Round
1027	Chronometer		RG	Round
3029	Chronometer		RG	Round
3255	Chronometer		YG	Square
3260	Chronometer		YG	Square
3689	Chronometer		YG	Square
3737	Chronometer		YG	Square
3762	Chronometer		YG	Round
3783	Chronometer		RG	Round
3894	Chronometer		YG	Square
4051	Chronometer		SS	Round
4117	Chronometer		RG	Round
4118	Chronometer		RG	Round
4134	Chronometer		RG	Round
4409	Chronometer		RG	Round
4411	Chronometer		YG	Round
4497	Chronometer		YG	Rectangular
4533	Chronometer		YG	Rectangular
4643	Chronometer		YG	Square
4816	Chronometer		YG	Round
4845	Chronometer		YG	Round
6512	Chronometer		YG	Round
8569	Chronometer		YG	Round
8651	Chronometer		YG	Round
8940	Chronometer		YG	Round

Ref.	Cal. Grade	Size	Case	Description
8952	Chronometer		YG	Round
9081	Chronometer		YG	Round
9164	Chronometer		YG	Round
9347	Chronometer		YG	Rectangular
1696	Extra Prima		WG	Rectangular
1852	Extra Prima		YG	Rectangular
1862	Extra Prima		SS	Rectangular
1618	Perpetual		GF	Round
3059	Precision		RG	Rectangular
3140	Precision		YG	Rectangular
3667	Precision		YG	Round
3861	Precision		SS	Rectangular
4513	Precision		SS	Rectangular
9659	Precision		YG	Round
912	Prima		YG	Square
1122	Prima		Silver	Round
3428	Prima		YG	Cushion
556	Ultra Prima		YG	Rectangular
1880	Ultra Prima		SSYG	Rectangular
2537	Ultra Prima		YG	Rectangular
2582	Ultra Prima		SSYG	Round
13			YG	Rectangular
162			YG	Cushion
478			SS	Rectangular
514			YG	Rounded
757			YG	Rectangular
758			YG	Rectangular
860			YG	Rectangular
870			YGWG	Rectangular
1328			YG	Rectangular
1370			Silver	Tonneau
1832			YG	Rectangular
1897			SS	Rectangular
1918			WG	Rectangular

Ref.	Cal. Grade	Size	Case	Description
1936			YG	Rectangular
1992			SS	Rectangular
2151			SSYG	Rectangular
2356			YG	Rectangular
2372			YG	Rectangular
2536			YG	Rectangular
2568			SS	Round
2734			SS	Round
2886			SS	Rectangular
3003			SSRG	Round
3028			RG	Round
3038			YG	Round
3265			SS	Round
3287			RG	Square
3456			YG	Rectangular
3571			SS	Round
3573			YG	Round
3684			SSYG	Square
3754			YG	Round
3777			YG	Rectangular
3782			RG	Round
3861			YG	Rectangular
3923			YG	Round
4029			YG	Rectangular
4100			YG/WG	Horseshoe
4101			YG	Horseshoe
4102			WG	Horseshoe
4107			SS/RG	Round
4108			YG	Rectangular
4119			YG	Round
4326			SS	Round
4330			YG	Rectangular
4366			SS	Square
4417			SS	Round
4446			RG	Round

Ref.	Cal. Grade	Size	Case	Description
4471			YG	Square
4542			SS	Round
4560			SS	Round
4612			WG	Oval
4613			WG	Oval
7000			SSYG	Square
7008			YG	Round, Canadian Market
7011			YG	Round, Canadian Market
7038			YG	Round, Canadian Market
7051			YG	Square
8094			YG	Square
8382			RG	Round
8612			RG	Square
9576			YG	Round
9578			YG	Square
9665			YG	Round
9720			WG	Square
9780			YG	Round
9798			WG	Round
9878			RG	Round

Antique Moon Phase & Chronographs

War-era Rolex chronographs are not well documented. During this time, there was little media advertising of luxury goods; and Rolex catalogs, and print advertisements are scarce.

Of those printed, very fewer survive. This lack of archival history makes verification and authentication of these early watches very difficult. Counterfeiters have taken full advantage of the opportuniyt this presents.

Rolex made heavy use of the same Valjoux movements as other chronograph makers of the time. These watchmakers included Longines, Heuer, and Breitling; each going to varying lengths to customize their Valjoux movements. This practice is known as *finishing*.

Rolex finished their movements by signing the balance cock and the train gear bridge. They also went to considerable effort to apply satin finishes and bevels to individual parts.

Finishing styles evolved over time, and each manufacturer favored different techniques. It takes an expert to identify Rolex finishing from different decades. Only a few of these experts exist, and they commonly work for the premium auction houses (if not Rolex itself).

Nearly all antique Rolex chronographs in collections today have at least some parts that were not made by Rolex. This makes the question of authenticity, originality, and correctness moot. Their value lies in the visual appeal of the dial and running order.

Dato-Compax Chronographs

A class of hand-wound chronographs produced between the 1940s and 1960s was known as the Dato-Compax. These have acquired the nickname, Jean Claude Killy.

Jean Claude Killy was a World Champion skier, who dominated the downhill slalom and giant slalom events in the 1960s. He also enjoyed a career as a race car driver and screen actor. He became a Rolex brand ambassador in the 1970s and went on to join the Rolex board of directors.

Five references bare the nickname Jean Claude Killy - refs. 4768, 4767, 5036, 6036 and 6236. Strangely, Rolex produced these references a decade or more before his skiing achievements.

The name Dato-Compax consists of two intricate complications. The date (Dato) and a chronograph (Compax). The term, Compax, was first used by Universal and Zenith around 1936. It referred to the number of complications of a movement. Later it came to refer to the arrangement of the triple sub dials.

The ref. 4768 was the shortest lived of the Killy Chronographs. Experts claim Rolex made only 220 units. It is the only Data-Compax without an Oyster case and featured a snap-on case back. The dial features only the text, *Rolex Chronographe*.

In 1947 Rolex replaced it with ref. 4767. This was a significant upgrade with an Oyster case and screw-down crown. It now had the dial text, "Oyster Chronographe." This is the first triple calendar chronograph in an Oyster case. The ref. 4767 lasted only a year.

It was replaced with ref. 5036, in 1948 which ran until 1951. The ref. 6036 replaced it a few years later around 1955. In the late 1950s the ref. 6236 arrived. It was to be the final Dato-Compax. It had a larger bezel reminiscent of today's three-piece case construction.

Jean Claude Killy, 1968
Triple Olympic Gold Medalist (Center)

The Dato-Compax arrived on the market shortly after the end of WWII. Rolex offered them in stainless steel, yellow gold and rose gold. The austere market conditions meant demand was soft. Sales were insufficient to sustain the high production costs of such a complicated watch.

These are still the most complicated watches ever produced by Rolex. The small production volume means they are scarce. When they come to auction, they attract considerable attention and command headline prices.

Dato-Compax Reference Summary

Ref.	Cal.	Dept Rating	Years	Case	Description
4767	V72	50m	1947 - 1948	SS	Twin-pusher, triple register, Oyster case, triple calendar
4768	V72		1947 - 1948	SS	Twin-pusher, triple register, triple calendar
4769	V72		1947 - 1948	YG	Twin-pusher, triple register, triple calendar
5034	720		1948 - 1951		
5036	720		1948 - 1951	YG	Twin-pusher, triple register, triple calendar
6036	72		1951 - 1955	SS	Twin-pusher, triple register, triple calendar
6234	72	50m	1955 - 1961	SS	Twin-pusher, triple register, Oyster case, screw down crown Tachymeter and telemeter on dial.
6236	72C		1958 - 1962	SS	

Centergraph & Zerograph Chronographs

Name	Ref.	Cal.
Zerographe / Centregraph	3346	10 ligne Hunter
Zerographe / Centregraph	3462	10 ligne Hunter

These two references (3346, 3462) were the first Oyster-cased, mono-pusher chronographs. They are 32mm in diameter and were the first of any chronograph to use the Rolex Oyster crown. They are also the first Rolex watches to feature a rotating bezel.

They were housed in a Bubbleback case and were an entirely in-house chronograph, using a 10 ligne Hunter movement, which was retrofitted with a fly-back chronograph complication. This was achieved by adding only ten additional parts to a conventional hunter movement plus a protruding case back to accommodate them.

Launched in the mid-1930s, they were made in small numbers and for only a few years. Little is known about them, since only a few have surfaced at auction (Phillips and Christie's) with little to no documentation.

At launch, the names Zerograph and Centergraph were used interchangeably on both references. As production settled, Zerograph was applied to ref. 3346 and Centergraph to ref. 3462.

The Zerograph (3346) has a rotating steel bezel used to measure elapsed minutes. A rotating bezel did not appear again until the Turn-O-Graph 20 years later in 1953. The Centergraph (3462) has a fixed polished bezel with a tachymeter on the edge of the dial.

Dials appear in both black and white. Some examples had California style dials (half Roman and half Arabic numerals).

These watches are extremely rare. To this day, they are the only fly-back mono-pusher chronograph ever made by Rolex. Only one other reference (a Bubbleback) has used a California dial.

Ref. 6062 Moonphase Special Note

This triple calendar moonphase model, offered Day, Date, Month and phase of the moon. It debuted at the Basel Watch Fair in 1950. Early advertisements describe it as a Cosmograph, yet this text does not appear on any the dials.

An example of ref. 6062 sold at auction in May 2017 for CHF 5M setting a world record for the most expensive Rolex watch. This record-breaking example featured a Bao Dai dial. Named after Vietnam's last emperor, it features diamond numerals.

There are only three documented examples of ref. 6062 with diamond dials. The Bao Dai is the only known example with the diamonds positioned on even numerals. Unlike the others, it has a diamond at the 12 o'clock position displacing the Rolex coronet. The coronet appears below the diamond in place of the upper dial text. The traditional Rolex Oyster Perpetual text appears below the day and month apertures.

For the 1950s, ref. 6062 was a masculine 36mm. It used a 9 ligne movement and was the first with a water-resistant, non-screw-down, Super Oyster crown. These predated the screw-down Twinlock and were often replaced during service.

Sold alongside the Dato-Compax, ref. 6062 appeared in stainless steel, yellow gold, and pink gold. Dials were available in black and white with unusual combinations of hour indexes. One of the most eye-catching is the Stelline dial, Italian meaning Starlet dial. It had eight five-pointed gold stars as hour markers and a blue or black moonphase sub-dial. Other configurations include combinations of stars, arrowheads, and diamonds.

Ref. 8171 Padellone Moon Phase Special Note

In 1949 Rolex introduced the ref. 8171 which acquired the nickname *Padellone*, Italian for, *large frying pan*.

This was a triple date moon phase watch made in steel and yellow gold only. It had a snap back case, engraved with a serial number and coronet. Scholars believe Rolex made less than 1,000 examples of ref. 8171.

By standards of the time, it was a substantial 38mm. It had sharply curved lugs protruding from the sides of the case emphasizing the size.

The Padellone featured an unusual cal. A295 automatic movement, which was not widely used in other references.

The dial has twin apertures displaying the day and month. An integrated sub-dial shows both a fan-shaped moon phase and a running seconds hand. A fourth hand points to the date on an outer chapter ring.

This is a gorgeous and well balanced looking watch. At auction, it changes hands for serious money.

Antique Chronographs Reference Summary

Ref.	Cal.	Period	Description
8237			Triple calendar, moon phase, twin-pusher, twin register
6062	780	1949 - 1953	Triple calendar, moon phase, twin-pusher, triple register
8171	A295	1949 - 1952	Triple calendar, moon phase, perpetual chronometer
1074	1560		Mono-pusher, twin register, cushion case
1223	1560		Mono-pusher, twin register, cushion case, telemeter
2021	16 1/2		Twin-pusher, twin register, tachymeter and telemeter
2022	V23		Mono-pusher, twin register, cushion case
2023	V23		Mono-pusher, twin register, round case
2057			Mono-pusher, twin register, cushion case
2226			Mono-pusher, twin register, boys size round case
2303	10 1/2		Mono-pusher, twin register, boys size round case
2507			Mono-pusher, twin register, round case
2508	V23		Twin-pusher, twin register, tachymeter and telemeter
2705			Twin-pusher, twin register, tachymeter and telemeter
2737			Twin-pusher, twin register at 12 and 6
2811	72A		Twin-pusher (round or oval), twin register, boys size round case
2917			Twin-pusher (square), twin register
2918	V23		Twin-pusher, twin register
2920	V23		Twin-pusher, twin register
3036			Twin-pusher (round), twin register
3055	69		Twin-pusher (oval), twin register, Full and Boys size round case
3082	V72		Twin-pusher (oval), twin register
3085			
3181			Twin-pusher (round), engine-turned bezel
3233			Twin-pusher, twin register, tachymeter and telemeter
3330	V22		Twin-pusher, twin register, tachymeter
3333	V22		
3335	V22		Twin-pusher (square), triple register, pulsemeter
3481			Twin-pusher (round) twin register, Mid size round case

Ref.	Cal.	Period	Description
3484			Twin-pusher, twin register
3525	12		Twin-pusher, twin register
3529	10 1/2		Twin-pusher, twin register, square case
3635			Twin-pusher, twin register
3642			Mono-pusher, twin register, Small round case
3668	13		Twin-pusher, twin register, engine turned bezel, screw down crown
3695			Twin-pusher, twin register
3735			Mono-pusher, twin register, enamel dial, hinged lugs and caseback
3827			Twin-pusher, triple register
3834	10		Twin-pusher, twin register, tachymeter and telemeter
3835			Twin-pusher, triple register, tachymeter and telemeter
3997			Twin-pusher, twin register
4048	V23		
4062	V23		Twin-pusher, twin register
4099			Twin-pusher, twin register
4100	13		Twin-pusher, twin register
4113	V55	1942 - 1942	Twin-pusher, twin register, split seconds, large case, Official Timer for Formula 1
4311			Twin-pusher, twin register
4313	V23		Twin-pusher, triple register
4332	V27		
4352			Twin-pusher (round), twin register
4500	V23		Twin-pusher, twin register, screw down crown
4537	V72		Twin-pusher, triple register
6032	72		Twin-pusher, twin register
6034	72		Twin-pusher, triple register, screw down crown
6232	72		Twin-pusher, twin register
6236	72B		Twin-pusher, triple register, triple calendar
6238	72B		Twin-pusher, triple register, polished bezel, screw down crown
6270	55		
7131	234		
7132	234		
7159	234		
7169	234		

Ref.	Cal.	Period	Description
8180	172		Twin-pusher, triple register, triple calendar
8206	69		Twin-pusher, twin register, square case
9162	V72	1954 -	Twin-pusher, triple register

7 PROFESSIONAL TOOLS

"First he wrought, and afterward he taught."
- Geoffrey Chaucer

In Rolex marketing terminology, these watches belong to the Professional Collection. Rolex adopted the name Professional for their collection of sport and tool watches around the year 2000.

The collector community however, still refers to them as Tool and Sport watches, and dislike the nomenclature for its similarity to Omega's Professional Collection (Speedmaster, Seamaster, & Railmaster).

While there are only eight model lines in the Professional collection, there are several versions within. Each of these has many small variations in seemingly insignificant details.

There are approximately 170 distinct references to consider since the Rolex tool watch was first introduced in 1952/3. This figure excludes semi-tool watches like the Turn-O-Graph and the Killy Chronographs, which are covered in other sections.

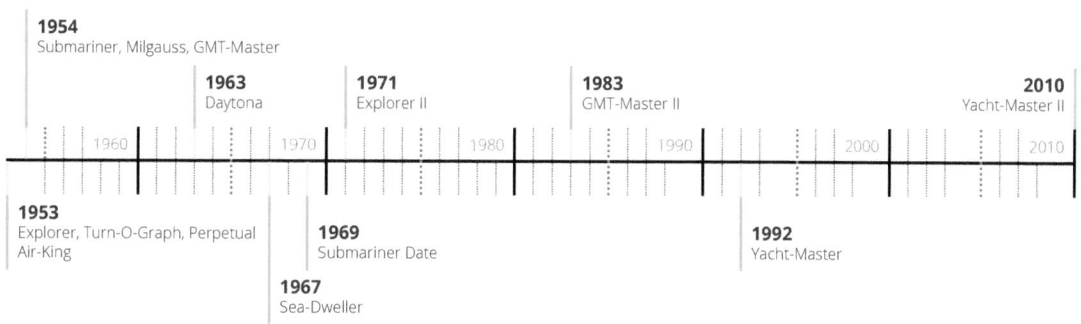

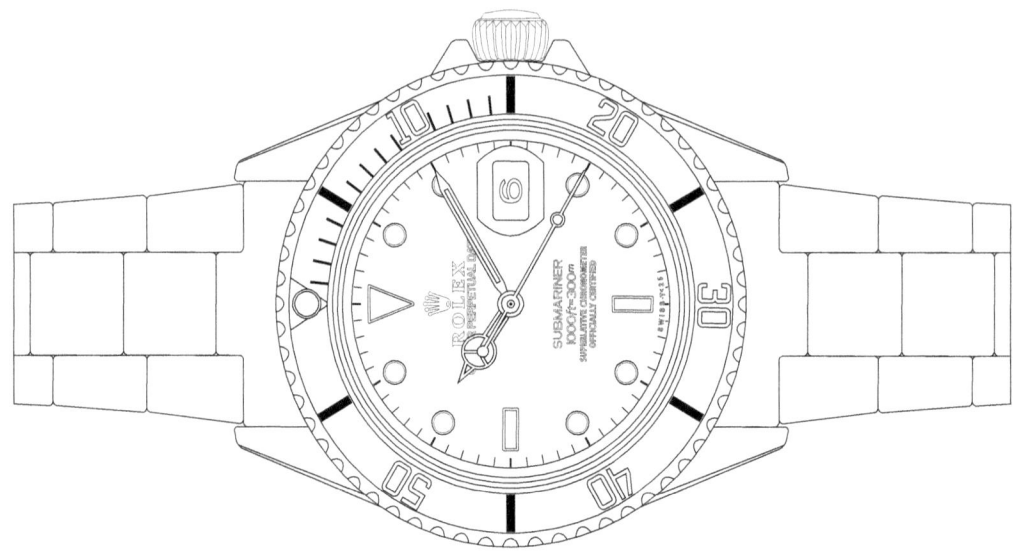

Oyster Perpetual Submariner

Launched in 1953 and presented at the Basel Watch Fair the following year, the Submariner was the first wristwatch to be waterproof to *100m / 330ft*. It was not, however, the first watch designed for diving. This honor goes to the Blancpain Fifty-Fathoms.

The Submariners rotating bezel is designed for measuring elapsed time underwater. While not an industry first it is elegantly executed by Rolex. It was this simple feature and not the water resistance which it shared with other collections, that marked the Submariner as a professional tool watch.

Arrival of the date feature in 1969 made the Submariner a mainstream watch appealing to a broader and more aspirational market. Purists still consider the no-date Submariners to be the most faithful to the original design concept and shun the date window and the magnifying cyclops lens.

The first Submariner references are the 6200, 6204 and 6205 which were small by today's standards (36mm).

These earliest examples are some of the hardest to validate and authenticate due to decades of wear, numerous owners and a large number of minor variations in their configurations.

Like vintage cars of the same era, most of these early references have needed extensive work to keep them running. This makes the widespread obsession with originality and authenticity subjective and dogmatic.

There are countless tiny variations in the four digit reference series of Submariners. Some had depth ratings printed meters-first for European markets while others had feet first.

Others had depth ratings printed in red, or with Explorer-style 3-6-9 hour markers. While the 3-6-9 style was intended for military orders, they made it to the commercial market and proved popular.

Other dial variations include gilt text, nipple indices, open and closed minute tracks, and gloss and matte lacquer finishes. Some had pencil-style hands, others had Plongeur style (only military orders).

Early bezels were friction fitted and bi-directional while later versions became clicking and unidirectional. Bezels were bi-directional until 1953 thanks to a patent owned by Blancpain for their Fifty Fathoms watch. Once the patent expired, the Submariner gained a unidirectional bezel beginning with the 55xx series.

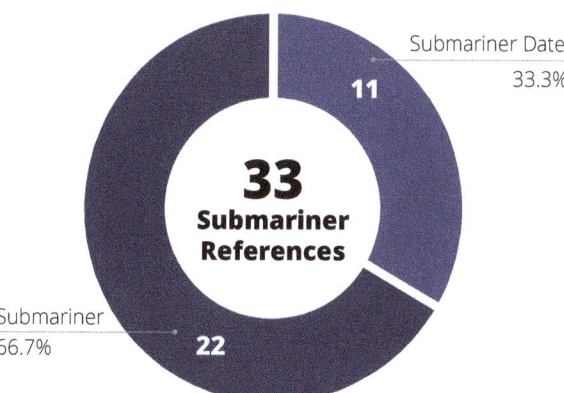

Submariner dial ref. 6204 with meters-first gilt dial and closed minute track

It's this sheer variety that makes Submariners so collectible. High demand and rising prices have encouraged unsavory practices, making it challenging to find an honest example.

Buying poor examples to restore is a costly, risky and lengthy proposition. These ill-advised projects of passion seldom make economic sense.

If you're motivated to take one on, expect restoration costs to match the already astronomical acquisition cost (unless you're equipped to do the work yourself).

Modern Classic iterations of the no date Submariner such as the 14060 and 16610, continue to be popular for daily wear. The clean dial symmetry and contemporary features make these watches attractive, practical and collectible. Prices are softer than their four-digit predecessors like the ref. 5513 and 5512.

The only four-digit reference with a date complication is the ref. 1680. This is a complex and long-running reference with seven dial variations during its lifetime. Only the ref. 1680 and 16800 (matte dial variation) qualify as *vintage*. Use of the vintage label is controversial for any reference that followed the matte 16800.

Bezel inserts are an essential part of the value and price of any steel sport watch. This is especially true for the Submariner. Service replacement bezels are identified by their thin font printing. Bezels with a large and broad-print font are considered original and correct for the ref. 1680.

The lume pip in the triangular zero marker is prone to detaching and getting lost. Replacements can be bought but matching the tritium to the patina of the dial and hands can be difficult. Some collectors opt for a luminova pip that will glow brightly, while others will just leave the hole, believing it to be more honest.

Faded (ghost) bezels should be evaluated against the condition of the case, dial and hands i.e. an aged bezel should be paired with an equally old bezel pip, case, dial and hands. Buyers should be looking for all over even and consistent aging.

Given the price premium of a well-worn and faded bezel insert, unscrupulous dealers are known to artificially age bezels with bleach and high temperature (a practice known as baking a bezel). These artificially aged bezels are usually devoid of the scratches and marks you'd associate with extensive outdoor use.

Modern Classic Submariner Date
Ref. 16800, COSC cal 3035

Modern Classic Submariner
Ref. 14060, non-COSC cal 30000

Modern Classic Submariner Date
Ref. 16610, COSC cal 3135

Buyers and collectors should avoid watches with mismatched wear patterns, as these will be difficult to resell. A baked bezel is of less concern if you plan to wear the watch for years to come, adding your own patina. If the intention is to buy and hold, select a Submariner that appeals to you personally and (politely) negotiate a price on the factors described in this guide.

Across the 33 Submariner references, 14 different movements (or calibers) have been used since 1952. Caliber 3135 is the most common. With so many references and variations within references, I will make individual notes on only those examples I believe to be most interesting to most new collectors.

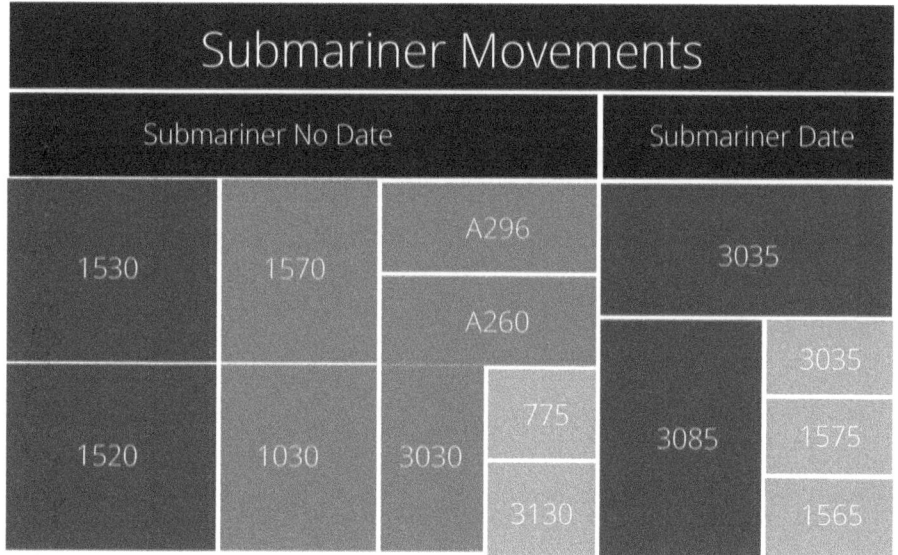

Submariners use 14 different calibers

Submariner Timeline

1954
ref.6204 Debut of the Submariner at the Basel Fair

1955
ref. 6538 Successor to 6204 Pre-Sub, with caliber 1030 movement.
ref. 6536 Successor of reference 6205 with big crown.
ref. 6536/1 Chronometer version of reference 6536 with caliber 1030.
ref. 6538 British Royal Navy choses the Submariner

1981
ref. 168000, 16610
The Submariner receives a unidirectional bezel so remaining diving time can only be shortened. Caliber 3085 is adopted.

1983
ref. 16613 The Submariner becomes available in "Rolesor", a two tone gold and steel

1962
ref. 5513 Updated crown guards and upgraded cal. 1530

2003
ref. 16610 LV
A green bezel is fitted to a 50th Anniversary Submariner which came to be known as the Kermit.

1963
ref. 5513 Updated with cal. 1520 introduced in the same year

1988
ref. 16610 Upgraded with caliber 3135

1979
ref. 16800 Submariner receives a sapphire crystal and water resistance is increased to 300 meters

1969
ref. 16618 Submariner available in 18k gold.

ref. 1680 Date window, plexi crystal with cyclops, red writing on the dial (till 1973) and cal. 1575.

2009
ref. 16613 LB
First Submariner fitted with a ceramic bezel, in rolesor (gold and stainless steel). Case lugs became fat and new bracelet added.

1959
ref. 5512 Crown guards, increased case diameter to 40mm from 36mm, "Superlative Chronometer, Officially Certified"
ref. 6538 "Superlative Chronometer, Officially Certified"

2010
ref. 16619
White gold Submariner with blue dial and ceramic bezel.
ref. 116610LN/LV
The LV is introduced with a green dial and green ceramic bezel.

1958
Font change on the bezel with 0 (zeroes) becoming square-ish
ref. 5510 Based on reference 6200 with caliber 1530 (1957)
ref. 5508 6536/1 with caliber 1530.

1956
A new design for the hands and the bezel gets 15 minute index markers.
ref. 6538/8 The 6538 receives the same case as reference 6200.
ref. 6536 A red triangle on the bezel to mark the zero position.

REF. 1680 RED SUBMARINER DATE

SPECIAL NOTES

The is one of the most desirable and collectible variations of the ref. 1680. These watches are known as Red Submariners due to the distinctive red dial text.

This is a complicated and expensive reference with many potential pitfalls. If you are new to vintage Rolex, it is inadvisable to take this reference on as your very first acquisition.

This hallmark red text was eventually replaced with white in later iterations of this reference. These are often referred to as, White 1680s.

The presence of a single line of red text commands a substantial price premium and an almost obsessive and rabid following. The text shape, ink texture and color, and overall character has been studied and debated in minute details.

Collectors continue to debate whether the ref.1680 is the most desirable vintage Submariner of all time, or just the most desirable featuring a date complication. Personal preference plays a large part in this debate.

It is common for white and red text dials to be swapped. Meaning that a red text dial may be found in a later case that is out of range of the expected serial numbers for Red Subs (or a white text dial may be found in a case which formerly belonged to a Red Sub).

Given the value of authentic Red Subs, collectors should assess the watch in microscopic detail and be aware of promiscuous dials. Also be prepared to encounter very high quality counterfeit dials in otherwise authentic watches.

Until a Red Sub can be examined in hand by an acknowledged Red Sub expert, a potential buyer should assume the watch is less than honest. In this case, obtain a commitment of 100% Authenticity from the seller and clarification of their return policy. Buyers will need time to have the watch appraised, and some recourse if undisclosed issues are identified.

Of the red Submariners, there are seven dial variants including a luminova service dial. All seven appear concurrently and overlapping during three years from the introduction in 1969 to 1972. The variations are minute and require good macro photos or a loupe to examine.

MK I Dial

These dials have a Meters-First depth rating and they appear in the serial range approximately 2.07M to 2.2M or roughly 1969 to 1970.

They use a thick, heavy font with closed 6's. Note the distinctive long curve of the letter f.

MK II Dial

These dials have a Meters-First depth rating. The serial range is approximately 2.2M to 2.45M or 1970.

They differ from the MK I by having a lighter, thinner font with open 6's. Note the sharper angular curve of the letter f and the alignment of the letter L of OFFICIALLY, beneath the letter E of SUPERLATIVE.

MK III Dial

This is the last of the dials with a Meters-First depth rating. Serial range is in the 2.2M to 2.45M range (1970) and overlaps with the MK II. It maintains the open 6s but with a thicker font. The red letting is over-printed on the white text below. Note the shorter, clipped top of the letter f.

MK IV Dial

This is the first red dial with a Feet-First depth rating. Serial numbers are in the range 2.45M to 3M, or 1970 to 1972.

Red letting is over-printed on the white text below. Note the distinctive open 6s of the depth rating which appear fuller, or bolder.

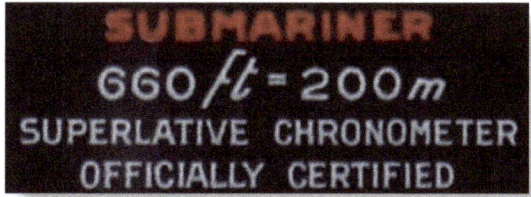

MK V Dial

The MK V dial as less pronounced but still open 6s. Serials are in the range 2M to 3M or 1970 to 1972. Red text is directly printed on the dial and not over-printed on the white text below. Note the flatter, almost box-shaped printing of the letter S.

MK VI Dial

The MK VI dial has closed 6's and a rounded fuller font. The S is notably more rounded than the MK V. These are seen in the 3M to the 4M serial range and were gone by 1975.

There is also a Red 1680 service dial that is identifiable with the SWISS marking at 6 o'clock indicating use of Luminova. These still glow.

Some dials of early ref. 1680 (Mark I, II & III) are prone to turning brown giving rise to the *Chocolate Submariner* moniker. Brown dials are a result of paint defects and highly desirable and collectible.

The red Submariner printing on Mark I, III and IV are known to be imperfect. It is not uncommon for white to appear around the lettering or through the red paint. These imperfections are recognized by the collector community and accepted as legitimate.

Casebacks from the range 2M to about 3.4M were stamped with a date code starting with II 69 (second quarter of 1969). This practice appears to end with II 72 in the 3M range. Watches from 1973 onward and Rolex service replacements, do not have a stamped date code on their case backs.

The movement used in the ref. 1680 is the caliber 1575 (the trailing 5 denoting the date complication). It is common for the auto winding rotor to be stamped 1570 as this part was interchangeable between the Submariner Date and the no-date Submariner.

This movement was also used in other less desirable and inexpensive references. Verifying that the movement is a cal.1575 doesn't mean it was the original one shipped from the factory. Only Rolex can match a case serial number to a movement serial number and confirm they left the factory together.

The ref.1680 has variation in the warranty papers it was sold with. The most desirable and valuable are punched papers. Handwritten or blank documents carry only a modest price premium.

Ref. 1680 White Submariner Date Special Notes

The white Submariner has not achieved the cult status or the prices of the red text predecessor. There are three acknowledged variations of the white dial ref.1680. All three are found in watches across the serial range.

MK I Dial

The white printed MK I dials are made by Lemrich. The back of the dial is stamped with a number with a 121 prefix. The L is directly below the coronet, and the = is below the A. The = appears aligned over the space between OFFICIALLY CERTIFIED on the bottom row of text.

MK II Dial

These white printed dials are made by Beyeler. The back of these dials had repeating text, Beyeler Geneve stamped across them. Note the letter L is shifted left below the coronet.

MK III Dial

These MK III dials are also made by Lemrich. The shifting of the L is more pronounced. The position of the = relative to the space between OFFICIALLY and CERTIFIED appears different from the MK I

 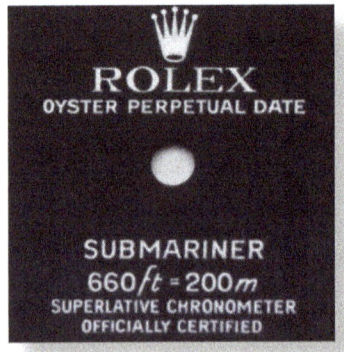 

White Submariner dials MK I, II & III

Ref. 5513 Submariner (No Date) Special Notes

The ref. 5513 was made from 1962 until 1990, one of the longest production runs of any Rolex. As a result, there are many good examples in circulation.

Like other long-running references, there were many minor variations as the model evolved. These included two different movements, the cal. 1530 and cal. 1520.

This reference has a strong James Bond 007 connection, which appeals to some collectors. George Lazenby wore a ref. 5513 with an Oyster bracelet in parts of *On Her Majesty's Secret Service*, as did Roger Moore in *Live and Let Die* and *The Man with the Golden Gun*.

The 5513 and 5512 were the first Submariners to receive the oversized 7mm crowns. These were to become standard issue on all subsequent Submariners.

The ref. 5513 appears with two-lines of text below the center point indicating neither of the movements offered (cal. 1530, 1520) were COSC certified, i.e. they were not chronometer-grade as determined by Controle Officiel Suisse des Chronomotres (COSC), or the Official Swiss Chronometer Testing Institute.

The ref. 5512, on the other hand, had four lines of text and *was* COSC certified. The 5512 features the *Superlative Chronometer, Officially Certified* (SCOC) text below the Submariner and depth rating. Production of the two references (5512 & 5513) overlapped.

The 5513 had three genres of dial style, each with several variants. The earliest iterations had gilt gloss dials from 1962 to 1966. The desirable matte dials and maxi variants were made from 1966 to around 1984, before reverting back to a gloss dial (with new white gold indexes).

Within the matte maxi dial genre, five distinct variants have come to be known as MK I to V. The distinctions between them come down to minor differences in text font and coronet shape and can require a loupe to detect.

Submariner ref. 5513 dial genre timeline

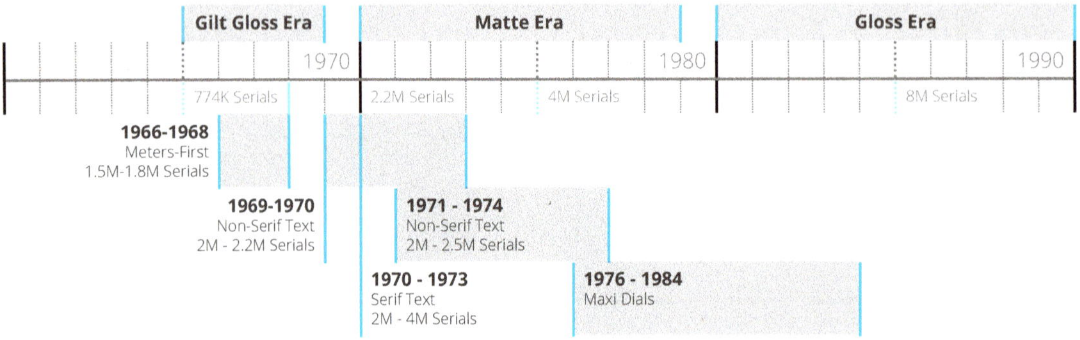

Gilt Gloss Era | **Matte Era** | **Gloss Era**

1970 | 1980 | 1990

774K Serials | 2.2M Serials | 4M Serials | 8M Serials

1966-1968
Meters-First
1.5M-1.8M Serials

1969-1970
Non-Serif Text
2M - 2.2M Serials

1971 - 1974
Non-Serif Text
2M - 2.5M Serials

1970 - 1973
Serif Text
2M - 4M Serials

1976 - 1984
Maxi Dials

Meters-First Matte dials started in 1966 around the 1.6M serial range and ran to around 1968. The tritium lume application on these is known to be inconsistent and variable.

The early versions had thin layers of lume that can be quite hard to detect and may require a loupe. In the middle of the production run, the lume appears to be applied more thickly and has a domed appearance typical of hand applied lume markers. By the end of this dial series, the tritium has a flat, more even appearance more consistent with pad printing techniques.

Non-serif dials followed in 1969 and ran to 1970, starting in the 2M serial range. Serif dials followed these, running until 1973 with serials in the 3M range. Then things returned to the non-serif style until around 1976.

Maxi dials started after 1976 and ran to 1984, and were subsequently replaced by the gloss dial with the white gold hour markers.

You can use the timeline above to verify the dial is an appropriate style and matches the expected serial number of a watch.

Green Submariners

Rolex is extremely conservative in its use of color, particularly their signature green. Green is reserved for anniversary celebration models. The 50th anniversary of the Submariner was celebrated with a special edition of the ref. 16610. If you're looking for something a little different, these green Submariners, affectionately known as Hulk and Kermit, are excellent choices.

Ref. 16610LV Kermit (2003 to 2010)

Developed to celebrate the Submariners 50th Anniversary, the Kermit, as it has come to be nicknamed, is distinguished by the green bezel insert. It is also the first instance of a Submariner with a maxi dial (enlarged hour indices). This version has slightly wider hands than the standard black-dial ref. 16610, though you'll need to be experienced with both to notice the difference.

The first models were issued in the autumn of 2003 with a 'Y' serial number in September, with low F serials following in October through December. Because of this, only a narrow range of watches are true anniversary models issued on the Submariner's 50th birthday. Acceptable serials for these range from high Y to low F numbers.

The Oyster case of the Kermit has no drilled lug holes. Some collectors claim to have seen early press pictures of the Kermit with drilled lug holes, and anecdotal evidence suggests prototypes had drilled lugs - as did the first production batch given to Rolex executives. Rumor has it these photos were released to throw off counterfeiters.

The Kermit was upgraded in 2010 with the six-digit 116610LV. Now out of production, it has become sought after and collectible as a future classic.

The Kermit commands a price premium over the standard black bezel version (16610) of the same year. If pursuing one of these, pay careful attention to the authenticity of the green bezel and the size (width) of the hands. It is possible to swap a black bezel on a standard 16610 for a green one (possibly after market) and pass it off as a 16610LV Anniversary Model with a price premium. A bezel swap is a simple undertaking requiring little more than a knife and masking tape. Swapping hands is possible too, but is a more involved job requiring watchmaker's tools and some know-how.

The LV designation should be indicated on the warranty card, along with the case serial number. The earliest versions, with the old style punched warranty papers, were apparently only marked with a V designation.

If you're going to buy a 16610LV, you are strongly advised to have it verified by an RSC or AD with a Rolex-trained watchmaker on staff.

Ref. 116610LV Hulk (2010 to Present)

The Hulk is an evolution of the anniversary Kermit, and the sunburst green maxi dial is a significant change to the five-digit Kermit it replaced. It has a Cerachrom bezel and the broader lugs of what has become known as the modern maxi case. It wears larger on the wrist and has an aggressive masculine character.

MILITARY SUBMARINERS

The sub genre of Submariners with military provenance is complex. Rolex watches purchased by the military are State property and issued to military personnel along with other specialized tools such as diving equipment.

Like all military equipment these government-owned watches bare military engravings and serial numbers. They never became the personal property of the soldiers that used them and any failure to return them after use to the quartermaster, could have severe consequences.

Eventually, some watches that survived active duty made their way into private ownership via military surplus auctions.

Government-issued examples are highly prized and should not be confused with those purchased privately by servicemen during their active service.

These personal purchases usually took place at exclusive retail outlets (often tax-free) such a the British NAFFI and the US China Fleet Club. While their owners bestow a military provenance on these watches, they are not Military Submariners in the strictest sense.

The third class of military Submariner is those gifted to soldiers by a foreign sovereign. Examples include the red Khanjar or Qaboos Sea-Dwellers, given by the Sultan of Oman to 90 SAS soldiers after the Battle of Mirbat in 1972.

The Ministry of Defense (MOD), is the official customer and first owner of British Military Submariners.

These unique gifts of appreciation have a military provenance unlike the government issued examples. Examples like this are pursued by both watch nerds and military history buffs.

Rolex supplied special issue Submariners to the British Ministry of Defense (MOD). These watches were procured for use by special forces of the Royal Navy and British Army. Specifically the Naval Special Boat Squadron (SBS) and the Army Special Air Service (SAS).

Tudor Submariners were issued to other elite military forces including the French, Canadian and Australian.

The term Milsub usually refers to only four specific Rolex references - ref. A/6538 (or 6538A), 5513, 5514 and 5517.

The most collectible and desirable is the ref.5517, produced in minimal volume. The ref. 5517 is a rare and valuable piece, which means they are also frequently counterfeited to a very convincing quality.

Thankfully, Milsubs are relatively well cataloged and documented, and Milsub specialists can verify them. Given the classified nature of the work performed by their owners, these records are closely held.

Ref. A/6538
(1957 to 1966)

The first orders for special issue Submariners came from the British Royal Navy from 1957 to 1966. These were for a modified version of the James Bond Goldfinger ref. 6538.

The ref. A/6538 had modifications including a larger (and taller) bezel made out of nickel silver instead of the 6538's plated brass. This modification allowed a frogmen better grip with wet, gloved hands. It also had fixed 2mm spring bars. Engravings on the case backs include the war department arrow, military branch and year of issue. From 1967 to 1971, the British Navy switched suppliers and adopted the Omega Seamaster 300.

Rolex sold a stock Submariner ref. 6538 to the Royal Canadian Navy beginning in 1956/7. These versions have an identification and service number engraved on the inside of the case back. The configuration is otherwise the same as the standard production Rolex Submariner.

Ref. 5513 & 5517
(1972 - 1979)

The second period of Milsubs was for modified ref. 5513 and 5517 and Rolex supplied approximately 1,200 units. About 180 of these examples are accounted for and attributed to known collectors.

The first batch of ref.5513 had case engravings between the 12 o'clock lugs. The second batch bore the same 5513 case engravings but with an additional 5517 stamp on the underside of the seven o'clock lug.

The third set bore the 5517 case engravings between the lugs. This third batch has the more legible, broadsword, or plongeur-style hands and an arrow style second hand. Rolex did not make these hands, and during servicing, they were often replaced with the Rolex Mercedes-style hands (Squelette).

All three batches featured a matte dial with a *600 ft = 200m* depth rating and a circled T denoting the use of Tritium lume. All their bezels had continually graduated markers for the full 60 minutes, and an anti-reflective satin case finish. The case had fixed bars to enhanced durability. These fixed bars allowed for use with NATO straps and could be affixed to a "dive board."

All the ref. 5513 and ref. 5517 casebacks have the military, Crown Property mark, and unique issue numbers.

Case backs for the Royal Navy SBS versions have a UK Ministry Of Defense (MOD) service code of 0552 along with a NATO code for dive watches of 923-7697. They will also have a Broad Arrow-style insignia with an issue number and year of issue.

Case backs for Army SAS versions have a MOD service code of W10. They also have three NATO code 6645 denoting a timing instrument, 99 for the UK and 923-7697 for divers watches. They will also have an issue number and a year of issue.

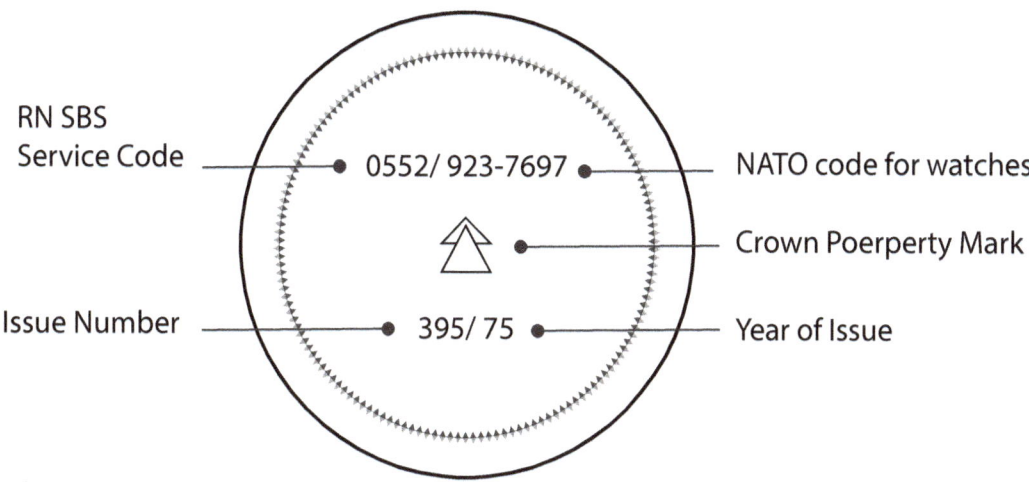

MOD military Submariner caseback engravings

Ref. 5514 COMEX

The ref. 5514 was made under contract specifically for COMEX and was never sold directly to armed forces of any foreign governments. The ref. 5514 was a modified ref. 5513 with a Helium Escape Valve (HEV).

Its designation as a Milsub is controversial and based on one example that came to auction at Christie's Auction House. This example had a dial marked A.R.A. which stands for Armada de la Republica Argentina or Argentine Navy. It had an ARA military issue number 68507-Ci.

Researchers at Christie's confirmed that COMEX commissioned this 5514 along with other COMEX dialed ref. 5514 watches. COMEX requested the inscription A.R.A. above the depth rating on the dial instead of their COMEX logo. These A.R.A-dialed ref. 5514s were issued to 16 Argentine naval divers, who were training at the COMEX Hyperbaric Experimental Centre in Marseilles, France in 1977.

It is likely that the Argentine military engraved issue numbers on the case backs upon their return to duty in Argentina.

Submariner Reference Summary

Ref.	Date	Cal.	Depth Rating	Case	Bezel	Years	Description
6200	N	775	200m/660ft	36mm SS	Numbered, LN	1953 - 1954	Big 8mm crown with Explorer style (3-6-9) hour markers on a gilt dial. May not feature "Submariner" branding. 200m depth rating with fatter case. Considered the very first Submariner.
6204	N	A260	100m/330ft	36mm SS	Numbered, LN	1953 - 1954	100m depth rating with thinner case than 6200. Pencil style hour hand. Seen with black honeycomb gilt dial.
6202	N	A296	100m/330ft	36mm SS	Numbered, LN	1953 - 1954	Pre-Submariner. Occasionally branded "Monometer"
6200	N	A296	200m/660ft	36mm SS	Numbered, LN	1953 - 1955	Big 8mm crown with Explorer style (3-6-9) hour markers and gilt dial. May not feature "Submariner". Fatter case for improved 200m depth rating. Considered the very first Submariner.
6205	N	A260	100m/330ft	36mm SS	Numbered, LN	1953 - 1957	Black honeycomb dial. 100m depth rating with thinner case than 6200. Early version had pencil hour hand and later versions the Mercedes hour hand. Also seen without crown guards
6536	N	1030	100m/330ft	36mm SS	Numbered, LN	1954 - 1958	No crown guards. May feature Explorer 3-6-9 hour markers with 2 or four line colored print such as red depth markings. Waterproof to 100m
6538	N	1030	200m/660ft	40mm SS	Numbered, LN	1957 - 1960	First to be rated to 660ft/200m. First to have Triplock Big Crown (8mm). Bezel introduced 15 minute markers and red triangle at 12 o'clock. The James Bond Dr. No ref. First use of Mercedes hands.
5510	N	1530	200m/660ft	36mm SS	Numbered, LN	1958 - 1960	Transitional reference, may feature Explorer 3-6-9 hour markers and depth rating to 200m. Two or four line colored print such as red depth markings. Fixed spring bars indicate military issue. Big crown (8mm)

Ref.	Date	Cal.	Depth Rating	Case	Bezel	Years	Description
5510	N	3030	200m/660ft	36mm SS	Numbered, LN	1958 - 1960	Transitional reference, may feature Explorer 3-6-9 hour markers and depth rating to 200m. Two or four line colored print such as red depth markings. Fixed spring bars indicate military issue. Big crown (8mm)
5508	N	1530	100m/330ft	36mm SS	Numbered, LN	1958 - 1965	May feature Explorer (3-6-9) hour markers with 2 or four line colored print such as red depth markings. May feature big or small crowns. Both COSC and non-chronometer movements. Gilt dial.
5514	N	1520	200m/660ft	40mm SS	Numbered, LN	1960 - 1978	Non-COSC COMEX
5517	N	1520	660ft/200m	40mm SS	Numbered, LN	1960 - 1978	Military Issue Only. Ordinance Markings. Plongeur Sword Hands.
5514	N	1570	200m/660ft	40mm SS	Numbered, LN	1960 - 1978	Non-COSC COMEX
5512	N	1520	200m/660ft	40mm SS	Numbered, LN	1960 - 1980	First Sub with crown guards. Later versions were COSC "Superlative Chronometer, Officially Certified"
5512	N	1530	200m/660ft	40mm SS	Numbered, LN	1960 - 1980	First Sub with crown guards. Later versions were COSC "Superlative Chronometer, Officially Certified"
5512	N	1570	200m/660ft	40mm SS	Numbered, LN	1960 - 1980	First Sub with crown guards. Later versions were COSC "Superlative Chronometer, Officially Certified"
5513	N	1520	200m/660ft	40mm SS	Numbered, LN	1960 - 1990	Some Royal Navy and some COMES. Dials change from gilt gloss to meters first matte dials around the 1.6 mil serial range or 1966.
5513	N	1530	200m/660ft	40mm SS	Numbered, LN	1960 - 1990	Some Royal Navy and some COMES. Dials change from gilt gloss to meters first matte dials around the 1.6 mil serial range or 1966.
5513	N	1570	200m/660ft	40mm SS	Numbered, LN	1960 - 1990	Some Royal Navy and some COMES. Dials change from gilt gloss to meters first matte dials around the 1.6 mil serial range or 1966.

Ref.	Date	Cal.	Depth Rating	Case	Bezel	Years	Description
1680	Y	1565	660ft/200m	40mm SS	Numbered, LN	1969 - 1981	Chronometer. Red & white text.
1680	Y	1575	660ft/200m	40mm SS	Numbered, LN	1969 - 1981	Chronometer. Red & white text.
1680	Y	3035	660ft/200m	40mm SS	Numbered, LN	1969 - 1981	Chronometer. White text only.
6540	N	1030	660ft/200m	40mm SS	Numbered, LN	1971 - 1978	UK Ministry of Defense issue. Plongeur sword hands, 60 min bezel markers (approx 1,200 units made including 6538A)
6538A	N	1030	200m/660ft	40mm SS	Numbered, LN	1971 - 1978	UK Ministry of Defense issue. Plongeur sword hands, 60 min bezel markers (approx 1,200 units made including 6540)
16800	Y	3085	660ft/200m	40mm SS	Numbered, LN	1977 - 1987	Upgraded 1680.
16803	Y	3085	660ft/200m	40mm SSYG	Numbered, LN	1977 - 1987	Two tone 16800
16808	Y	3085	660ft/200m	40mm YG	Numbered, LN	1977 - 1987	Gold 16800
168000	Y	3135	1000ft/300m	40mm SS	Numbered, LN	1987 - 1988	Transitional reference, first to feature 906L stainless steel.
16618	Y	3085	1000ft/300m	40mm YG	Numbered, LN	1987 - 2010	18k Gold version of the 16610
16610	Y	3135	1000ft/300m	40mm SS	Numbered, LN	1987 - 2010	Successor to the 16800 and 168000. Final Sub with aluminum bezel and first Sub to adopt Luminova and etched rehaut.
16613	Y	3135	1000ft/300m	40mm SSYG	Numbered, LN	1987 - 2010	Two Tone version of the 16610
16618	Y	3135	1000ft/300m	40mm YG	Numbered, LN	1987 - 2010	18k Gold version of the 16610
14060	N	3030	1000ft/300m	40mm SS	Numbered, LN	1989 - 2012	Introduction of sapphire crystals, white gold surrounds on hour markers. Tritium lume aging nicely.
14060M	N	3130	1000ft/300m	40mm SS	Numbered, LN	2000 - 2012	A transitional reference with uprated movement as denoted by "M". Last reference to feature drilled lugs.
16610LV	Y	3135	1000ft/300m	40mm SS	Numbered, LV	2003 - 2010	Kermit with green bezel and black dial

Ref.	Date	Cal.	Depth Rating	Case	Bezel	Years	Description
116610LN	Y	3135	1000ft/300m	40mm SS	Numbered Cerachrom, LN	2010 -	First cerachrom bezel and maxi dial and case. Slightly wider minute hand and Chromalight lume.
116610LV	Y	3135	1000ft/300m	40mm SS	Numbered Cerachrom, LV	2010 -	Hulk with ceramic green bezel and dial.
116613LB	Y	3135	1000ft/300m	40mm SSYG	Numbered Cerachrom, LB	2010 -	Two tone with blue bezel and dial.
116613LN	Y	3135	1000ft/300m	40mm SSYG	Numbered Cerachrom, LN	2010 -	Two tone 116610 with black bezel and dial.
116618LB	Y	3135	1000ft/300m	40mm YG	Numbered Cerachrom, LB	2010 -	Gold 116610 with blue bezel and dial.
116618LN	Y	3135	1000ft/300m	40mm YG	Numbered Cerachrom. LN	2010 -	Gold 116610 with black bezel and dial
116619LB	Y	3135	1000ft/300m	40mm WG	Numbered Cerachrom, LB	2010 -	White Gold with blue bezel and dial.
114060	N	3130	1000ft/300m	40mm SS	Numbered, LN	2012 -	Introduction of Super Luminova and the engraved rehaut.

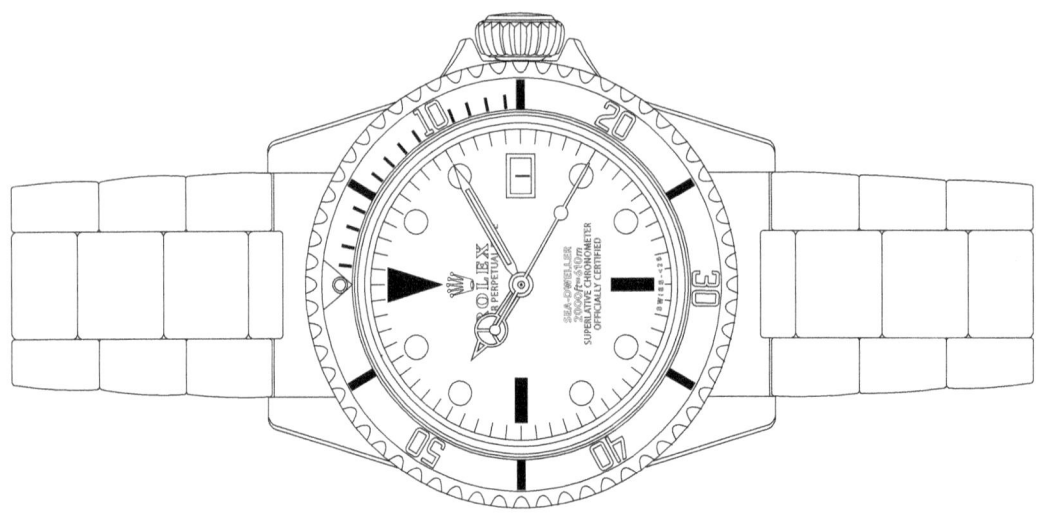

Oyster Perpetual Sea-Dweller

The Sea-Dweller has an ambiguous and complex history. It debuted as a brand in 1967 after several years of development and rigorous testing. Born of the Submariner, the Sea-Dweller is a more substantial and more serious diving tool developed in collaboration with the French marine engineering and commercial diving company, Comex SA.

The early Submariner ref. 5513 provided the platform for the first Sea-Dwellers. The helium escape valves (HEV) on the side of the Oyster case distinguishes them as Sea-Dwellers.

These early versions are numbered, with caseback engravings indicating where they were issued.

A small number of the first Sea-Dwellers were distributed to retail outlets and co-branded with jewelers like Tiffany's. Only a few of these have surfaced. They are curious examples of hardcore professional tool watches sold at unlikely, high-end, refined luxury jewelers. These co-branded Sea-Dwellers command a collectors price premium and continue to be controversial.

As the Submariner grew to become the recreational scuba divers watch, the Sea-Dweller was for the professional saturation diver. They are set apart by technical specifications such as the Sea-Dweller's enhanced case back for improved depth rating and on later models, visual cues like the 60-minute markers around the bezel.

The date complication was not a modern convenience but a useful instrument during dives and decompression. Many of these dives and subsequent decompression lasted many days and even weeks.

Each Sea-Dweller reference had several distinct variants with a variety of dial differences, caseback engravings, and movements. All feature a helium escape valve on the 9 o'clock side of the Oyster case. The Sea-Dweller is the only Rolex to feature caseback engravings, and it has more rows of dial text than any other Rolex.

Sea-Dwellers Variants

Ref.1665			Ref.116660	Ref.16600
Double Red	Great White	Single Red	Deepsea	Sea-Dweller
				Ref.116600
				Sea-Dweller 4000
Ref.16660			Deepsea DeepBlue	12660	126660
Triple 6 gloss	Triple 6 matte				

Sea-Dweller reference variations

Ref. 1665 Double Red Sea-Dweller Special Note

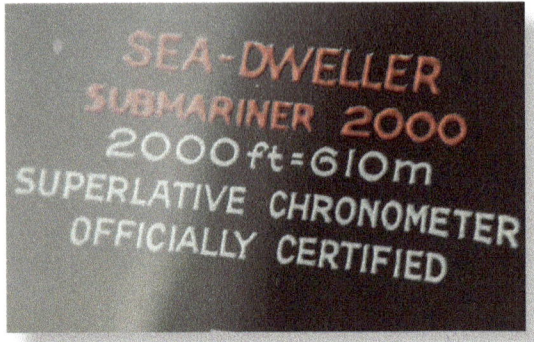

The Double Red Sea-Dweller ref.1665 was the first commercially available Sea-Dweller, and for collectors, it is the most coveted. Its official name is the Sea-Dweller Submariner 2000. The dial has this name printed as two rows of red text, giving it the nickname the Double Red Sea-Dweller or DRSD for short.

The reference ran for an impressive ten years (1967 until 1977) and during this run, five distinct dial variations appeared.

MK I Dial (1.6M - 2.2M)

This appeared on the earliest examples before the granting of the HEV patent. MK I dials appear with a caseback engraved Patent Pending. The MK I dial has red lettering that is a consistent size and weight. The Rolex coronet is of a thicker style consistent with other Professional watches of the period.

MK II Dial (1.6M - 3.5M)

This dial can be paired with the caseback engravings that read Patent Pending or Patented. The font size and weight of the red lettering differ with the SEA-DWELLER appearing larger and heavier than the SUBMARINER 2000 text below it.

MK III Dial (2.6M - 4.0M)

This dial is distinguished from the MK II by an updated coronet which appears longer and less thick.

MK IV Dial (3.0M - 5.2M)

This last version has a thicker and heavier font across both White and Red lettering. It also has a pronounced coronet. This dial should be matched with a date wheel featuring closed rather than open 6s and 9s.

In addition to dial variations, there were two distinct styles of caseback engravings. Earliest versions of the Sea-Dweller have a caseback with ROLEX written horizontally across the outside surface. Following versions beginning with the Great White in 1977, have their engravings appearing around the circumference caseback.

Ref. 1665 caseback variations

Stamped on the inside of the caseback, is the model number and a partial serial number (last three digits). Later models have the full serial number. Some also have a stamped production date indicating quarter and year (e.g. II 72 for Q2 1972).

Helium gas escape valve

Sea-Dweller ref. 1665 Great White

Ref. 1665 Great White Sea-Dweller Special Note

In 1977 the ref.1665 received a minor dial makeover with white lettering replacing the red. Also gone was a reference to the Submariner. By this stage, the Sea-Dweller was an established and independent product line, not just a heavy duty Submariner.

The Great White 1665 continued in production until the early 1980s. Production overlapped with its replacement, the newer 16660 which launched in 1978. For several years, the Great White 1665 was sold alongside its descendant the 16660 as inventory was run down.

The Sea-Dweller ref. 1665 Great White set the standard for Sea-Dweller design aesthetics until the release of ref. 126600 in 2017 (with the return of red lettering).

Like its predecessor the DRSD, the Great White featured five dial variants. Frustratingly, the collector community has numbered them 0 to 4, rather than 1 to 5 like the DRSD. This choice is a result of the discovery of the earlier MK0 after the MK1

MK 0 Dial

This is by far the rarest of the Great White dials and has SEA-DWELLER text that is longer and wider than the depth rating printed below it. Also of note is the closed 6 on the depth rating, *2000 ft = 600m*. This closed font 6 won't match the date wheel's open font 6's.

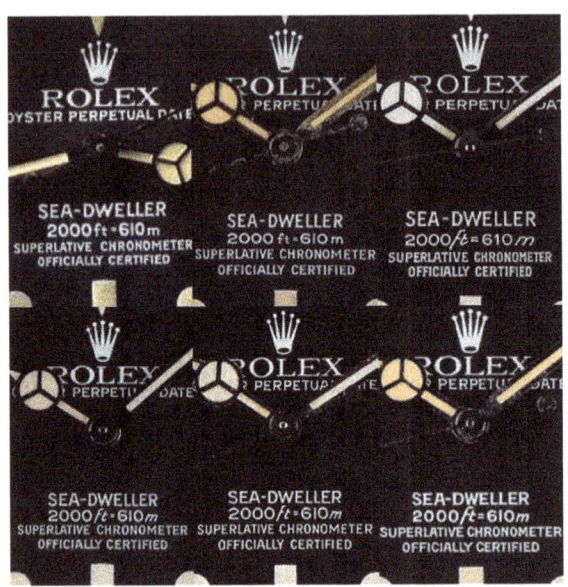

Sea-Dweller ref. 1665 dial variations
Top : MK 0, MK I, MK II
Bottom: MK III, MK IV, MK V

MK I Dial (6.1M - 6.2M)

The SEA-DWELLER and depth rating text, line up and appear fully justified, unlike on the MK 0. Also, the 6 on the depth rating now appears closed.

MK II Dial (5.7M - 6.2M)

This is a rail dial, with the C of Chronometer aligned with the C of Certified below it. The depth rating units (ft, m) now appear in italics.

MK III Dial (6M - 6.8M)

Unlike the rail dial (MK II) the Cs are not aligned, and the fonts appear different.

MK IV Dial

This is hard to distinguish from the MK III, with the difference being a differently shaped 6 in the depth rating and a smaller R at the end of Chronometer.

Comex Sea-Dwellers

While the following references have been co-branded with Comex, it is still correct to have Submariners and Sea-Dwellers with HEVs and no overt Comex dial branding.

These examples will have caseback engravings indicating their special issue designation. Comex dive watches were never sold through retail outlets and will have no other co-branding.

- Submariner Comex 5513
- Submariner Comex 5514 (154 Units)
- Submariner Comex 1680
- Submariner Comex 16800
- Submariner Comex 168000
- Submariner Comex 16610
- Sea-Dweller Comex 1665
- Sea-Dweller Comex 16600
- Sea-Dweller Comex 16660

Ref. 116660 Deepsea Sea-Dweller Special Note

In 2008 Rolex introduced the Sea-Dweller DEEPSEA ref.116660. This reference is not vintage or even modern classic, but an essential part of the Sea-Dweller story. It was a significant upgrade to the modern classic ref. 16600 and introduced the Ringlock System. This innovation sets the DEEPSEA apart from the Sea-Dweller by setting the depth rating to 12,800ft.

The Ringlock system is a combination of three innovations. These included a grade 5 titanium case back capable of flexing under incredible pressure. It also had a 5mm thick sapphire crystal positioned above an inner steel ring. This Ringlock system reset the bar for professional dive watches, and as such has become a potential collectible.

Deepsea Sea-Dweller Deepblue James Cameron Edition

The James Cameron Deepblue is a thoroughly contemporary watch. However, some characteristics mark it as a sleeper, and potentially a highly collectible reference in the future.

As far as commemorative special edition watches go, this one is unusual in that it celebrates both a record-breaking achievement and the person who performed it. Rolex commissioned it to celebrate James Cameron's successful descent to the deepest point on our planet, located at 10,900m below the surface of the Pacific Ocean. This record-setting dive was the second significant trip to the bottom of the Pacific accompanied by a special project Rolex.

The Deepsea Challenge (DCV1) reached the bottom of the Mariana Trench on March 26th, 2012.

PROFESSIONAL TOOLS

It was built in Australia by the research and design company Acheron Project Pty Ltd. It carried scientific sampling equipment and high-definition 3D cameras. The submersible also featured a robotic arm, and attached to it was the Rolex Deepsea Challenge Concept Watch.

The concept watch was a super-sized version of the standard Deepsea, created in only a few weeks and numbering only 5 or 6 units. It had a diameter of 51.4mm and a thickness of 28.5mm; 14.3mm of which was a unique sapphire crystal.

The submersible and its special watch reached the ocean's deepest point after two hours and 36 minutes of descent from the surface.

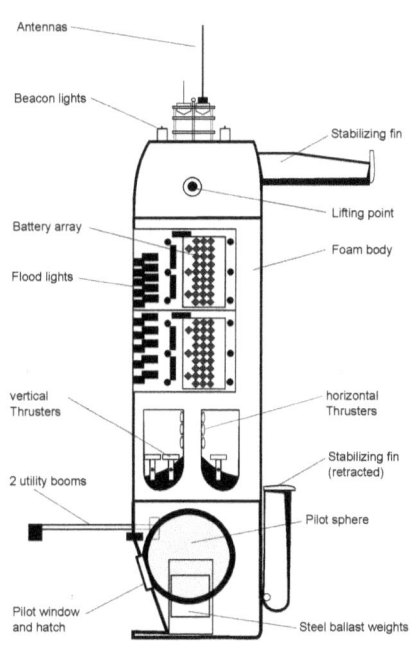

General assembly drawing of DCV1, Circa 2012

The commercial Deepblue version of the concept watch has a distinctive blue and black gradient dial with vibrant green colored DEEPSEA text. This color is the same green as that of the Deepsea Challenge submersible.

Rolex designed the James Cameron Sea-Dweller DEEPBLUE for water resistance of 12,000m. This rating is over three times that of the Deepsea.

The first available version of the Rolex Deepsea Sea-Dweller Deepblue (ref. 116660) is an homage to the concept watch. It is currently the highest performing dive watch made by Rolex. It is also the largest (17.7mm thick and 44mm diameter) with a

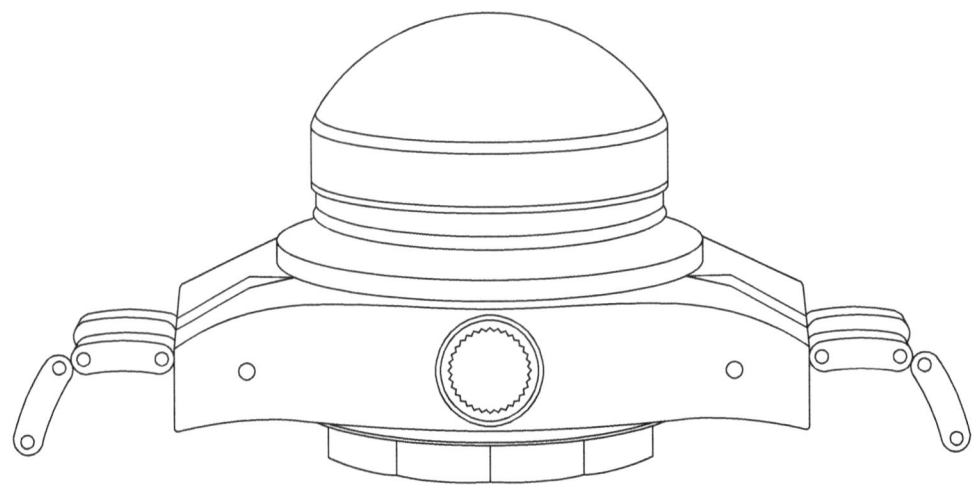

5mm thick crystal and a titanium caseback, featuring a patented Ring Lock System. Combined they enable massive water resistance to 3,900m.

Curiously, the Deepblue shares the same reference number as the black-dialed Deepsea (ref. 116660). Critics of the Deepblue claim it is too large and top-heavy, requiring a wider redesigned Oyster bracelet.

The Rolex Deepsea Sea-Dweller Deepblue was revised in 2017 and replaced with ref. 126600. Rolex redesigned the Oyster case with thinned (narrower) lugs but with a broader lug width of 22mm. This design adjustment resolved the top-heavy criticisms of the 116660.

52 years earlier on January 23rd 1960, the Trieste deep-diving research bathyscaphe, with its crew of Jacques Piccard and US Navy Lieutenant Don Walsh, achieved a similar feat. Reaching a depth of 10,911 meters (35,797 ft). It was accompanied by the custom-built Rolex Deepsea Special 1 (opposite).

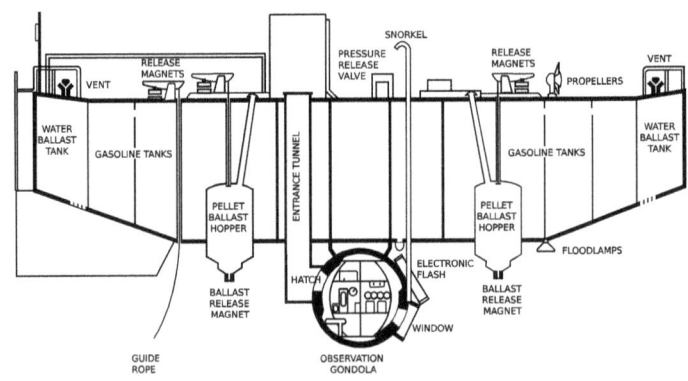

General assembly drawing of Trieste, Circa 1959

Sea Dweller Reference Summary

Name	Ref.	Cal.	Depth Rating	Years	Case	Description
Single Red	1665	1575	500m/1,650ft	1967 - 1968	40mm SS	Prototype with only 12 examples known, derived from the Submariner 5514.
Double Red	1665	1575	610m/2,000ft	1967 - 1977	40mm SS	Included red text "Submariner 2000". Inside caseback engraved with last three digits of serial number and production quarter and year.
Great White	1665	1575	610m/2,000ft	1977 - 1983	40mm SS	
Triple 6 matte	16660	3035	1,220m/4000ft	1978 - 1989	40mm SS	Case back engraving gained an extra coronet.
Triple 6 gloss	16660	3035	1,220m/4000ft	1985 - 1989	40mm SS	Adopted white gold surrounds and dropped the hyphen between "Sea" and "Dweller". Prone to crazing/spidering. Tritium Dial (marked 'T<25')
Sea-Dweller	16600	3135	1,220m/4000ft	1989 - 2008	40mm SS	1998 - 1999 Luminova Dial (marked 'Swiss') 1999 - 2002/3 Super Luminova Dial with lug holes (marked 'Swiss Made') 2002/3 - 2008 Super Luminova dial no lug holes (marked 'Swiss Made')
Deepsea	116660	3135	3,900m/12,800ft	2008 - 2018	44mm SS	17.6mm thick
Deepsea D-Blue	116660	3135	3,900m/12,800ft	2014 - 2018	44mm SS	James Cameron Edition with Deepblue dial
Sea-Dweller 4000	116600	3135	1,220m/4,000ft	2014 - 2017	40mm SS	14.8mm thick
Sea-Dweller	126600	3235	1,220m/4,000ft	2017 -	43mm SS	Cyclops & Red Text with black dial. 50th Anniversary Edition
Sea-Dweller	126660	3235	3,900m/12,800ft	2017 -	43mm SS	Cyclops & Red Text with Black and Deepblue dial

Oyster Perpetual Yacht-Master

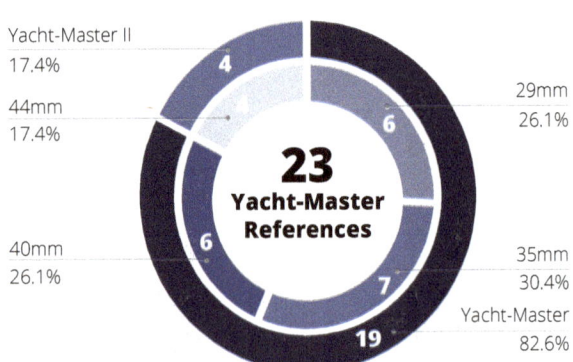

While the Yacht-Master is a new and modern watch, still in production, early examples are becoming sought-after classics.

The larger and more technical Yacht-Master II has a design aesthetic that divides opinion and has sold in modest volumes. These characteristics of low sales volume and polarized customer opinion are markers of future collectability. Interestingly, customers responded to the early Cosmograph Daytona and Explorer II in the same way - divided opinion, resulting in low production volume. The Yacht-Master is a series that long-term collectors should keep a close eye on.

Yacht-Master

The Yacht-Master debuted at the Basel Fair in 1992 with the reference 16628 in 18kt gold, a 3135 movement, and a typical 40mm Oyster case. Subsequent iterations included a Mid-Size (35mm) and Ladies Size (29mm) versions. The model received an update in 2012 with the six-digit reference 116622, and again in 2015 with the ref. 116655.

The Yacht-Master was conceived as a precious-metal, luxury take on the Submariner. It has since become a distinct product line with a specific sporting niche. Available in gold and platinum cases they are substantial on the wrist, and the signature sunburst or platinum dials are eye-catching. The platinum versions are proving the most popular. The hands are fatter than the Submariner's which improves the visual balance and overall aesthetic. The red second-hand complements the red dial text, and the bi-directional bezel has a matching platinum insert with raised and polished numbers. The Oyster case is highly polished on all surfaces (no satin finish). This distinctive fully-polished look is unique to the Yacht-Master.

All Yacht-Masters use the ubiquitous Oyster bracelet with the newest version, ref. 116655 (2015) offered on a rubber Oysterflex strap. This model is the first Rolex has delivered on a rubber strap.

Yacht-Master Regatta II

The Rolex Yacht-Master Regatta II (to use its full name) is a particularly polarizing design. At 44mm in diameter, it requires a muscular and tanned forearm to pull off. This model is a highly specialized niche instrument featuring a unique (to Rolex) regatta 10-minute countdown and fly-back chronograph.

The start-up sequence for this compilation is convoluted, involving a bezel twist, depressing the reset pusher and (counter intuitively, considering it's likely to get wet) unscrewing the crown. Presumably, yachtsmen can perform this feat while staying in control of their yacht, battling the wind and waves and still being first across the starting line(!).

Yacht-Master II ref. 116680

Yacht-Master Reference Summary

Name	Ref.	Cal.	Year	Case
Yacht-Master	68623	2135	1994	35mm YGSS
Yacht-Master	69623	2135	1994	29mm YGSS
Yacht-Master	68628	2135	1994	35mm YG
Yacht-Master	69628	2135	1994	29mm YG
Yacht-Master	68628	2235	1994	35mm PLSS
Yacht-Master	69682	2235	1994	29mm RG
Yacht-Master	168622	2235	1999	35mm PLSS
Yacht-Master	169622	2235	1999	29mm PLSS
Yacht-Master	168622	2235	1999	35mm SS
Yacht-Master	168623	2235	1999	35mm YGSS
Yacht-Master	168628	2235	1999	35mm YG
Yacht-Master	169622	2235	1999	29mm PLSS
Yacht-Master	169623	2235	1999	29mm YGSS
Yacht-Master	16628	3135	1992	40mm YG
Yacht-Master	16628	3135	1992	40mm YG
Yacht-Master	16622	3135	1999	40mm PLSS
Yacht-Master	16623	3135	2005	40mm YGSS
Yacht-Master	116622	3135	2012	40mm PLSS
Yacht-Master	116655	3135	2015	40mm RG
Yacht-Master II	116680	4161	2010	44mm SS
Yacht-Master II	116681	4161	2010	44mm SSRG
Yacht-Master II	116688	4161	2010	44mm YG
Yacht-Master II	116689	4161	2010	44mm WG

Oyster Perpetual Explorer

With such a long and rich history, the Explorer collection of watches has been subject to evolution and multiple revisions.

There are 14 different calibers used in approximately 24 references. Other models share many of these calibers too, making it challenging to ensure antique and vintage examples are original. Despite this (or because of it), Explorers are incredibly desirable and highly collectible with prices to match. The Explorer is considered, *The Thinking Mans Rolex*.

The Rolex Explorer resulted from 20 years of research in extreme conditions. This development involved equipping alpine expeditions in the 1930s, long before the historical conquering of Everest. Rolex was one of several watchmakers sponsoring mountaineers with timing instruments and funding.

The goal of this sponsorship was to create the ultimate mountaineer's tool watch, capable of surviving low-pressure altitude and temperatures as low as -50C (-58F).

Contrary to popular perception Sir Edmund Hillary did not wear an Explorer during his Everest expedition. He was wearing a Smiths watch, and a Rolex was one of two worn by Sherpa Tenzing Norgay on that first summit of Everest on May 29th, 1953. Rolex based Norgay's Explorer on an existing tough-wearing Bubbleback, modified for the expedition.

Pre-Explorers

In 1952, the references 6098 and 6150 (cal. A296) provided the platform for Explorer development. They had white dials and alpha style hands and did not bear the name Explorer yet. A year later in 1953, these models evolved into the references 6298 and ref. 6350. Both now had the iconic Explorer 3-6-9 Arabic dials and Mercedes-style hands.

Before conquering Everest in May 1953, Rolex did not use the Explorer trademark, despite registering it in Geneva on January 26th of that same year.

Ref 6350

Rolex designed the ref.6350 for explorers and mountaineers, by building in the ability to survive significant temperature variations and the low pressure of high altitudes. It had a readable dial that performed well in poor visibility, a strengthened case, and lubricants able to tolerate temperature variations from -20 C to +40C. Rolex added Explorer to the dials of ref. 6350 after 1953.

Sir Edmund Hillary and Sherpa Tenzing Norgay, 1953

Ref 6150 & 6610

In 1959 ref.6610 replaced the pre-Explorer ref.6150 which ceased production. These references were indistinguishable from one another, except for the new cal. 1030 movement in the ref.6610. This new movement design allowed for a flatter case back compared to the Bubbleback style of the ref.6150. Collectors cite these two references as the first real Oyster Perpetual Explorers.

Explorer Reference Summary

Name	Ref.	Cal.	Start	End	Bezel	Size
Explorer	6150	A296	1952	1959	Smooth (Polished)	36mm
Air King or Explorer	5501	1520	1953		Smooth (Polished)	34mm
Explorer	6298	1030	1953		Smooth (Polished)	36mm
Explorer	6298	A296	1953		Smooth (Polished)	36mm
Explorer	6299	A296	1953		Smooth (Polished)	36mm
Explorer	6350	A296	1953		Smooth (Polished)	36mm
Air King or Explorer	5500	1520	1957		Smooth (Polished)	34mm
Air King or Explorer	5507	1520	1958		Smooth (Polished)	34mm
Explorer	6610	1030	1959		Smooth (Polished)	36mm
Explorer	1016	1560	1963	1989	Smooth (Polished)	36mm
Explorer	1016	1570	1963	1989	Smooth (Polished)	36mm
Air King or Explorer	5507	1520			Smooth (Polished)	34mm
Air King or Explorer	5504	1530			Smooth (Polished)	34mm
Air King or Explorer	5701	1535			Smooth (Polished)	34mm
Explorer	8044	1030			Smooth (Polished)	36mm
Explorer	8045	1030			Smooth (Polished)	
Explorer	14270	3000			Smooth (Polished)	36mm
Explorer	114270	3130			Smooth (Polished)	36mm
Explorer	214270	3132			Smooth (Polished)	39mm

Explorer II Reference Summary

Name	Ref.	Cal.	Case	Years	Description
Explorer II	1655	1570	39mm SS	1971 - 1981	Big orange 24-hour arrow hand
Explorer II	1655	1575	39mm SS	1971 - 1981	Big orange 24-hour arrow hand
Explorer II	16550	3085	40mm SS	1985 - 1989	Red and black GMT arrow hand
Explorer II	16570	3185	40mm SS	1989 - 2012	Red and black GMT arrow hand
Explorer II	16570	3186	40mm SS	1989 - 2012	Red and black GMT arrow hand
Explorer II	216570	3187	42mm SS	2012 -	Anniversary big orange GMT arrow hand

Oyster Perpetual Explorer II

Of the four models which bear the Explorer II branding, only ref. 1665 is considered vintage. The five-digit references that followed are Modern Classics.

Rolex unveiled the Explorer II ref. 1655 in a 39mm Oyster case. In a departure from the mountaineering focus of the original Explorer, this watch was built for cave explorers (aka spelunkers or speleologists) who spent extended periods in darkness and required both a date and AM-PM indicator.

The first 1655s have a large and very distinctive, bright orange 24-hour hand. These were red in later 1655s, but they still aged to orange, meaning that all 1655 24-hour hands look orange today.

The ref.1655 was not a commercial success. Some attribute this to two shortcomings. The orange hand could not be set independently and was limited to showing AM and PM as a 24-hour clock. Also, the fixed bezel prevented the complication from working as a timer or tracking dual time, as a GMT-Master could.

The ref.1665 is highly sought after today, even gaining unique nicknames. The first is Freccione derived from the Italian word for arrow, a reference to the orange arrow-tipped hand. The second is the Steve McQueen Rolex, despite zero evidence he ever owned one.

While there is an ardent following, the 1970s dial aesthetic is an acquired taste. The disco-dial as it has come to be known, is iconic to the 70s, unique among the tool watches and instantly recognizable.

There were seven dial variations produced during the lifespan of the ref.1655. The dial maker Stern, produced five of the variants while Beyeler made the two service replacement dials. The service dials remained available after the watches production ended, and were stockpiled to service the watches over the following decades.

Explorer II ref. 1655
orange 24-hour hand and unique straight seconds-hand.

Ref. 1655 Dial Variants

Fig. Ref. 1655 MK I Dial

MK I Dial (1971-1972)

The first iteration of the ref. 1655 had a wide coronet, with a rounded foot on the R of Rolex. The base of the dial was marked T SWISS T below the 6 o'clock marker to indicate the use of tritium lume on the dial.

MK II Dial (1972-1977)

The second series had the coronet appearing more splayed, with more substantial dots on the points of the coronet. Nicknamed the Frog Foot, this style of coronet also appears on Explorer ref.1016.

Another difference between the MK I and MK II Explorer II dials is the spacing of the word PERPETUAL which is narrower on the MK II. The top of the letter L lines up with the bottom right stroke of the letter X in ROLEX (on the MK I, the A of PERPETUAL sits below the X). The base of the dial is marked T SWISS T below the 6 o'clock marker, indicating tritium lume.

Fig. Ref. 1655 MK II Dial

MK III Dial (1974 - 1977)

This version is what collectors term a *Rail Dial*. The name refers to the alignment of the text, SUPERLATIVE CHRONOMETER OFFICIALLY CERTIFIED on the bottom half of the dial. The letter Cs in words CHRONOMETER and CERTIFIED are aligned, leaving a distinctive vertical gap in the middle of the two lines of text. Similar Rail Dials also appear on some ref. 1665 Sea-Dwellers. The coronet differs from the MK II by being better defined and more symmetrical. It is marked T SWISS T on the outer bottom edge.

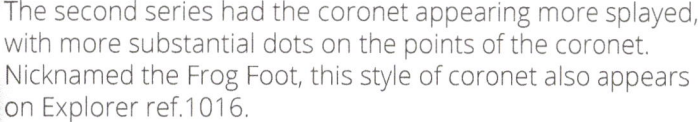

Fig. Ref. 1655 MK III Dial

Fig. Ref. 1655 MK IV Dial

Fig. Ref. 1655 MK V Dial

MK IV Dial (1977-1980)

The coronet on the MK IV is narrower and taller than the MK III, and the text alignment of the lower dial text is the same as the MK II.

The most noticeable change is the text at the bottom edge of the dial, which now reads T SWISS < 25 T in a serif font.

MK V Dial (1979-1984)

The last of the production dials also had the T SWISS < 25 T at the bottom edge of the dial, but without serifs on the lettering (sans-serif font).

The coronet is narrower than the MK IV and has a larger, more open oval at the bottom. This coronet is very similar to those on the Maxi-dial Submariner ref. 5513.

MK VI & MK VII Dials (from 1984)

The MK VI service dial was the last to use tritium T SWISS <25 T and the MK VII was the first to use Luminova (SWISS)

Ref. 1655 Bezel Variations

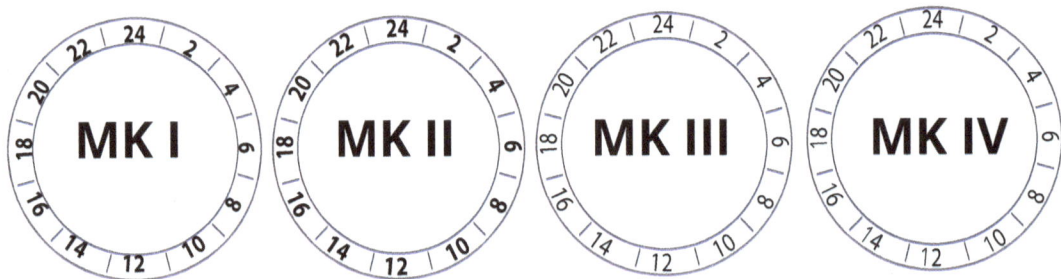

Fig. Explorer II ref.1655 bezels. Artist rendering to emphasize variations.

There are four bezel variations plus a service version. The differences are in the font size (weight) and the alignment of numerals.

MK I Bezel (1971 - 1973)

These appeared with a thick, bold font and the base of the numerals sit close to the inner edge of the bezel. The MK I bezel is correct for both MK I and MK II dials.

MK II Bezel (1973 - 1977)

These used a similar thick bold font with numerals aligned around the center of the bezel ring, rather than sitting on the inner edge. These bezels have appeared on some MK I dial watches but mostly on watches with MK III and MK IV dials.

MK III Bezel (1977 - 1980)

These used a thinner font with numerals positioned centrally on the bezel. The MK III bezel is correct for MK III and MK IV-dialed watches.

MK IV Bezel (after 1980)

The numerals on this bezel use a thin font, like the MK III bezel. A noticeable difference is a long hook on the 1s. The MK IV bezel is correct for MK V-dialed watches.

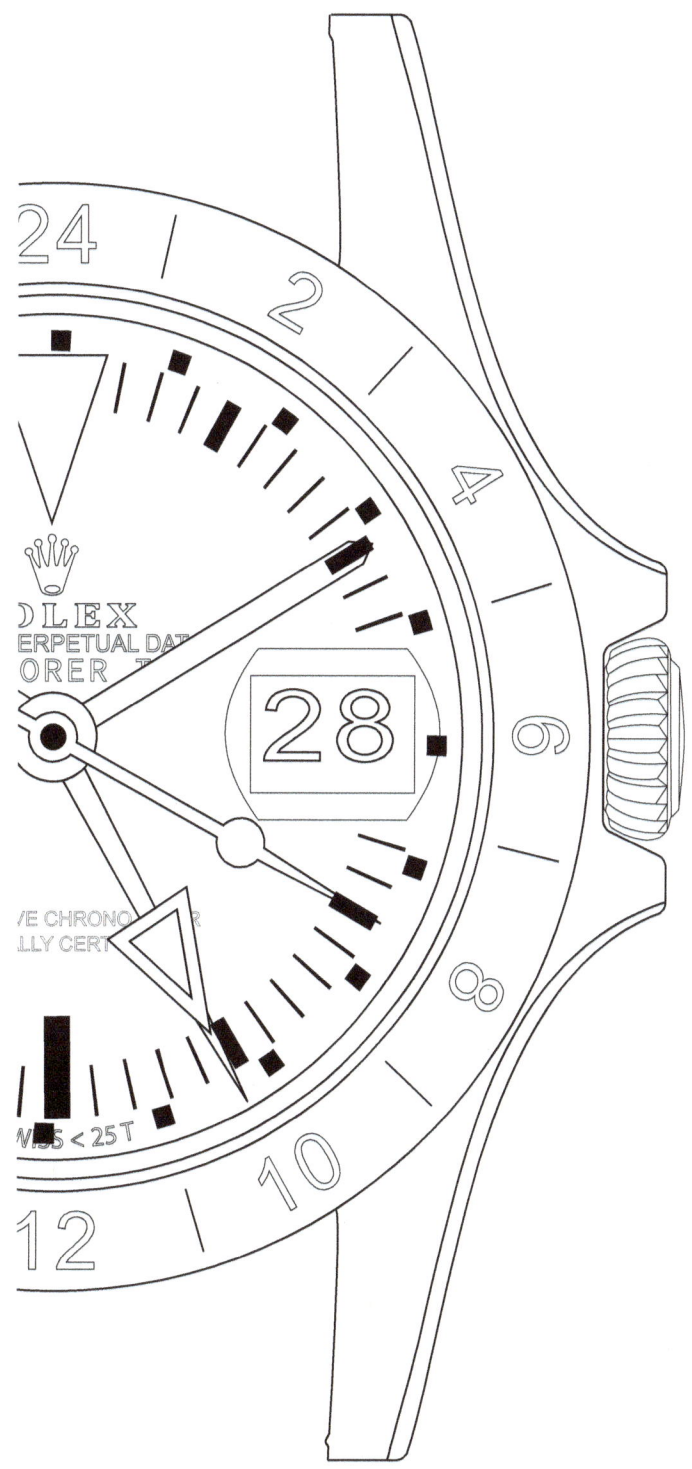

Ref 16550 (1985)

Rolex introduced the ref.16550 with a larger 40mm Oyster case and a sapphire crystal. Ref.16550 was a transitional reference in all respects and offered in black and white Rail Dials. It had white gold surrounds to the hour markers and adopted the GMT-Master-style GMT hands. The new movement shared with the GMT-Master now allowed the GMT hand to be independently set, enabling dual time zones.

The white dial version has come to be known as the Polar Explorer, and a paint defect has turned them a pleasing cream color today. Polar Explorers command a considerable price premium over the black dial variants. Rolex corrected this paint defect before the end of the production run and introduced it along with changes to hour makers, which changed from white gold to black. These revised dials may well have been brought forward into the production of ref.16550 from its pending successor, the ref. 16750.

Ref 16570 (1989)

Cosmetically, this reference differed from its predecessor by the black color of the hour marker surrounds. The main difference justifying the new reference number was an upgraded movement cal. 3185.

Subsequent revisions of this reference saw enhancements like Luminova, a laser-etched rehaut and the no-holes case (elimination of drilled lugs).

Ref 216570

This modern version has an enlarged 42mm Oyster case with an upgraded caliber 3187. The new dial has maxi-style hour markers and Chromalight lume, but the most obvious visual change is the return of the orange, Big Triangle style GMT hand reminiscent of the ref. 1665.

Oyster Perpetual Milgauss

The Milgauss is a rather obscure model that remains somewhat below the radar. In recent years, it has gained more traction with collectors and prices for vintage references in any condition are rising.

The earliest examples are easily mistaken for an Oyster Perpetual. Contemporary examples are less prone to this thanks to some unique design cues.

In 1956, Rolex introduced the Oyster Perpetual Milgauss, ref. 6451, intended for scientists and engineers working in power plants, medical facilities, and research labs.

The name comes from the Latin *mille*, meaning one-thousand, and *gauss*, the unit of measure for magnetism.

The watch was developed and tested in the 1950s by the European Organization for Nuclear Research (CERN), the world's preeminent particle physics laboratory. The design was a technological breakthrough solving a real problem for timekeeping in these electrically and magnetically polluted environments.

Reference 6541 was very similar in appearance to the Rolex Submariner, which had proved to be a winning design. The movement was enclosed in a Faraday cage of ferromagnetic alloy, making it resistant to magnetism up to 1000 gauss.

The original Milgauss sold in modest volume, presumably because this was a small professional niche in the 1950s. Today they are rare and sought after by collectors.

In stainless steel only, the Milgauss is discreet and low-key, yet instantly recognizable by vintage enthusiasts.

The Milgauss has a short history compared to other Professional models. Only two updates were released, ref.6541 and a modified 1019, in the 1960s and 1970s. The updates introduced a silver dial option. Some 1019s were also released without the unique lightning-bolt second hand, though many had it added later during service.

For 20 years consumers largely ignored the Milgauss. Then in 2007, Rolex revived their *scientist's watch* releasing three new references starting with model ref. 116400.

Due to the internal magnetic shield, the Milgauss is thicker than other Professional watches, including the similarly designed Submariner. As with all Rolex Oyster cases, the Milgauss is waterproof up to 100 meters (330 feet).

A 50th-anniversary model features a black dial with a distinctive green-tinted sapphire crystal. This Glace Verte (GV) model is named for its tinted glass and is the only Rolex to feature it. The GV is also the only sapphire crystal without a Laser Etched Coronet (LEC), as the green tint makes it too hard to see, even under magnification.

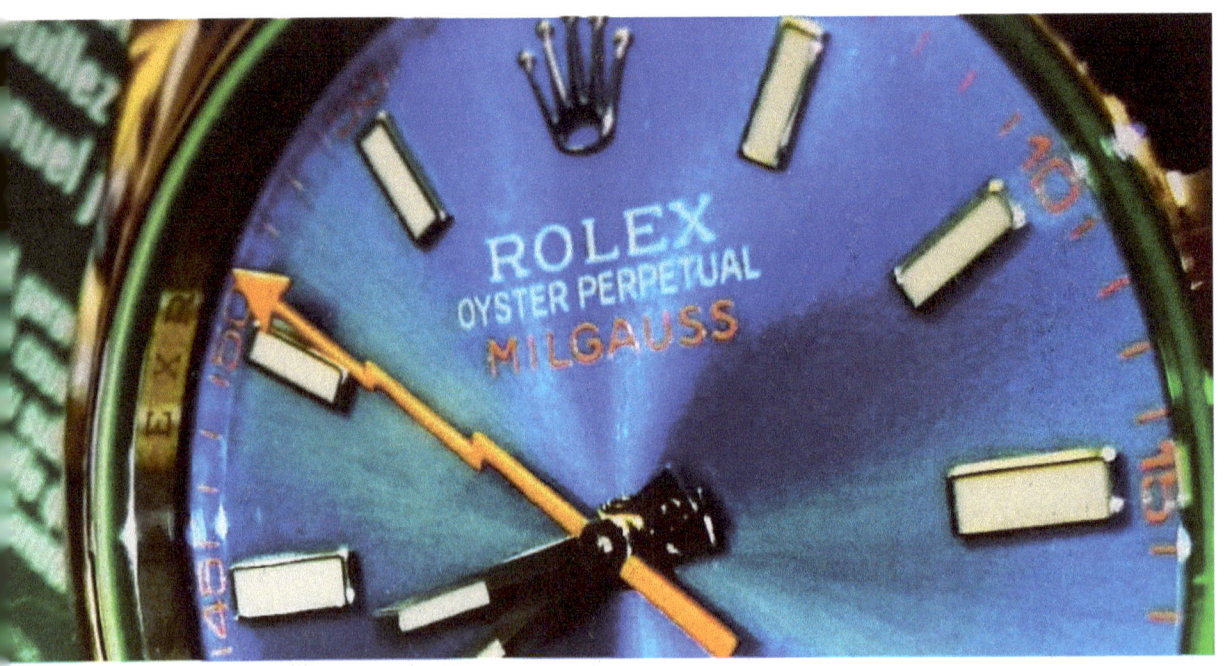

Milgauss Reference Summary

Name	Ref.	Cal.	Years	Bezel	Case	Description
Milgauss	6543	1080	1953 - 1956	Numbered, LN	38mm SS	Only 80-200 thought to exist. 19mm Lugs.
Milgauss	6541	1080	1956 - 1960	Numbered, LN	38mm SS	Introduced the lightning bolt second hand and bigger 20mm Lugs. Includes a full ferromagnetic Faraday cage
Milgauss	6019		1960 - 1963	Polished (Smooth)	38mm SS	Silver or Black matte dial, straight second hand and smooth bezel. A silver CERN dial exists with no luminous markers exists
Milgauss	1019	1580	1963 - 1988	Polished (Smooth)	38mm SS	CERN dial variant also available.
Milgauss	116400	3131	2007 -	Polished (Smooth)	40mm SS	Black, White and Blue (2014) dial variants
50th Anniversary Milgauss	116400GV	3131	2016 -	Polished (Smooth)	40mm SS	50th Anniversary green tinted crystal. Does not have the Laser Etched Crystal

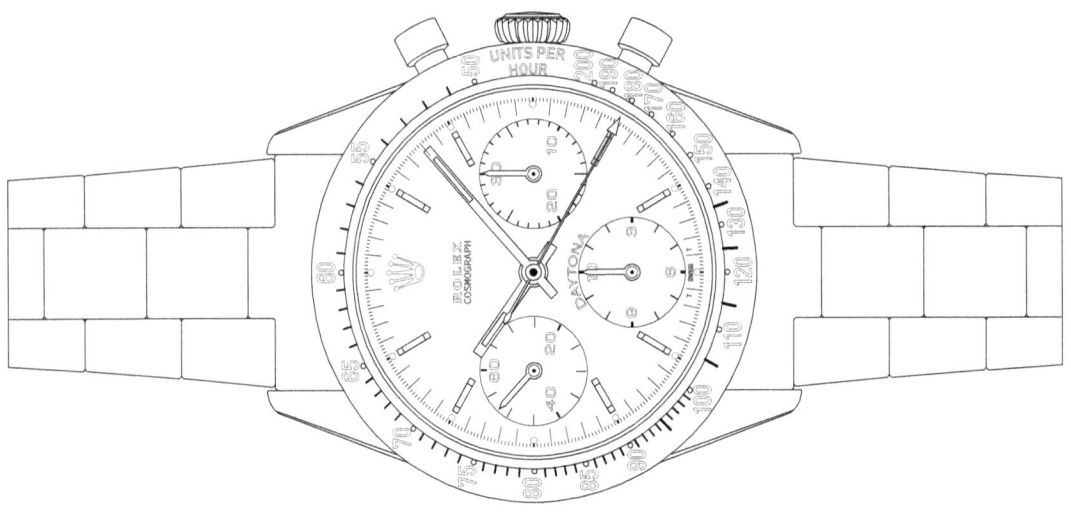

Cosmograph Daytona

A chronograph is a stopwatch integrated with a conventional time-of-day watch, and Rolex has been making these since the 1930s.

Rolex chronographs have evolved through three distinct eras. 1) The four digit reference Valjoux era, 2) The five-digit reference Zenith era, and 3) The contemporary six-digit reference, in-house era.

Rolex offered the now typical two pusher configuration starting in 1937 with Valjoux movements. These are all based on numerous variants of the caliber 72. In the 1980s Rolex adopted the Zenith El Primero movement in the 16000 series models. In 2000 Rolex debuted their in-house caliber 4130 in their six-digit model references.

Although we commonly associate the name Cosmograph with the pre-Daytona, it was the triple-date Moonphase dress watch that used it first. Cosmos is a reference to the night sky illustrated on the moon phase sub dial.

The vintage Cosmograph and early Daytonas are extremely technical to service and highly challenging references to collect. With countless dial variations and numerous reference iterations, they make the other tool watches straight-forward by comparison.

Headline-making auction prices continue to attract both admirers and nefarious dealers. Most collectors now acknowledge that the majority of pre-Daytonas in circulation do not have entirely original dials. An underground cottage industry has been tampering with dial text for several decades in the pursuit of higher prices. In particular, after market red text is being added to dials, creating an abundance of Daytona Big Reds. Writing is also being removed to create the Rolex-only, Solo Dials. Experts refrain from public judgment, as most cannot be definitively confirmed and Rolex maintains their customary silence on the matter.

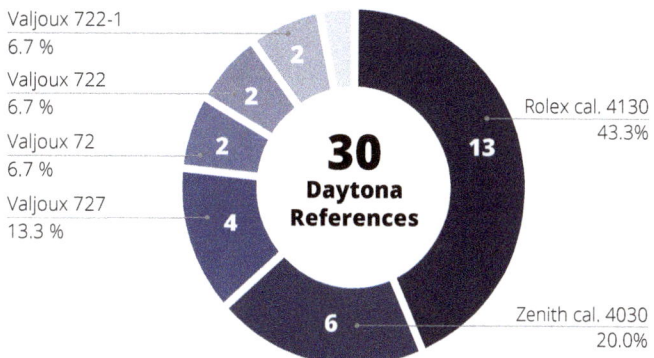

Pre-Cosmograph

The ref. 6234 was launched in 1955 and did not yet bear the Cosmograph name. This model was an evolution of the Dato-Compax chronographs of the antique period. It had both a tachymeter and a telemeter scale printed on the outer edge of the dial, under the crystal. Tachymeters measure speed and telemeters distance, both equally important to race car drivers as downhill skiers (see Antique section, Dato-Compax). Both instruments used either imperial (mph) or metric (kph) measures but not both.

The ref. 6234 was made at the rate of about 500 per year until production ended in 1961. Ref. 6234 was not a commercial success. However, the roughly 3,000 units made during the seven-year production run makes them a scarce and desirable reference today.

Cosmograph Daytona

Dial printing on the first Cosmograph Daytona (ref.6239 in 1963) was evolutionary. These watches began life as a Rolex Cosmograph, with the Daytona name added the following year (1964). These first Cosmograph references appeared with double Swiss dials, double Swiss underline dials, and double T-Swiss-T dials. There is no generally accepted explanation why these dials had these duplicate markings and all these variations appear within a narrow range of serial numbers.

The screw down pushers arrived in the 1970s with ref.6263, introducing waterproofing. These pushers were in response to owners ruining their watches by trying to run the chronograph under water. This addition initially claimed to waterproof the watch to 50m/165ft, but by the 1980s, was uprated to 300m/330ft.

An unusual feature of the 6263, is that it used higher grade versions of the Valjoux 23 movement in precious metal cases. The 18K gold cases had chronometer grade movements, while the stainless steel versions did not. This practice continued until the use of Superlative Chronometer, Officially Certified started to appear on dials

Cosmograph ref. 6263 with Panda dial.

in the 1970s.

Valjoux movements continued to power Cosmograph Daytonas until 1987 when Rolex switched suppliers to Zenith and their automatic El Primero movement. Renamed cal. 4030 this powered the Daytona ref. 16520, until 1987.

By this stage, the name had evolved from Cosmograph Daytona, to Daytona Cosmograph, to just Daytona.

Rolex switched to their in-house cal. 4130, with the launch of ref. 116520 in 2000. After 80 years, this was Rolex's first in-house chronograph.

The cal. 4130 required changes to the sub dial configuration and placement of the minute and hour counters moved to the left and right positions. The seconds counter moved from the left side of the dial to the bottom, and the two horizontal sub dials shifted to seven degrees above the center point. Some speculate this was an anti-counterfeiting measure rather than a technical engineering requirement.

Vintage and Classic Daytonas have been the subject of extensive research, with numerous books written about them in recent years. These three titles are particularly noteworthy -

- Rolex Daytona Manual Winding by Osvaldo Patrizzi and Guido Mondani (ISBN 978-88-940669-9-9)

- Rolex Daytona Story by Osvaldo Patrizzi and Guido Mondani (AISN B009HQ87PS)

- THE ULTIMATE ROLEX DAYTONA - Miniature edition by Pino Abbrescia, Fabio Santinelli, Paolo Gobbi and Naomi Ornstein

Ref. 6239 Cosmograph
Special Note

Rolex introduced the first Cosmograph ref. 6239 in 1963. It had a modest 36.5mm diameter and did not yet officially bare the name Daytona. It acquired the nickname thanks to Rolex becoming the official timekeeper at the Daytona Raceway in Florida.

The ref.6239 had been redesigned for race car drivers and found informal celebrity endorsement with Paul Newman.

This ref. 6239 has come to be known as the Paul Newman Daytona and was the first reference to use inverse colors for sub-dials. This color scheme has come to be known as a panda dial, with the inverse color combination being the reverse-panda dial. All previous chronograph dials are monotone. Like the first of most new models, it has several variations in dials, bezels, and movements. Valjoux 72B, 722 and 722-1 are all correct for the ref. 6239.

This Cosmograph was the first chronograph to have the tachymeter scale moved from under the glass on the dial, to outside the watch on the bezel. Singer made the dials for the 6239 and stamped the backs with Singer Brevets AV. The first series had serial numbers starting around 923,000, and they featured a satin-finish bezel. These had uniquely calibrated tachymeter scales known as the *275 Intermediate*. The intermediate-style tachymeter reads 300, *275*, 250, 255, and so on.

With the next iteration around 1964, Rolex removed the 275 indicator along with the small dash or hash markers, replacing them with dots or pips which are easier to read.

Also gone was the satin brushed finish, replaced with a mirror-polish finish. Dials were marked SWISS only and accompanied by an underline below the top dial text. This small horizontal line is thought to indicate the use of tritium lume, before the formal adoption of T SWISS T markings in 1964.

The name Daytona appears on dials below the text, Rolex Cosmograph. These are often described as floating logos as the Daytona name has an off-set vertical spacing with the Cosmograph text above, and appears to float in space. Floating logos disappear by 1966.

Rolex scholars estimate total production of ref.6239 at about 105,000 units.

Ref. 16500 Daytona Series
Special Note

Running from 1988 to 2000, this modern classic Daytona is increasingly sought after by collectors. It features the high performance Zenith caliber 400 (El Primero) which has been heavily customized by Rolex for use in this series of chronographs. 200 distinct modifications were made before becoming known as the Rolex caliber 4030, a Superlative Chronometer Officially Certified (SCOC). With modern screw-down crown and pushers it is waterproof to 100m, like the other tool watches in the Professional collection.

While some owners claim the dial is busy and hard to read, it is a practical watch suitable for daily wear. Prices for this reference vary considerably based on the six reference variations, with the stainless steel ref. 16520 being the most desirable.

The first versions appear on R-serial numbers from 1987 to late 1988. These were made in small volume and are quite rare. Their dials usually feature the floating Cosmograph with Officially Certified Chronograph text, and the bezel is calibrated, 200, 180, 160 etc.

To complicate matters, exceptions have been seen with intermediate bezels showing the 225 indicator from the Cosmograph predecessors. These unusual combinations are considered official as they've appeared in Rolex marketing materials. This Daytona was offered on a 78360 bracelet that is fully brushed, with no polished links.

The second version appears on L-serial numbers from 1989 to early 1990. It differs from the first R-serial series, with a bezel calibrated 400, 300, 250, 220 etc. Dials do not have Officially Certified Chronometer text. These were made in small numbers and are very rare.

The third versions appear on E, X, and N-serial numbers from early 1990 to late 1991. They differ from the second version by dial markings only. These have Superlative Chronometer Officially Certified text and an unusual inverted digit 6 in the lower sub dial. Numerals are printed with a more rounded font style and the minute track has shorter markers.

The fourth version appears on N, C, and S-serial numbers from late 1991 to early 1993. While the dial is the same as the third series, it was available on a new bracelet ref. 78390 with polished center links. This version is thought to have been produced in larger volume than the third series. With a larger supply on the pre-owned market, prices are lower than earlier versions.

The fifth versions appear on S, W, T, and U-serial numbers from early 1993 to late 1998. This version was made in higher volume and are not rare. It features a typical tritium dial with the digit 6 on the sub dial now being the right way up. The minute track markers appear fatter and more prominent.

The sixth and final series on U, A, and early P-serial numbers are from late 1998 to early 2000. The only difference being the Luminova dial.

Cosmograph Daytona Reference Summary

Ref.	Cal.	Depth Rating	Years
6238	72B	0	
6239	72	0	1963 - 1987
6239	722	0	1963 - 1987
6239	722-1	0	1963 - 1987
6240	722	50m	1965 - 1969
6241	722-1	0	1968 -
6241	645	0	1969 -
6262	727	0	1970 - 1970
6263	727	100m/330ft	1971 - 1987
6264	727	100m/330ft	1970 - 1980
6265	727	100m/330ft	1970 - 1980
16515	4030	100m/330ft	1991 - 1999
16518	4030	100m/330ft	1991 - 1999
16519	4030	100m/330ft	1991 - 1999
16520	4030	100m/330ft	1991 - 1999
16523	4030	100m/330ft	1991 - 1999
16528	4030	100m/330ft	1991 - 1999
116503	4130	100m/330ft	2000 - 2016
116505	4130	100m/330ft	2000 - 2016
116508	4130	100m/330ft	2000 - 2016
116509	4130	100m/330ft	2000 - 2016
116515	4130	100m/330ft	2000 - 2016
116518	4130	100m/330ft	2000 - 2016
116519	4130	100m/330ft	2000 - 2016
116520	4130	100m/330ft	2000 - 2016
116523	4130	100m/330ft	2000 - 2016
116528	4130	100m/330ft	2000 - 2016
116589	4130	100m/330ft	2000 - 2016
116598	4130	100m/330ft	2000 - 2016
116599	4130	100m/330ft	22000 - 2016
116500 LN	4130	100m/330ft	2016 -
116515 LN	4130	100m/330ft	2016 -
116518 LN	4130	100m/330ft	2016 -
116519 LN	4130	100m/330ft	2016 -

Oyster Perpetual Air-King

The Air-King brand has a long aviation pedigree and is one of the longest-running product lines in Rolex history.

The first Air-King appeared in 1945 and arrived as a conscious effort to merge predecessors featuring names like Air Lion, Air Tiger, and Air Giant. These monikers had been in use on various Bubbleback Rolex Oyster Perpetuals since the early 1930s.

They became popular among WWII pilots of the British Royal Air Force since they proved more reliable, accurate and readable than the RAF-issued timepieces.

Rolex reused references across model lines. Because of this, it is correct for a ref. 5500 to appear in both product lines with either Air-King or Explorer dials.

These dual-reference models are challenging to validate with the conversion from one to the other being a matter of a simple dial swap. For example, a prized 3-6-9 Explorer dial fitted to a less desirable Air King 5443, can net an unscrupulous dealer a tidy profit.

There's a lot to learn and love about the Air-King. Broadly speaking (and there are exceptions) the 4000 series reference numbers are WWII era watches from the 1940s. The 6500 series appear in the early 1950s. The 5000 series references appear in the mid-1950s and run until the late 1970s. The line was dormant during the 1980s before reappearing again in the early 1990s as a five-digit reference (14000 series).

The first Air-King references used manual wind Aegler Hunter movements like cal. A720 and A296. These included ref. 4925 and 4365 (also a dual-reference) and 4499.

In the 1950s Rolex released Air-Kings with what are considered Rolex in-house movements like the cal. 1030, 3000, 1520, 1530, 3130 and the modern cal. 3131.

The first auto-winding, Oyster Perpetual Air-King was ref.6552 with cal. 1030 which arrived in 1953.

The iconic Air-King ref. 5500 appeared in 1957 with cal.1530 and 1520 and lasted 37 years. It is one of the longest-running references in the Rolex lineup.

The ref. 5500 is a robust and reliable watch that can be serviced by any competent, independent watchmaker. With supply still plentiful, prices are reasonable making this a popular choice for a first vintage Rolex.

Confusingly the ref. 5500 was introduced in 1957 then again with the same reference number in 1970 but with an upgraded chronometer movement, cal. 1570.

The Air-King line of watches mainly used manual wound movements, but in the 1950s adopted automatic self-winding movements (Perpetuals).

Some of these Perpetuals featured a date complication and were branded, Air-King Date. These automatics had thicker Oyster case dimensions.

The manually-wound Air-Kings used Precision and Super Precision-class movements. These references are considered desirable for their slimmer case profiles.

Through the 1950s and 1960s the Air-King formula remained unchanged, as the 34mm (Mid Size) Oyster complemented the larger Datejust (36mm).

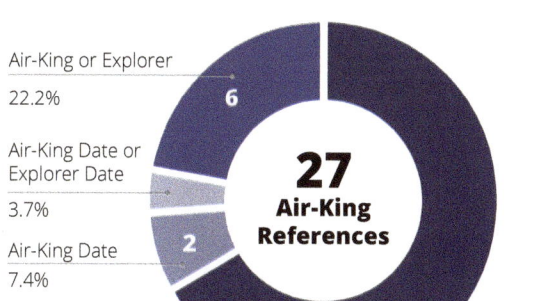

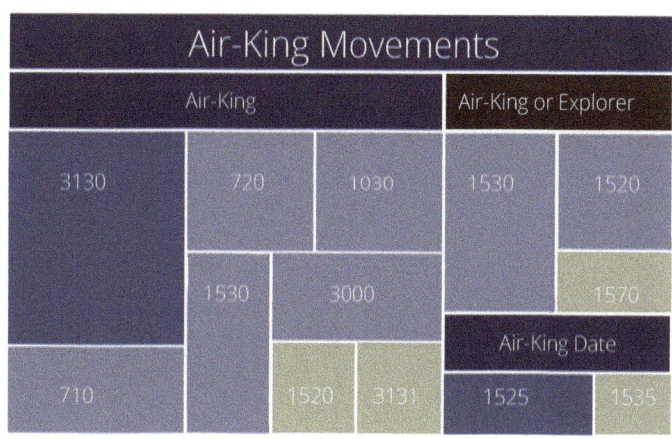

*Air-King movements by reference
i.e. number of references using each caliber*

During the 1970s the Air King line received movement upgrades to the chronometer cal. 1570, and eventually achieved full COSC certification in 2007.

Rolex retired the Air-King in 2014. By this time it had become a thoroughly contemporary watch, offered in 26mm, 31mm, 34mm, and 36mm sizes. The decision to retire the Air-King was to make way for the Rolex Oyster Perpetual and avoid the two lines competing in the same market segment.

Airmen of No. 80 Squadron RAF with a Hawker Hurricane in the Western Desert, during Operation Crusader

The Air-King was relaunched with a radical and modern reinterpretation in 2016 with ref. 116900. This new interpretation is also a highly polarizing design and has all the hallmarks of a future classic collectible.

Air King Reference Summary

Name	Ref.	Cal.	Start	Bezel		Description
Air King	1401	710	1943	Engine-Turned	34mm SS	Precision
Air King	4365	710	1945	Smooth (Polished)	34mm SS	Pre Air-King Air Giant, Precision
Air King	4925	720	1945	Smooth (Polished)	34mm SS	
Air King	4499	720	1946	Smooth (Polished)	34mm SS	
Air King	6552	1030	1953	Smooth (Polished)	34mm SS	First automatic Air-King, Precision
Air King	6652	1030	1953	Smooth (Polished)	34mm SS	Transitional to the 5500
Air King or Explorer	5500	1520	1957	Smooth (Polished)	35mm SS	Baton hands, Precision
Air King or Explorer	5500	1530	1957	Smooth (Polished)	35mm SS	Super Precision
Air King	5502	1530	1958	Smooth (Polished)	35mm GF	Precision
Air King	5506	1530	1958	Smooth (Polished)	34mm GF	Super Precision
Air King Date	5700	1525	1958	Smooth (Polished)	34mm SS	Precision
Air King Date or Explorer	5701	1535	1958	Fluted	34mm SSYG	Precision
Air King or Explorer	5501	1520	1958	Fluted	35mm SSYG	Precision
Air King or Explorer	5501	1530	1958	Fluted	35mm SSYG	Super Precision
Air King or Explorer	5504	1530	1958	Smooth (Polished)	35mm SS	Super Precision
Air King or Explorer	5500	1570	1970	Smooth (Polished)	34mm SS	COSC
Air King	5520	1520	1974	Smooth (Polished)	34mm GF	Precision
Air King Date	5520	1525	1974	Smooth (Polished)	34mm GF	Quickset date
Air King	14000	3000	1989	Smooth (Polished)	34mm SS	COSC
Air King	14010	3000	1989	Engine-Turned	34mm SS	COSC
Air King	14000M	3130	2000	Smooth (Polished)	34mm SS	COSC
Air King	14010M	3130	2000	Engine-Turned	34mm SS	COSC
Air King	114200	3130	2007	Smooth (Polished)	40mm SS	COSC
Air King	114210	3130	2007	Engine-Turned	40mm SS	Precision
Air King	114234	3130	2007	Fluted	40mm WG	COSC
Air King	116900	3131	2017	Smooth (Polished)	40mm SS	COSC

Oyster Perpetual GMT-Master

This iconic reference boasts an incredible history marked by technological innovation. Many subtle design variations add to the mystique, making this reference enjoyable to learn about and challenging to collect.

The GMT-Master has well-documented connections to early jet aviation and pioneering space flight. The James Bond 007 (Honor Blackman) and Magnum PI (Tom Selleck) associations only add to the romance.

All versions of the GMT feature a bi-directional bezel. These were friction fit (non-clicking) until the arrival of the five-digit references with their 120 click bezel. It is correct for transitional models like the 16750 to have the older-style friction fit, non-clicking bezels.

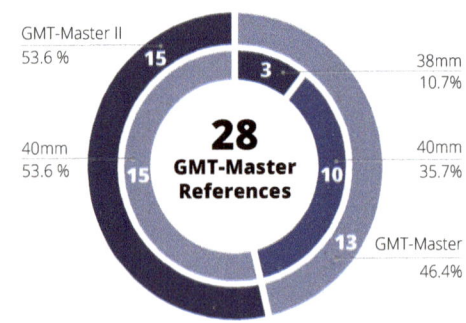

GMT Master references

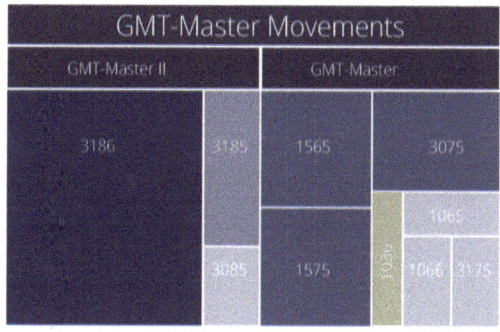

Ref 6542 (1954 - 1959)

Fidel Castro liked his Rolex watches and his GMTs in particular.

Many photographs show him wearing two different Rolex on the same wrist. He set one to local time in Havana, and the other displayed the time in Moscow.

Castro frequently gave Rolex watches to his commanders and associates. These were essential equipment for field commanders and crucial for coordinating and synchronizing military operations. In a pre-quartz era, the precision of a Rolex tool watch was an obvious choice.

The first GMT arrived with a gilt dial, radium Bakelite bezel and no crown guards. The bezel used a fragile Bakelite (acrylic plastic) insert which is prone to cracking and was only available in red and blue.

In 1959 the ref.6542 was subject to an embarrassing recall due to the high levels of radioactivity from the radium in the Bakelite bezels. The US Atomic Energy Agency demanded the recall securing the ref.6542's place in GMT folklore. A few examples that went unreturned are still in existence and command significant collector premiums. Even examples with replaced bezels are rare and sell for high prices.

The reference 6542 was famously worn by Pussy Galore (Honor Blackman) in the 1964 James Bond classic, *Goldfinger*.

Ref 1675 (1959 - 1979)

Che Guevara appears in many pictures with his GMT-Master ref.1675. It was a gift from fellow communist leader, Fidel Castro.

Che Guevara was killed on October 9th, 1967 by CIA operative Felix Rodriguez. He removed Guevara's Rolex GMT-Master from the wrist of his corpse, and it remains in his possession to this day.

The ref.1675 introduced crown guards starting with pointed crown guards

(PCG). This case was known as the *Cornine* case (Italian for little antlers). It was later updated and featured the rounded ones that became standard.

The ref.1675 was the first Rolex sports watch available with a choice of either the Oyster (ref, 7206, 7836, 78360) or Jubilee (ref. 6251, 62510) bracelets.

In 1966 this model was updated with a matte dial finish and printed lettering. The first gilt dial examples sell for a significant premium over the later white-letter matte dial versions. The earliest examples had gilt lettering and closed chapter rings (minute tracks).

Before 1970 the 24hr-hand had a small triangle arrow tip. This style of arrow hand lasted into the early white-letter matte dial period. After 1970 it switched to the larger, arrow style used today.

Rolex launched the ref.1675 with a red and blue bezel insert (BLRO, bleu rouge, Pepsi). A black option (LN, Lunette Noire) was introduced late in the models' life cycle. The bezel is friction fitted and does not click.

This reference was COSC certified and was the first GMT-Master to use the text, *Superlative Chronometer Officially Certified*.

Variations include a two-tone ref. 1675/3 and a solid 18k gold ref. 1675/8. These featured unique nipple-style index markers and an applied gold coronet (made of gold and fixed to the dial like the hour markers). The applied coronet is unique to the four-digit 1675/3 and 1675/8. With the arrival of the five-digit reference, Rolex replaced the applied crown with a gilt version, matching the dial text.

A typical ref. 1675 seldom has perfectly matched hand and dial lume patina.

There were six matte dial variants from MK 0 to MK V. MK I, MK II, and MK V are thought to have sub-variants. The variations in font style text alignment are very subtle and require considerable practice to recognize.

Ref 16750 (1979 - 1988)

This reference arrived with movement caliber 3075, and introduced a convenient quickset date and hacking feature. Due to the new movement, the dial and hands are not backward compatible with ref.1675. The hand stack changed, with the hour hand moving to the bottom of the pile, unlike ref.1675 where the red 24-hour hand is at the bottom. Like the earlier ref.1675, the GMT-hand was fixed and could not be independently set. Reading second time zones required the bezel to be rotated to align with the 24-hour hand. The bezel assembly and colors were the same as ref.1675.

Ref. 16750 GMT-Master with glossy dial.

The dials were matte finished with tritium lume until about 1983. Rolex then switched to the modern gloss finish with white gold index surrounds. The first versions of these glossy dials omitted the word, Date, reading only *Oyster Perpetual*.

Rolex offered black or brown dials on the two-tone and solid gold references (16753 & 16758). These dials were the last to feature the nipple-style indexes and the first to have the gilt coronet (as opposed to an applied coronet). Rolex offered the ref.16750 on either Oyster or Jubilee bracelets.

Ref 16760 (1983 - 1987)

Reference 16760 is the first GMT Master II, and it launched with caliber 3085. This reference was the first GMT-Master to feature a sapphire crystal. Production overlapped with its predecessor, the ref.16750. The new cal. 3085 extended the hacking and quickset date to include quickset of the 24-hour hand, too. This improvement allowed calculation of a third timezone. Collectors dubbed this reference the Fat Lady, or the Sophia Loren, thanks to the thicker and fuller Oyster case needed to accommodate the new movement.

Rolex made this reference only in stainless steel, and the bezel was available in two colors - black (LN) or black and red bezel, (LNRO, lunette noire rouge, Coke). There was no blue and red option (BLRO). The colored bezel insert is interchangeable with that of the GMT-II 16710 and the GMT 16700.

Ref 16700 (1988 -1998)

The 16700 launched with caliber 3175. Dials featured Tritium lume (with the corresponding T<25 markings) until about 1998 when Luminova was adopted. Although the 16700 was the replacement for the 16750, it did not have a quick set 24-hour hand.

Rolex offered the ref.16700 in stainless steel only but with a choice of two bezel colors- red and blue (BLRO, bleu rouge, Pepsi) or black (LN, lunette noire).

The date wheel had open 6s and 9s like its predecessors, until about 1992 when the font change to the modern closed font style.

Ref 16710 (1989 -2007)

This reference features caliber 3185. It came with Tritium dials (and the T<25 dial markings) until about 1997, then switched to Luminova (and the SWISS dial markings) in 1998 and then Super Luminova (with SWISS MADE) in 2000.

Curiously, there was a short run of Luminova dials marked with the tritium indicator T<25, produced in 1998. This contradiction (tritium markings and Luminova lume) can be mistaken for a relumed or fake dial.

GMT-Master II ref. 16710 BLRO, (Pepsi) 1990.

The ref. 16710 is functionally the same as the reference it replaced - ref. 16760 except it had a slimmer Oyster case. In 2000, Rolex introduced Solid End Links (SELs) to eliminate the notorious bracelet rattle. In 2003, Rolex marked crystals with a Laser Etched Crown (LEC).

In 2007 caliber 3186 was introduced, around Z & M serial number range. Examples of the transitional ref.16710 with the cal.3186 movements are rare and sought after. In the same year, the case was redesigned to eliminate visible spring bar holes in the lugs. The bracelets for these SEL-models had notched end links for removing the spring bars. They are also permanently attached to the bracelet.

In 2005, starting in the D-serial range, the dial font evolved to a non-serif font giving rise to the Stick Dial. The term refers to the Roman numerals in GMT-Master II. With the serif gone they resemble two parallel sticks. These dials lasted through the Z and M serial range. Rolex discontinued the reference in 2008.

The 16710 was available in stainless steel, two-tone (16713) and solid gold (16718) with all three bezel options (Black LN, Coke LNRO & Pepsi BLRO).

GMT Master Reference Summary

Name	Ref.	Cal.	Depth Rating	Years	Bezel	Case
GMT	6542	1036 (1954-1959)	50m/165ft	1954-1959	Numbered, Bakelite, BLRO	38mm SS
First GMT derived from the Turn-O-Graph (6202) featured a Bakelite bezel, no crown guards. Worn by Pussy Galore in Goldfinger 1964						
GMT	6542	1065 (1957-1959)	50m/165ft	1954-1959	Numbered, Bakelite, BLRO	38mm SS
First GMT derived from the Turn-O-Graph (6202) featured a Bakelite bezel, no crown guards. Worn by Pussy Galore in Goldfinger 1964						
GMT	6542	1066 (1957-1959)	50m/165ft	1954-1959	Numbered, Bakelite, BLRO	38mm SS
First GMT derived from the Turn-O-Graph (6202) featured a Bakelite bezel, no crown guards. Worn by Pussy Galore in Goldfinger 1964						
GMT	1675/3	1565 (1959-1965)	50m/165ft	1959-1979	Numbered, BLRO, LN	40mm SSYG
Two Tone version of the 1675 featuring black or brown nipple dial with applied coronet.						
GMT	1675	1565 (1959-1965)	50m/165ft	1959-1979	Numbered, BLRO, LN	40mm SS
First Rolex sports watch available on both the Oyster (ref 78360) and Jubilee (ref 62510) bracelet. Prior to 1970 the 24hr hand had a "small" triangle arrow.						
GMT	1675/8	1565 (1959-1965)	50m/165ft	1959-1979	Numbered, BLRO, LN	40mm YG
Solid gold version of the 1675 featuring black or brown nipple dial with applied coronet.						
GMT	1675/3	1575 (1965-1980)	50m/165ft	1959-1979	Numbered, BLRO, LN	40mm SSYG
Two Tone version of the 1675 featuring black or brown nipple dial with applied coronet.						
GMT	1675	1575 (1965-1980)	50m/165ft	1959-1979	Numbered, BLRO, LN	40mm SS
First Rolex sports watch available on both the Oyster (ref 78360) and Jubilee (ref 62510) bracelet. Prior to 1970 the 24hr hand had a "small" triangle arrow.						
GMT	1675/8	1575 (1965-1980)	50m/165ft	1959-1979	Numbered, BLRO, LN	40mm YG
Solid gold version of the 1675 featuring black or brown nipple dial with applied coronet.						
GMT	16750	3075	100m/330ft	1979-1988	Numbered	40mm SS
Early versions omitted "Date" from the dial. New movement introduced hand stack change. 1986 saw change to glossy dial with white gold surrounds.						

Name	Ref.	Cal.	Depth Rating	Years	Bezel	Case
GMT	16753	3075	100m/330ft	1979-1988	Numbered	40mm SSYG
Two tone version of the 16750 (Tigers Eye)						
GMT	16758	3075	100m/330ft	1979-1988	Numbered	40mm YG
Solid gold version of the 16750						
GMT-II	16760	3085	100m/330ft	1983-1987	Numbered, LNRO	40mm SS
Fat Lady, Sophia Loren. First GMT-Master II with thicker case, sapphire crystal and white gold indexes. Coke & Black Bezel only.						
GMT	16700	3175	100m/330ft	1988-1998	Numbered, BLRO, LN	40mm SS
Tritium up to 1997 and Luminova from 1998. Date wheel had open 6s and 9s until 1992/3. Available in Pepsi and Black bezel only.						
GMT-II	16710	3186	100m/330ft	1989-2007	Numbered, BLRO, LNRO, LN	40mm SS
Initially tritium then switching to Luminova in 1998. Case and movement revised in 2007.						
GMT-II	16713	3186	100m/330ft	1989-2007	Numbered, LN	40mm SSYG
Two tone version of 16710						
GMT-II	16718	3186	100m/330ft	1989-2007	Numbered, LN	40mm YG
Solid gold version of 16710						
GMT-II	16710	3185 (1988-1992)	100m/330ft	1989-2007	Numbered, BLRO, LNRO, LN	40mm SS
Initially tritium then switching to Luminova in 1998. Case and movement revised in 2007.						
GMT-II	16713	3185 (1988-1992)	100m/330ft	1989-2007	Numbered, LN	40mm SSYG
Two tone version of 16710						
GMT-II	16718	3185 (1988-1992)	100m/330ft	1989-2007	Numbered, LN	40mm YG
Solid gold version of 16710						
GMT-II	116710	3186	1000ft/300m	2008-	Numbered, Cerachrom	40mm SS
Introduction of Maxi Case, ceramic bezel and rehaut engraving						
GMT-II	116713	3186	1000ft/300m	2008-	Numbered, Cerachrom	40mm SSYG
Two tone version of 116710						
GMT-II	116718	3186	1000ft/300m	2008-	Numbered, Cerachrom	40mm YG

Name	Ref.	Cal.	Depth Rating	Years	Bezel	Case
Solid gold version of 116710						
GMT-II	116719	3186	1000ft/300m	2014-	Numbered, Cerachrom	40mm WG
White gold Pepsi (BLRO)						
GMT-II	116758	3186	1000ft/300m	2014-	Numbered, Cerachrom	40mm YG
Jeweled version						
GMT-II	116759	3186	1000ft/300m	2014-	Numbered, Cerachrom	40mm WG
Jeweled version						
GMT-II	116760	3186	1000ft/300m	2014-	Numbered, Cerachrom	40mm SS
Jeweled version						
GMT-II	126710	3285	1000ft/300m	2017-	Numbered, Cerachrom, BLRO, LN	40mm SS

CLASSICS & CROSSOVERS

"Fashion passes, style remains"
- Coco Chanel (1883-1971)

The Rolex Classic Collection is neither formal and dressy (like the Cellini collection) nor professional and sporting. They are versatile crossover watches that are robust and equally appropriate to pair with formal wear as they are with sports-wear. They share the waterproof and accuracy specifications of the Professional collection, but also feature jewel-set bezels and precious metals.

The brand trademarks in this category are some of the oldest in the Rolex stable, spanning antique, vintage and classic genres. Surviving examples are plentiful, making them attractively priced and an excellent entry point into vintage Rolex ownership.

For most collectors, the Rolex Oyster is all about the world-famous, waterproof Oyster case, with its rounded mid case, integrated lugs, screw-down crown and proprietary threaded case back.

In common vintage parlance, the term and trademark Oyster refers to the case style. Few know that the Rolex Oyster was also used to brand a collection of significant watches before the arrival of the iconic Oyster case.

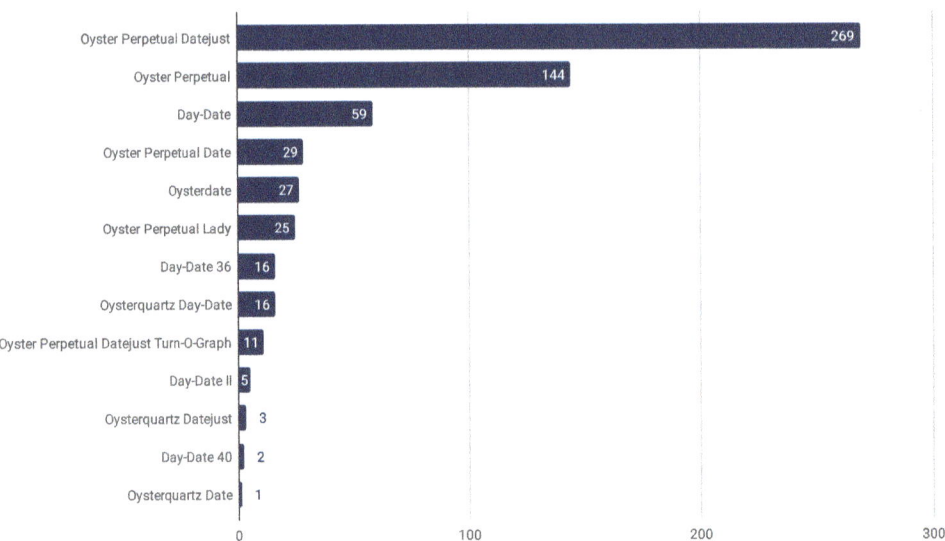

Oyster Case

Cultural norms today make no distinction between men's and women's watch sizes. Today, women proudly wear men's size Rolex's, but neither men nor women have yet to show much interest in women's antique and vintage Rolex's.

There is virtually no collector interest in Ladies sized Oysters, and the market is very soft. Ladies-size watches currently sell for scrap metal and gem value.

However, there is growing appreciation among male collectors for smaller watches.

36mm down to 34mm Oyster cases wear well on smaller wrists and are particularly comfortable if you have a pronounced wrist bone. Combined with clever design cues like thin bezels, tapered hands, and indexes, these smaller cases are said to wear larger than their size.

For antique and vintage examples produced up to the mid-1950s, 33mm to 34mm is considered a Men's Size and was quite large at the time. There are four classes of Oyster case - Full, Ladies, Mid and Boys sizes.

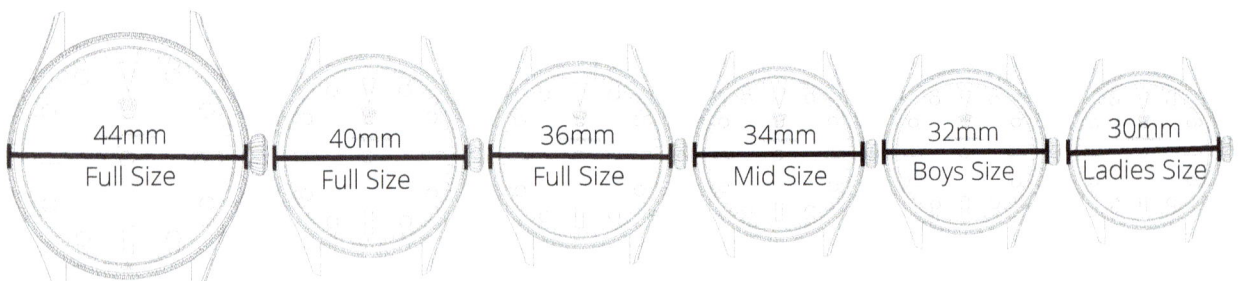

ROLEX OYSTER WATCHES

In 1926, the Rolex Oyster models made up a Collection. These early models fall in the antique rather than the vintage category.

Initially there were four models, including an octagonal and a cushion-shaped case. Each was available in gents (32mm) and ladies (28mm) sizes in yellow and white gold.

In 1927, Mercedes Gleitze wore a 28mm ladies, octagonal Rolex Oyster around her neck during her famous 35km cross-channel swim attempts. She became one of the first Rolex brand ambassadors to feature in early advertising and marketing.

The octagonal Oyster proved less popular than the cushion case, and Rolex dropped it from the catalog after a few years. Rarity now makes them the more desirable model among collectors.

A few years later it was a 36mm men's cushion case on the wrist of Sir Malcolm Campbell when he broke his land speed record for the 9th and final time in 1935.

Rolex adopted the simple, two-piece Oyster case, in the 1930s. Then continued to improve the Oyster design with the inventions of the Twinlock and Triplock crowns in 1953 and 1970. It was these innovations that provided the platform for the success of the subsequent sport and professional models so beloved of the vintage era.

The term Oyster is a registered trademark, and Rolex guarantees all Rolex Oysters to be waterproof to a depth of at least 50m.

This guarantee is extended to 100m for the Explorer, to 300m for the Submariner and 1220m for the Sea-Dweller.

The original Rolex Oyster collection is therefore limited to these antique models bearing only the words, Rolex Oyster on the dial.

Mercedes Gleitze, distance swimmer and Rolex ambassador. Circa 1930

OYSTER PRECISION

Rolex watch dials featuring the text, Precision, Extra Precision or Super Precision are not product lines, but a classification of the accuracy of the movement. A variety of case styles in addition to the Oyster, contain Precision grade movements.

The terms Precision, Extra Precision or Super Precision are successors to the earlier Prima, Extra Prima, and Ultra Prima classifications, which appeared on Bubblebacks and pocket watches.

These movements were not submitted for independent certification but were tested in-house (for reasons known only to Rolex). These are not COSC certified movements.

Rolex has a long history of using independent testing labs, reflected by their use of the word Chronometer on early (antique) dials. Rolex changed the term in the 1930s to *Officially Certified Chronometer* which appears on early Bubblebacks. In the 1950s this became *Superlative Chronometer*.

The Controle Officiel Suisse des Chronometres (COSC) was formed in 1973 and adopted by Rolex as their official testing authority. Certified movements had dials featuring the words, *Superlative Chronometer Officially Certified*.

Like the early pre-Oysters, Rolex awarded the Ultra Prima or Super Precision designation to the top 10% most consistent and accurate movements. The remaining 90% were assigned either Extra Prima (or Extra Precision) or Prima (or Precision).

Prima markings appear on pre-Oyster and Bubbleback cases. Precision appears on Oyster cases with movements derived from the base caliber 1200.

The reputation of these non-COSC (not chronometer grade) movements for being lower quality is unfounded. Seasoned watchmakers will attest to the accuracy these movements can attain. They can be made to achieve accuracy within COSC

Above: Sir Malcolm Campbell sporting his cushion case Rolex Oyster.

Below: Testing the Napier Railton Bluebird at Pendine Sands, Wales. Circa 1927.

standards (-4 / +6 secs per day) and even meeting Rolex's own target of -1/+5 secs per day.

Manual wound Precision movements were sold alongside COSC-certified Perpetual (automatic) chronometers until they were phased out in the 1980s. Mechanically simple and very robust, Rolex produced the 1200 series from early 1954 up until late 1984.

- Cal. 1210 18,000bps 1954 - 1964

- Cal. 1215 18,000bps (Date) 1954 - 1964

- Cal.1225 21,600bps (Date) 1967 - 1984

Product lines like Oyster Precision (no date), Oysterdate, Date, some early Speedkings and Air Kings contain these 1200-series manual movements. All had waterproof Oyster cases offered in three sizes. In sales catalogs these were described as Ladies: 23mm x 8.5mm, Mid-Size: 30 mm x 11 mm, and Men's: 34.5mm x 10.3mm

Pros and Cons

Current prices for these references are soft, and there are bargains to be had. The price-to-value proposition is compelling.

These are hand-wound watches and require daily winding. While some owners love this, others don't. If you can spare the minute, it takes each day to turn the crown a dozen times these pieces will keep you on schedule throughout your day.

The cases are slimmer and lower-profile than the automatic Perpetual models of similar age. Many claim they're more comfortable to wear and sit lower on the wrist (helpful if you have a pronounced wrist bone). They're equally as water resistant as automatic models and finished to similarly high standards.

There is an urban myth circulating on watch forums suggesting that daily use of the crown causes accelerated deterioration of the crown tube, resulting in crossed threads and a loss of water resistance. Whether or not there's any evidence to support this, crown tubes are inexpensive and easily replaced.

With accuracy and reliability being a non-issue, the joy of owning an Oyster Precisions comes down to case size and dial style.

Above: The Rolex Oyster Precision ref. 6422 with waffle-texture dial and Explorer-style hour markers. The Oyster case shows signs of service polish.

Below: Caliber 1215 with unevenly aged service components (ratchet & crown wheels). The regulator is set to the minimum position, suggesting the movement is running fast and may be ready for a service.

Precision references most commonly feature thin, polished bezels, but can be found with the machine-turned bezels. These thin bezels accentuate their dials, giving the illusion of a larger watch, hence their reputation for wearing larger than their size.

Given their long production run, dials from these watches are available in a wide variety of styles and colors. These range from 1950's arrowhead hour markers with alpha-style hands, to 1980's double-bars with baton hands. Some dials feature unusual and collectible markings, such as the Meters-First water resistance rating.

Earlier references have a distinctive vintage look and feel that is subdued yet iconic. Dials, in particular, reflect the style trends of their era.

While significant price appreciation is unlikely, prices have been stable for several years. These watches are not investments, but reasonably-priced, functional jewelry, that happens to be comfortable to wear and fun to collect.

If you like a low-key, classy, vintage Rolex, there are few better references to start with than one of these.

Contemporary Oyster Perpetual with bronze sunburst dial and broad baton-style hands and markers.

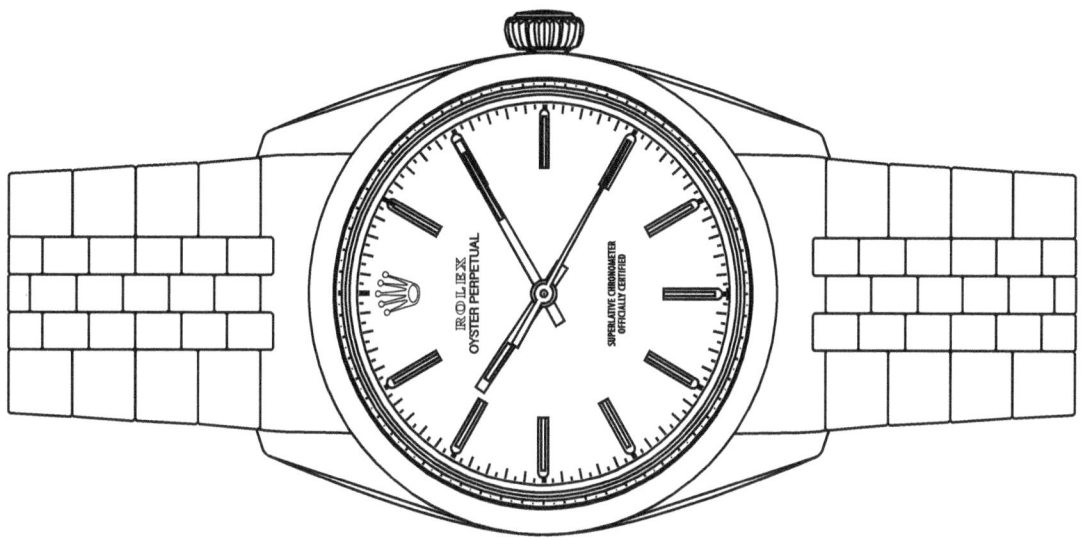

Oyster Perpetual

The story of the Oyster Perpetual is intimately related to that of the Bubbleback from which it evolved. From the 1950s onwards the Rolex Oyster Perpetual collection has been positioned and priced as the entry-level Rolex. The simple three-hand design, devoid of embellishments or complications, continues to be a commercially successful formula.

Perpetual is a trademark reserved and used for the automatic self-winding movement. This innovation emerged in the 1930s and was not exclusive to Rolex. Other Swiss watchmakers were designing self-winding movements with sleeker and more integrated solutions, allowing slimmer case profiles.

The Rolex solution was to retrofit an auto-winding rotor to existing manual winding movements. This approach allowed for a manual wind to top up the reserved power, and provided owners with a level of reassurance and comfort that other fully automatic watches did not.

The legacy manual-wind capability was skillfully exploited and marketed as a desirable feature. While not the most technically sophisticated solution, it proved a winner commercially.

It also had the added advantage of being entirely familiar to watchmakers accustomed to the manual-winding movement that lay beneath the rotor. The Perpetual proved not only robust but simple and inexpensive to service.

Dial designs have evolved subtly, reflecting tastes and styles across the decades. Collectors today have a vast range to select from depending on the decade of interest.

Most popular are the textured waffle dials with the Explorer-style 3-6-9 hour markers. These reflect the design aesthetic of the 1950s and include arrowhead or shark tooth-shaped hour markers. Examples from this period usually have dauphine or alpha-shaped hands.

When choosing a watch from this collection, be sure the style and color of the hands match the dial furniture. With so many in circulation, many examples have been customized to owners particular tastes.

There are approximately 140 references in the Oyster Perpetual line, offered in Full-Size (38mm), Mid-Size (32-34mm) and Ladies-Size (26-32mm).

There are a further 80 references across the Oyster Perpetual Date, Oyster Perpetual Lady, and Oysterdate models.

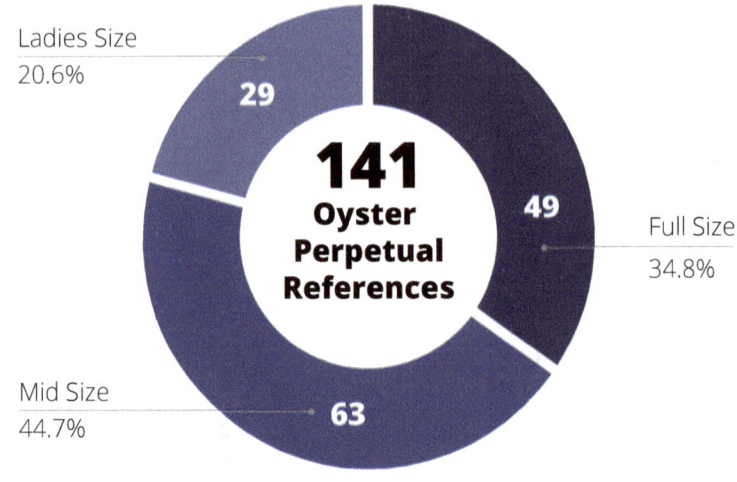

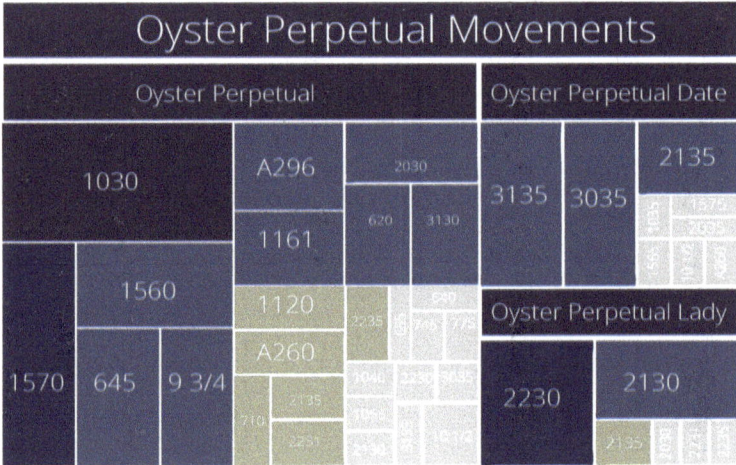

Oyster Perpetual Date

Sometimes known as the Rolex Date it is often confused with the larger Datejust.

It made its debut in the 1950s following the 1945 launch of the larger Datejust. At 34mm it is 2mm smaller than the Datejust but the same size as the Oysterdate and Air-King from which it was born.

The smaller case allows for a narrower 19mm lug width and subsequently a thinner bracelet. The Rolex Oyster Perpetual Date is available on both Oyster and Jubilee bracelets and has a wide variety of bezel and dial combinations.

The modern version is known as the Rolex Oyster Perpetual Date 34 and now belongs to the Datejust Collection. Early predecessors like the Oysterdate were considered independent product lines and not part of the Datejust collection.

Oysterdate

The Oysterdate is the original Mid Size Rolex. The name was applied to mid size Oyster cases as early as 1951. By 1966 it became Oyster Perpetual - Date - before losing the hyphens in the late 1970s and becoming Oyster Perpetual Date. Use of the Oysterdate name seems to have entirely disappeared by 1970.

The Oysterdate name was applied liberally to several classes of watches. Most were manual-winding Precision-class movements like the ref. 6694.

A few had automatic, chronometer-grade, Perpetual movements with Officially Certified Chronometer or Ritetime on the dial (e.g. ref. 6518). The only trait they had in common was the 32mm and 34mm cases, which came to be known as Boys Size and Mid Size.

The date complication is slow-setting, meaning that if the watch goes unwound and stops, then setting the correct date involves winding the crown the long way around past midnight. The date wheel, with its open 6s and 9s, is known as *roulette style*, with odd dates printed in black and even dates in red.

The reason for this is a mystery. Urban legend suggests it originates from post-war rationing when certain supplies were available on alternate days, and this was a convenience to keep track. Whatever the reason, it is an attractive and unusual feature.

Today, collectors seek out the Oysterdate for their rarity and the 1950s design aesthetic. These details include alpha and dauphine hands and tapered indexes (arrowhead, shark tooth and diamond shaped). Waffle textured dials and 3-6-9 indexes are also correct and are as popular today as they were in the 50s.

Oysterdate Perpetual

The Oysterdate Perpetual such as the ref. 6518 uses cal.1035 with its beautiful butterfly-style rotor.

Caliber 1035 is a chronometer-grade movement and timed to COSC standards, and their dials will bear the *Officially Certified Chronometer* text.

This caliber is the same cal. 1030 (with no date complication) used in the early GMT-Master and Submariner, and both these Professional watches command considerably higher prices.

Oysterdate Perpetuals are being cannibalized to provide parts for these other, more expensive models. The Oysterdate Perpetual is rare and becoming more so.

Oyster Perpetual Reference Summary

Name	Ref.	Cal.	Bezel	Size
Oyster Perpetual	3064	620	Polished (Smooth)	Full Size
Oyster Perpetual	6290	640	Polished (Smooth)	Full Size
Oyster Perpetual	6598	745	Polished (Smooth)	Full Size
Oyster Perpetual	6098	775	Polished (Smooth)	Full Size
Oyster Perpetual	6599	1030	Fluted	Full Size
Oyster Perpetual	6614	1030	Polished (Smooth)	Full Size
Oyster Perpetual	6634	1030	Polished (Smooth)	Full Size
Oyster Perpetual	6611	1055	Fluted	Full Size
Oyster Perpetual	1007	1560	Engine Turned	Full Size
Oyster Perpetual	1008	1560	Engine Turned	Full Size
Oyster Perpetual	1013	1560	Fluted	Full Size
Oyster Perpetual	1018	1560	Fluted	Full Size
Oyster Perpetual	1010	1560	Polished (Smooth)	Full Size
Oyster Perpetual	1012	1560	Polished (Smooth)	Full Size
Oyster Perpetual	1014	1560	Polished (Smooth)	Full Size
Oyster Perpetual	1024	1560	Polished (Smooth)	Full Size
Oyster Perpetual	1004	1570	Engine Turned	Full Size
Oyster Perpetual	1009	1570	Engine Turned	Full Size
Oyster Perpetual	1005	1570	Fluted	Full Size
Oyster Perpetual	1011	1570	Fluted	Full Size
Oyster Perpetual	6301	1570	Fluted	Full Size
Oyster Perpetual	1003	1570	Polished (Smooth)	Full Size
Oyster Perpetual	1006	1570	Polished (Smooth)	Full Size
Oyster Perpetual	1025	1570	Polished (Smooth)	Full Size
Oyster Perpetual	14203	3035	Fluted	Full Size
Oyster Perpetual	14233	3130	Fluted	Full Size
Oyster Perpetual	14238	3130	Fluted	Full Size
Oyster Perpetual	116000	3130	Polished (Smooth)	Full Size
Oyster Perpetual	116619LB	3135	Numbered	Full Size
Oyster Perpetual	6210	10 1/2	Polished (Smooth)	Full Size
Oyster Perpetual	6023	10.5"	Engine Turned	Full Size
Oyster Perpetual	3458	9 3/4"	Engraved	Full Size

Name	Ref.	Cal.	Bezel	Size
Oyster Perpetual	3794	9 3/4"		Full Size
Oyster Perpetual	6110	A260	Polished (Smooth)	Full Size
Oyster Perpetual	6099	A296	Engine Turned	Full Size
Oyster Perpetual	6202	A296	Numbered	Full Size
Oyster Perpetual	5028	A296	Polished (Smooth)	Full Size
Oyster Perpetual	6088	A296	Polished (Smooth)	Full Size
Oyster Perpetual	6332	A296	Polished (Smooth)	Full Size
Oyster Perpetual	1020			Full Size
Oyster Perpetual	1035			Full Size
Oyster Perpetual	1420			Full Size
Oyster Perpetual	1423			Full Size
Oyster Perpetual	3496			Full Size
Oyster Perpetual	4021			Full Size
Oyster Perpetual	4984			Full Size
Oyster Perpetual	5052			Full Size
Oyster Perpetual	5065			Full Size
Oyster Perpetual	6021			Full Size
Oyster Perpetual	6119			Full Size
Oyster Perpetual	6509	1120	Fluted	Ladies
Oyster Perpetual	6504	1120	Polished (Smooth)	Ladies
Oyster Perpetual	6507	1120	Polished (Smooth)	Ladies
Oyster Perpetual	6623	1161	Engine Turned	Ladies
Oyster Perpetual	6619	1161	Fluted	Ladies
Oyster Perpetual	6618	1161	Polished (Smooth)	Ladies
Oyster Perpetual	6724	2030	Engine Turned	Ladies
Oyster Perpetual	6718	2030	Polished (Smooth)	Ladies
Oyster Perpetual	6723	2030	Polished (Smooth)	Ladies
Oyster Perpetual	6719	2130	Fluted	Ladies
Oyster Perpetual	177210	2135	Engine Turned	Ladies
Oyster Perpetual	76243	2135	Engine Turned	Ladies
Oyster Perpetual	79160	2230	Engine Turned	Ladies
Oyster Perpetual	176234	2231	Fluted	Ladies
Oyster Perpetual	177200	2231	Polished (Smooth)	Ladies
Oyster Perpetual	79190	2235	Engine Turned	Ladies

Name	Ref.	Cal.	Bezel	Size
Oyster Perpetual	79240	2235	Engine Turned	Ladies
Oyster Perpetual	3272			Ladies
Oyster Perpetual	3352			Ladies
Oyster Perpetual	3686			Ladies
Oyster Perpetual	4686			Ladies
Oyster Perpetual	7603			Ladies
Oyster Perpetual	7608			Ladies
Oyster Perpetual	7609			Ladies
Oyster Perpetual	7618			Ladies
Oyster Perpetual	7619			Ladies
Oyster Perpetual	7623			Ladies
Oyster Perpetual	7624			Ladies
Oyster Perpetual	761833			Ladies
Oyster Perpetual	5016	620	Polished (Smooth)	Mid Size
Oyster Perpetual	6050	620	Polished (Smooth)	Mid Size
Oyster Perpetual	6084	620	Polished (Smooth)	Mid Size
Oyster Perpetual	3716	635	Polished (Smooth)	Mid Size
Oyster Perpetual	6085	645	Engine Turned	Mid Size
Oyster Perpetual	6107	645	Engine Turned	Mid Size
Oyster Perpetual	6284	645	Engine Turned	Mid Size
Oyster Perpetual	6285	645	Engine Turned	Mid Size
Oyster Perpetual	6303	645	Engine Turned	Mid Size
Oyster Perpetual	6102	645	Polished (Smooth)	Mid Size
Oyster Perpetual	6334	645	Polished (Smooth)	Mid Size
Oyster Perpetual	6082	710	Polished (Smooth)	Mid Size
Oyster Perpetual	4270	710	Polished (Smooth)	Mid Size
Oyster Perpetual	6565	1030	Engine Turned	Mid Size
Oyster Perpetual	6569	1030	Engine Turned	Mid Size
Oyster Perpetual	6582	1030	Engraved	Mid Size
Oyster Perpetual	6567	1030	Fluted	Mid Size
Oyster Perpetual	6593	1030	Fluted	Mid Size
Oyster Perpetual	5552	1030	Polished (Smooth)	Mid Size
Oyster Perpetual	6532	1030	Polished (Smooth)	Mid Size
Oyster Perpetual	6546	1030	Polished (Smooth)	Mid Size

Name	Ref.	Cal.	Bezel	Size
Oyster Perpetual	6564	1030	Polished (Smooth)	Mid Size
Oyster Perpetual	6566	1030	Polished (Smooth)	Mid Size
Oyster Perpetual	6580	1030	Polished (Smooth)	Mid Size
Oyster Perpetual	6584	1030	Polished (Smooth)	Mid Size
Oyster Perpetual	6585	1030	Polished (Smooth)	Mid Size
Oyster Perpetual	6590	1030	Polished (Smooth)	Mid Size
Oyster Perpetual	6556	1040	Polished (Smooth)	Mid Size
Oyster Perpetual	6551	1161	Fluted	Mid Size
Oyster Perpetual	6549	1161	Polished (Smooth)	Mid Size
Oyster Perpetual	1038	1570	Engine Turned	Mid Size
Oyster Perpetual	1507	1570	Engine Turned	Mid Size
Oyster Perpetual	6751	2030	Fluted	Mid Size
Oyster Perpetual	6748	2030	Polished (Smooth)	Mid Size
Oyster Perpetual	14208	3130	Polished (Smooth)	Mid Size
Oyster Perpetual	14203M	3130	Polished (Smooth)	Mid Size
Oyster Perpetual	14208M	3130	Polished (Smooth)	Mid Size
Oyster Perpetual	115234	3135	Fluted	Mid Size
Oyster Perpetual	6011	9 3/4"	Engine Turned	Mid Size
Oyster Perpetual	4362	9 3/4"	Polished (Smooth)	Mid Size
Oyster Perpetual	5018	9 3/4"	Polished (Smooth)	Mid Size
Oyster Perpetual	6018	9 3/4"	Polished (Smooth)	Mid Size
Oyster Perpetual	6090	A260	Polished (Smooth)	Mid Size
Oyster Perpetual	6092	A260	Polished (Smooth)	Mid Size
Oyster Perpetual	6539	A296	Mid Size	Mid Size
Oyster Perpetual	8053		Engine Turned	Mid Size
Oyster Perpetual	8055		Engine Turned	Mid Size
Oyster Perpetual	8058		Engine Turned	Mid Size
Oyster Perpetual	8075		Engine Turned	Mid Size
Oyster Perpetual	8077		Engine Turned	Mid Size
Oyster Perpetual	8079		Engine Turned	Mid Size
Oyster Perpetual	1023		Fluted	Mid Size
Oyster Perpetual	8011		Polished (Smooth)	Mid Size
Oyster Perpetual	8074		Polished (Smooth)	Mid Size
Oyster Perpetual	8076		Polished (Smooth)	Mid Size

Name	Ref.	Cal.	Bezel	Size
Oyster Perpetual	8078		Polished (Smooth)	Mid Size
Oyster Perpetual	8080		Polished (Smooth)	Mid Size
Oyster Perpetual	4857			Mid Size
Oyster Perpetual	5173			Mid Size
Oyster Perpetual	6016			Mid Size
Oyster Perpetual	6342			Mid Size
Oyster Perpetual	7701			Mid Size
Oyster Perpetual	7708			Mid Size
Oyster Perpetual	7748			Mid Size
Oyster Perpetual	7751			Mid Size

Oyster Perpetual Lady Date Reference Summary

Name	Ref.	Cal.	Bezel
Oyster Perpetual Lady	54439	2030	Fluted
Oyster Perpetual Lady	67233	2130	Engine Turned
Oyster Perpetual Lady	67193	2130	Fluted
Oyster Perpetual Lady	67194	2130	Fluted
Oyster Perpetual Lady	67198	2130	Fluted
Oyster Perpetual Lady	67190	2130	Jewel Set
Oyster Perpetual Lady	67180	2130	Polished (Smooth)
Oyster Perpetual Lady	67183	2130	Polished (Smooth)
Oyster Perpetual Lady	67188	2130	Polished (Smooth)
Oyster Perpetual Lady	67197	2130	Fluted
Oyster Perpetual Lady	67230	2135	Engine Turned
Oyster Perpetual Lady	69628	2135	Numbered
Oyster Perpetual Lady	76030	2230	Engine Turned
Oyster Perpetual Lady	76233	2230	Engine Turned
Oyster Perpetual Lady	76094	2230	Fluted
Oyster Perpetual Lady	76193	2230	Fluted
Oyster Perpetual Lady	76198	2230	Fluted
Oyster Perpetual Lady	76080	2230	Polished (Smooth)
Oyster Perpetual Lady	76183	2230	Polished (Smooth)
Oyster Perpetual Lady	76188	2230	Polished (Smooth)
Oyster Perpetual Lady	176200	2230	Polished (Smooth)
Oyster Perpetual Lady	76180	2230	Fluted
Oyster Perpetual Lady	77438	2230	Fluted

Oyster Perpetual Date Reference Summary

Name	Ref.	Cal.	Bezel	Size
Oyster Perpetual Date	4467	10 1/2	Polished (Smooth)	Full Size
Oyster Perpetual Date	6917	2035	Fluted	Ladies
Oyster Perpetual Date	69160	2135	Polished (Smooth)	Ladies
Oyster Perpetual Date	69173	2135	Fluted	Ladies
Oyster Perpetual Date	69174	2135	Fluted	Ladies
Oyster Perpetual Date	69190	2135	Engine Turned	Ladies
Oyster Perpetual Date	69240	2135	Engine Turned	Ladies
Oyster Perpetual Date	1560	1565	Polished (Smooth)	Mid Size
Oyster Perpetual Date	1565	1575	Polished (Smooth)	Mid Size
Oyster Perpetual Date	5075			Mid Size
Oyster Perpetual Date	6335	A260		Mid Size
Oyster Perpetual Date	6534	1035	Fluted	Mid Size
Oyster Perpetual Date	15000	3035	Polished (Smooth)	Mid Size
Oyster Perpetual Date	15010	3035	Engine Turned	Mid Size
Oyster Perpetual Date	15037	3035	Fluted	Mid Size
Oyster Perpetual Date	15038	3035	Engine Turned	Mid Size
Oyster Perpetual Date	15053	3035	Engine Turned	Mid Size
Oyster Perpetual Date	15200	3135	Polished (Smooth)	Mid Size
Oyster Perpetual Date	15203	3135	Polished (Smooth)	Mid Size
Oyster Perpetual Date	15210	3135	Engine Turned	Mid Size
Oyster Perpetual Date	15223	3135	Fluted	Mid Size
Oyster Perpetual Date	15233	3135	Engine Turned	Mid Size
Oyster Perpetual Date	15238	3135	Fluted	Mid Size
Oyster Perpetual Date	15505	3035	Polished (Smooth)	Mid Size
Oyster Perpetual Date	15505	3035	Polished (Smooth)	Mid Size
Oyster Perpetual Date	115200	3135	Polished (Smooth)	Mid Size
Oyster Perpetual Date	115210	3135	Engine Turned	Mid Size
Oyster Perpetual Date	115234	3135	Fluted	Mid Size
Oyster Perpetual Date	15058	3035		

Oysterdate Reference Summary

Name	Ref.	Cal.	Bezel	Size
Oysterdate	1570	1570	Fluted	Full Size
Oysterdate	1600	1570	Polished (Smooth)	Full Size
Oysterdate	1601	1570	Fluted	Full Size
Oysterdate	1603	1570	Fluted	Full Size
Oysterdate	6075	295	Engine Turned	Full Size
Oysterdate	6423	1210	Engine Turned	Full Size
Oysterdate	6424	1215	Polished (Smooth)	Full Size
Oysterdate	6605	1065	Fluted	Full Size
Oysterdate	6519	1135	Polished (Smooth)	Ladies
Oysterdate	6522	1100	Polished (Smooth)	Ladies
Oysterdate	6523	1100	Engine Turned	Ladies
Oysterdate	6525	1100	Fluted	Ladies
Oysterdate	1500	1570	Polished (Smooth)	Mid Size
Oysterdate	1501	1570	Engine Turned	Mid Size
Oysterdate	1503	1570	Polished (Smooth)	Mid Size
Oysterdate	1505	1570	Fluted	Mid Size
Oysterdate	1507	1570	Other	Mid Size
Oysterdate	1550	1570	Polished (Smooth)	Mid Size
Oysterdate	6430	1225	Polished (Smooth)	Mid Size
Oysterdate	6466	1210	Polished (Smooth)	Mid Size
Oysterdate	6494	1210	Polished (Smooth)	Mid Size
Oysterdate	6518	1035	Polished (Smooth)	Mid Size
Oysterdate	6524			Mid Size
Oysterdate	6534	1030	Polished (Smooth)	Mid Size
Oysterdate	6627	1161	Fluted	Mid Size
Oysterdate	6694			Mid Size
Oysterdate	6964			Mid Size

Oysterquartz

Despite this being a quirky and unusual reference it played a significant role in Rolex history. Rolex had been researching electronic watches since the early 1950s and was awarded their first electro-mechanical watch patent in 1952.

Over the three decades from 1960 and 1990 Rolex was awarded 50 patents. 21 of these were for electronic watches and digital displays. Rolex's investment in quartz technology was significant.

Rolex introduced its first commercially available quartz watch in 1970. The Quartz Date 5100 shared the Beta 21 movement used by other Swiss companies, including Omega and Enicar.

Assembly of the Beta 21 took place across multiple manufacturing facilities, with limited modifications for each brand's specifications.

Sixteen different Swiss watch companies began selling Beta 21 quartz watches in 1970, including Rolex with the Quartz Date 5100.

After making only 1,000 units of the Beta 21, Rolex started to develop their own quartz movement for the watch that would become the Oysterquartz.

In 1977, Rolex introduced their first entirely in-house quartz movements for the Datejust ref. 5035 and Day-Date ref. 5055 Oysterquartz models. These were COSC certified, which is very unusual for quartz movements.

At launch, these were remarkable technological achievements created with a level of fit and finish befitting the milestone achievement. Rolex designed and built these 11 jewel movements like mechanical movements with bridges, plates and lever escapements. They used the latest CMOS circuitry, a 32khz oscillator, and an analog thermal compensator.

Quartz movements are vulnerable to extreme temperatures, and a trimmer feature was incorporated to allow watchmakers to compensate for drift of the quartz crystals. It is very unusual to find quartz movements designed to be watchmaker serviceable in this way.

Rolex offered many dial options. These include malachite, lapis, silver, blue, black,

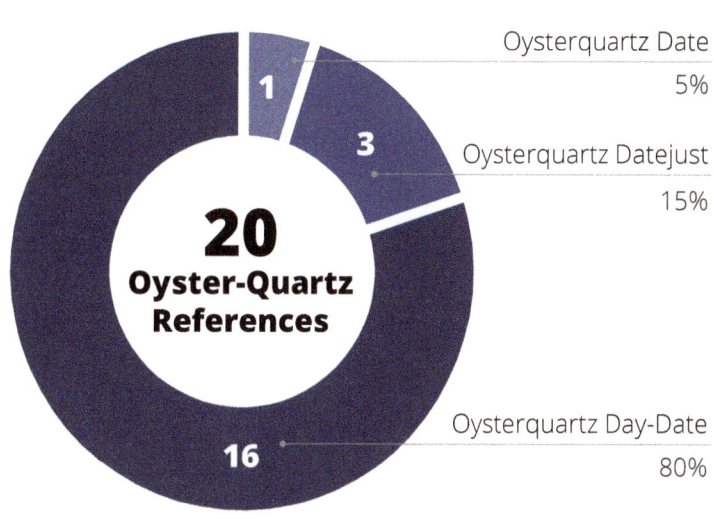

champagne, gold, tapestry stripes, diamond-set, Stella enamel in several colors, wood, and others. Most of these exotic dials were for the premium Day-Date Oysterquartz which was also available with jeweled dials, bezels, and bracelets.

The Oysterquartz models ran for 25 years, and Rolex made fewer than 25,000 units. Rolex dropped the ref.17000 from their catalog in 2002 but continued to offer the two-tone and solid gold models until 2003, when stocks were finally depleted.

In 1972 Rolex withdrew from the CEH consortium and began developing their own quartz movement and the watch that would house it, the Oysterquartz.

THE FIRST QUARTZ DATE REF. 5100

The ref. 5100 emerged from a co-development and collaboration agreement called Centre Electronique Horloger (CEH). The resulting quartz movement called the Beta 21, was deployed straight into the Quartz Date ref. 5100.

It featured an integrated bracelet and a sapphire crystal; also firsts for Rolex. Rolex could not fit the Beta 21 movement into the Oyster case without modifications. As such it was described as water resistant and not waterproof. The Rolex Quartz Date never received a depth rating.

The 5100 debuted on June 5, 1970. Initial orders exceeded expectation, with the planned production run of 1,000 watches selling out before production even began. All 1,000 serially-numbered 5100s were sold between 1970 and 1972. Today, collectors highly prize a ref.5100 complete with box and papers.

Oysterquartz Reference Summary

Name	Ref	Cal	Start	End	Bezel	Case	Description
Oysterquartz Date	5100	Beta 21	1970	1972	Fluted	YG	Very first Oysterquartz model
Oysterquartz Datejust	17000	5035	1977	2001	Polished (Smooth)	SS	Very last of the Oysterquartz models Non-CO-SC
Oysterquartz Datejust	17013	5035	1977	2001	Fluted	SSYG	Jubilee bracelet Non-COSC
Oysterquartz Datejust	17014	5035	1977	2001	Fluted	WG	Jubilee bracelet
Oysterquartz Day-Date	1901	5055			Fluted		
Oysterquartz Day-Date	1902	5055			Pyramid		
Oysterquartz Day-Date	1903	5055			Pyramid		Diamond
Oysterquartz Day-Date	1904	5055					Diamond
Oysterquartz Day-Date	1905	5055					Baguette diamonds
Oysterquartz Day-Date	1907	5055					
Oysterquartz Day-Date	1914	5055					
Oysterquartz Day-Date	1916	5055					
Oysterquartz Day-Date	19018	5055	1977	2001	Fluted	YG	Gem set dials, bezels and bracelets
Oysterquartz Day-Date	19019	5055	1977	2001	Fluted	WG	Gem set dials, bezels and bracelets
Oysterquartz Day-Date	19028	5055	1977	2001	Pyramid	YG	Gem set dials, bezels and bracelets Pyramid hour markers
Oysterquartz Day-Date	19038	5055	1977	2001	Pyramid	YG	Gem set dials, bezels and bracelets Pyramid hour markers and pyramid bracelet
Oysterquartz Day-Date	19048	5055	1977	2001		YG	Gem set dials, bezels and President bracelets
Oysterquartz Day-Date	19049	5055	1977	2001		WG	Gem set dials, bezels and President bracelets
Oysterquartz Day-Date	19068	5055	1977	2001		YG	Gem set dials, bezels and President bracelets
Oysterquartz Day-Date	19148	5055	1977	2001		WG	Gem set dials, bezels and Karat bracelets

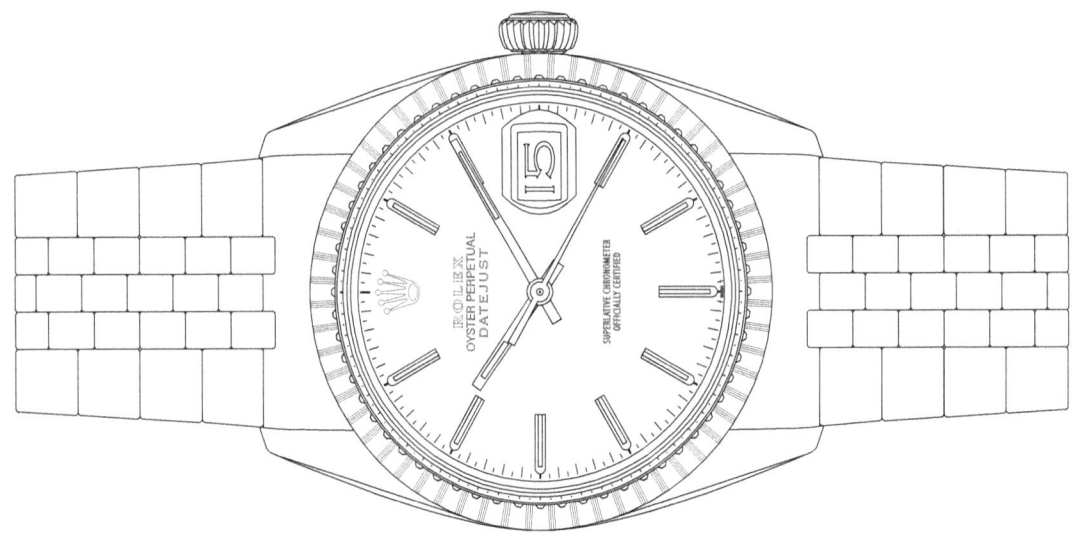

Oyster Perpetual Datejust

The first Datejust was ref. 4467 introduced in 1945. While it officially marked the company's 40th anniversary, it also unofficially marked the end of WWII. It is remarkable that Rolex was able to design, develop and manufacture this watch amid the chaos of the war that raged throughout Europe.

The name Datejust is a reference to the quick-changing date, which jumped to the next date on the stroke of midnight, rather than rolling over slowly. As such, the date was always just right. This seemingly simple innovation was a milestone development in the watch industry at the time.

The ref. 4467 also introduced the fluted-style bezel and the new Jubilee bracelet. The iconic cyclops magnifier over the date aperture was added nine years later in 1954.

The 36mm size was substantial for the time, and Rolex later added a Mid-Size 34mm version and a ladies size 28mm. These early examples were Bubblebacks with convex casebacks. It wasn't until the introduction of cal. 1065 in 1957 that the Datejust got its flat caseback.

The Datejust was a commercial success, thanks to the accurate COSC certified Perpetual movement, waterproof Oyster case and the new-fangled date complication. Rolex went on to make approximately 280 variations of the Datejust in three case sizes, using 25 different movements and numerous bezel combinations.

In 2009 Rolex released the Oyster Perpetual Datejust II in a larger 41mm Oyster case. In 2016, this was followed by the Oyster Perpetual Datejust 41. While the Oyster case size was the same, it had smaller hour indexes and a thinner bezel, giving the illusion of a much larger watch.

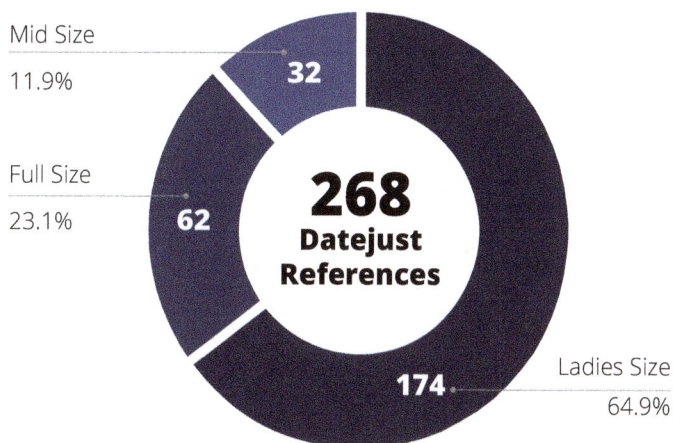

To say the Datejust model line is long-lived is an understatement. Rolex made these models in large quantities, and the pre-owned market is awash with them. They have numerous dial variations reflecting the design aesthetic of the era.

A few of these dials can be found with the prized red text and in some cases waterproof depth ratings too.

Dial textures include waffle, striped, tapestry, linen and embossed. The pie-pan dial is a popular variant with vintage collectors, as are the rare all-stainless-steel versions.

The ref.6105 is particularly unusual for being a left-hander, with the winding crown at the 9 o'clock position.

When buying a vintage Datejust, you'd be well advised not to obsess over originality and correctness, as these watches were often customized by the AD when first sold. Dealers would swap dials and hands at a customer's request. Look for one in good condition and running order, then select what appeals to you aesthetically. If you follow the advice in this guide, these can be well-bought at modest prices.

Datejust Turn-O-Graph

In 1955, Rolex introduced the Datejust Turn-O-Graph model with a novel rotating bezel. It was the genesis for the Rolex Submariner and the Rolex GMT-Master. The Turn-O-Graph became popular with pilots as a navigation tool even before the formal launch of the GMT-Master later in 1955.

The first reference was the 6202, which had a steel Oyster case with a gilt and glossy dial, luminous Mercedes-style hands, luminescent hour markers and a black bezel calibrated to 60 minutes.

Collectors and scholars acknowledge the ref. 6202 was the first Rolex tool watch, the first aviator's watch and the first offered in steel and gold two-tone. This luxury version was initially considered too avant-garde and sold in very modest numbers.

In 1954 several design changes were made with the new ref.6309. A date complication was added, along with a cyclops date magnifier, and a new engine-turned bezel with markers every five and ten minutes.

The movement was also revised with cal. 743, replacing the original cal. A260.

The US Air Force informally adopted the Turn-O-Graph, awarding it to pilots returning from the Vietnam and Korean Wars. Later it was formally adopted and issued to the U.S. Air Force's Thunderbird aerobatic team, hence the nickname, Thunderbird.

The Turn-O-Graph was assigned to the Datejust collection in 1964 in an attempt to make way for the Submariner and GMT-Master. In hindsight, this proved a misguided choice as the Turn-O-Graphs timing bezel on a dressy Datejust was an unusual and inconsistent style combination.

The Turn-O-Graph was revised and reissued in 2000 with cal, 3135, a fluted bezel, distinctive red dial text, and a red seconds hand. This reissued version was a dressier, more luxurious take on the original, but it still failed to find its niche in the publics mind.

After 11 references and 58 years, the Turn-O-Graph was finally retired in 2011. It maintains a second-tier place in Rolex history, and never made a big impression on the public, despite being endorsed by fighter pilots.

Prototype Bell X-1 rocket plane, undergoing shakedown tests. An early Oyster Datejust Bubbleback sat on the wrist of Chuck Yeager when he broke the sound barrier in 1947.

Turn-O-Graph Reference Summary

Ref.	Cal.
6309	710
6609	1065
1626	1570
1625	1570
16268	3035
16253	3035
116264	3135
116263	3135
116261	3135
16264	3135
6202	A260

Datejust Reference Summary

Ref.	Cal.	Bezel	Size	Description
86409		Smooth (Polished)	Full Size	Pearlmaster
1600	1570	Fluted	Full Size	
1601	1570	Fluted	Full Size	
1603	1570	Engine Turned	Full Size	
1605	1570	Engine Turned	Full Size	
1607	1570	Bark	Full Size	
1611	1570	Bark	Full Size	
1620	1570	Polished (Smooth)	Full Size	
1622	1570	Engine Turned	Full Size	
1623	1570	Fluted	Full Size	
1624	1570	Fluted	Full Size	
1630	1570	Fluted	Full Size	
5030	710	Polished (Smooth)	Full Size	
5031	710	Engine Turned	Full Size	
6031	710	Fluted	Full Size	Perpetual, Chronometer, Ovettone
6074	710	Polished (Smooth)	Full Size	Perpetual, Chronometer, Ovettone
6075	A295	Fluted	Full Size	Perpetual, Chronometer, Ovettone
6104	A296	Polished (Smooth)	Full Size	
6105	745	Engine Turned	Full Size	
6155	1570	Engine Turned	Full Size	
6304	A296	Polished (Smooth)	Full Size	
6305	A296	Fluted	Full Size	
6604	1065	Polished (Smooth)	Full Size	
6605	1065	Fluted	Full Size	
6909	2030	Engine Turned	Full Size	
6914	2135	Engine Turned	Full Size	
6923	2030	Engine Turned	Full Size	
7518	234	Engine Turned	Full Size	
8029	390	Polished (Smooth)	Full Size	
16000	3035	Fluted	Full Size	
16013	3035	Fluted	Full Size	

Ref.	Cal.	Bezel	Size	Description
16014	3035	Engine Turned	Full Size	
16018	3035	Fluted	Full Size	
16030	3035	Fluted	Full Size	
16078	3035	Bark	Full Size	
16200	3135	Polished (Smooth)	Full Size	
16203	3135	Polished (Smooth)	Full Size	
16220	3135	Fluted	Full Size	
16233	3135	Fluted	Full Size	
16234	3135	Fluted	Full Size	
16238	3135	Fluted	Full Size	
68188	2135	Fluted	Full Size	
79079	2235	Polished (Smooth)	Full Size	
116034	3130	Fluted	Full Size	
116138	3135	Fluted	Full Size	
116139	3135	Fluted	Full Size	
116188	3135	Jewel Set	Full Size	
116189	3135	Jewel Set	Full Size	
116199	3135	Jewel Set	Full Size	
116200	3135	Polished (Smooth)	Full Size	
116201	3135	Polished (Smooth)	Full Size	
116203	3135	Polished (Smooth)	Full Size	
116208	3135	Polished (Smooth)	Full Size	
116231	3135	Fluted	Full Size	
116233	3135	Fluted	Full Size	
116234	3135	Fluted	Full Size	
116238	3135	Fluted	Full Size	
116243	3135	Jewel Set	Full Size	
118399	3235	Jewel Set	Full Size	
126301	3235	Polished (Smooth)	Full Size	
126303	3235	Polished (Smooth)	Full Size	
126331	3235	Fluted	Full Size	
126333	3235	Fluted	Full Size	
6251	710	Fluted	Ladies	
6527	1160	Bark	Ladies	

Ref.	Cal.	Bezel	Size	Description
6824	2030	Polished (Smooth)	Ladies	
6825	2035	Engine Turned	Ladies	
6826	2030	Fluted	Ladies	
6828	2035	Jewel Set	Ladies	
6900	2030	Fluted	Ladies	
6901	2035	Bark	Ladies	
6902	2030	Bark	Ladies	
6903	2135	Fluted	Ladies	
6906	2135	Jewel Set	Ladies	
6907	2030	Jewel Set	Ladies	
6908	2035	Fluted	Ladies	
6910	2135	Jewel Set	Ladies	
6911	2030	Jewel Set	Ladies	
6912	2030	Fluted	Ladies	
6913	2030	Jewel Set	Ladies	
6915	2135	Jewel Set	Ladies	
6917	2030	Fluted	Ladies	
6925	2030	Jewel Set	Ladies	
6926	2135	Jewel Set	Ladies	
6927	2030	Jewel Set	Ladies	
6928	2135	Jewel Set	Ladies	
6930	2030	Fluted	Ladies	
6931	2135	Engine Turned	Ladies	
6935	2030	Fluted	Ladies	
7828	2135	Fluted	Ladies	
7906	2030	Fluted	Ladies	
7907	710	Fluted	Ladies	
7908	2030	Jewel Set	Ladies	
7912	1157	Jewel Set	Ladies	
7913	1156	Jewel Set	Ladies	
7915	2030	Jewel Set	Ladies	
7918	2135	Engine Turned	Ladies	
7927	1475	Fluted	Ladies	
8030	390	Fluted	Ladies	

Ref.	Cal.	Bezel	Size	Description
8031	1475	Polished (Smooth)	Ladies	
8032	1156	Jewel Set	Ladies	
8035	3035	Engine Turned	Ladies	
16239	3135	Jewel Set	Ladies	
18029	2130	Jewel Set	Ladies	
67243	2130	Engine Turned	Ladies	
68158	2135	Jewel Set	Ladies	
68159	2135	Jewel Set	Ladies	
68238	2135	Jewel Set	Ladies	
68240	2135	Polished (Smooth)	Ladies	
68243	2135	Polished (Smooth)	Ladies	
68246	2135	Polished (Smooth)	Ladies	
68258	2135	Jewel Set	Ladies	
68266	2135	Jewel Set	Ladies	
68268	2135	Jewel Set	Ladies	
68273	2135	Fluted	Ladies	
68274	2135	Fluted	Ladies	
68278	2135	Fluted	Ladies	
69068	2135	Jewel Set	Ladies	
69069	2135	Jewel Set	Ladies	
69078	2135	Jewel Set	Ladies	
69079	2135	Jewel Set	Ladies	
69088	2135	Jewel Set	Ladies	
69089	2135	Jewel Set	Ladies	
69126	2135	Jewel Set	Ladies	
69128	2135	Jewel Set	Ladies	
69136	2135	Jewel Set	Ladies	
69138	2135	Jewel Set	Ladies	
69139	2135	Jewel Set	Ladies	
69158	2135	Jewel Set	Ladies	
69160	2135	Polished (Smooth)	Ladies	
69163	2135	Polished (Smooth)	Ladies	
69166	2135	Polished (Smooth)	Ladies	
69168	2135	Jewel Set	Ladies	

Ref.	Cal.	Bezel	Size	Description
69173	2135	Fluted	Ladies	
69174	2135	Fluted	Ladies	
69178	2135	Jewel Set	Ladies	
69190	2135	Engine Turned	Ladies	
69198	2135	Jewel Set	Ladies	
69240	2135	Jewel Set	Ladies	
69258	2135	Jewel Set	Ladies	
69268	2135	Jewel Set	Ladies	
69278	2135	Engine Turned	Ladies	
69279	2135	Fluted	Ladies	
69288	2135	Jewel Set	Ladies	
69298	2135	Jewel Set	Ladies	
69299	2135	Jewel Set	Ladies	
69308	2135	Jewel Set	Ladies	
69318	2135	Jewel Set	Ladies	
76243	2230	Fluted	Ladies	
78246	2235	Polished (Smooth)	Ladies	
78248	2235	Polished (Smooth)	Ladies	
78266	2235	Engine Turned	Ladies	
78273	2235	Fluted	Ladies	
78274	2235	Fluted	Ladies	
78278	2235	Jewel Set	Ladies	
78279	2235	Jewel Set	Ladies	
78288	2235	Jewel Set	Ladies	
79068	2235	Jewel Set	Ladies	
79078	2235	Jewel Set	Ladies	
79088	2235	Jewel Set	Ladies	
79089	2235	Jewel Set	Ladies	
79126	2135	Jewel Set	Ladies	
79136	2135	Jewel Set	Ladies	
79138	2235	Jewel Set	Ladies	
79158	2235	Jewel Set	Ladies	
79160	2235	Polished (Smooth)	Ladies	
79163	2235	Polished (Smooth)	Ladies	

Ref.	Cal.	Bezel	Size	Description
79166	2135	Jewel Set	Ladies	
79168	2135	Polished (Smooth)	Ladies	
79173	2235	Fluted	Ladies	
79174	2135	Fluted	Ladies	
79178	2235	Fluted	Ladies	
79190	2235	Polished (Smooth)	Ladies	
79193	2235	Fluted	Ladies	
79240	2235	Fluted	Ladies	
80285	2235	Jewel Set	Ladies	
80298	2235	Jewel Set	Ladies	
80299	2235	Jewel Set	Ladies	
80309	2235	Jewel Set	Ladies	
80318	2235	Jewel Set	Ladies	
80319	2235	Jewel Set	Ladies	
80328	2235	Polished (Smooth)	Ladies	
80329	2235	Jewel Set	Ladies	
80359	2235	Jewel Set	Ladies	
177234	2235	Fluted	Ladies	
178158	2235	Jewel Set	Ladies	
178159	2235	Jewel Set	Ladies	
178238	2235	Fluted	Ladies	
178239	2235	Fluted	Ladies	
178240	2235	Polished (Smooth)	Ladies	
178241	2235	Polished (Smooth)	Ladies	
178243	2235	Polished (Smooth)	Ladies	
178245	2235	Polished (Smooth)	Ladies	
178246	2235	Polished (Smooth)	Ladies	
178248	2235	Polished (Smooth)	Ladies	
178269	2235	Polished (Smooth)	Ladies	
178271	2235	Fluted	Ladies	
178273	2235	Fluted	Ladies	
178274	2235	Fluted	Ladies	
178275	2235	Fluted	Ladies	
178278	2235	Fluted	Ladies	

Ref.	Cal.	Bezel	Size	Description
178279	2235	Fluted	Ladies	
178286	2235	Jewel Set	Ladies	
178288	2235	Jewel Set	Ladies	
178313	2235	Jewel Set	Ladies	
178343	2235	Jewel Set	Ladies	
178344	2235	Jewel Set	Ladies	
178383	2235	Jewel Set	Ladies	
178384	2235	Jewel Set	Ladies	
179136	2235	Jewel Set	Ladies	
179138	2235	Jewel Set	Ladies	
179158	2235	Jewel Set	Ladies	
179159	2235	Jewel Set	Ladies	
179160	2235	Polished (Smooth)	Ladies	
179161	2235	Polished (Smooth)	Ladies	
179163	2235	Polished (Smooth)	Ladies	
179165	2235	Polished (Smooth)	Ladies	
179166	2235	Jewel Set	Ladies	
179168	2235	Polished (Smooth)	Ladies	
179171	2235	Fluted	Ladies	
179173	2235	Fluted	Ladies	
179174	2235	Fluted	Ladies	
179175	2235	Fluted	Ladies	
179178	2235	Fluted	Ladies	
179179	2235	Fluted	Ladies	
179239	2235	Fluted	Ladies	
179298	2235	Polished (Smooth)	Ladies	
179313	2235	Jewel Set	Ladies	
179368	2235	Jewel Set	Ladies	
179459	2235	Jewel Set	Ladies	
197173		Fluted	Ladies	
228348	3255	Jewel Set	Ladies	
279135	2236	Jewel Set	Ladies	
279160	2236	Polished (Smooth)	Ladies	
279171	2236	Fluted	Ladies	

Ref.	Cal.	Bezel	Size	Description
279173	2236	Fluted	Ladies	
279381	2236	Jewel Set	Ladies	
6624	1160	Polished (Smooth)	Mid Size	
6800	2030	Polished (Smooth)	Mid Size	
6815	2030	Polished (Smooth)	Mid Size	
6823	2030	Polished (Smooth)	Mid Size	
7815	2030	Jewel Set	Mid Size	
7823	234	Fluted	Mid Size	
7824	2135	Polished (Smooth)	Mid Size	
7825	2030	Jewel Set	Mid Size	
7826	2030	Jewel Set	Mid Size	
7827	2135	Polished (Smooth)	Mid Size	
7926	1475	Polished (Smooth)	Mid Size	
8065	3035	Engine Turned	Mid Size	
8066	1156	Jewel Set	Mid Size	
8067	3035	Polished (Smooth)	Mid Size	
15505	3035	Polished (Smooth)	Mid Size	
68248	2135	Polished (Smooth)	Mid Size	
68279	2135	Fluted	Mid Size	
68286	2135	Jewel Set	Mid Size	
68288	2135	Jewel Set	Mid Size	
77014	2230	Fluted	Mid Size	
77080	2230	Polished (Smooth)	Mid Size	
77518	2235	Fluted	Mid Size	
78240	2235	Jewel Set	Mid Size	
78243	2235	Polished (Smooth)	Mid Size	
78286	2235	Jewel Set	Mid Size	
81158	2235	Jewel Set	Mid Size	
81208	2235	Polished (Smooth)	Mid Size	
81298	2235	Jewel Set	Mid Size	
81315	2235	Jewel Set	Mid Size	
81318	2235	Jewel Set	Mid Size	
81319	2235	Jewel Set	Mid Size	
81338	2235	Jewel Set	Mid Size	
18958	5055			

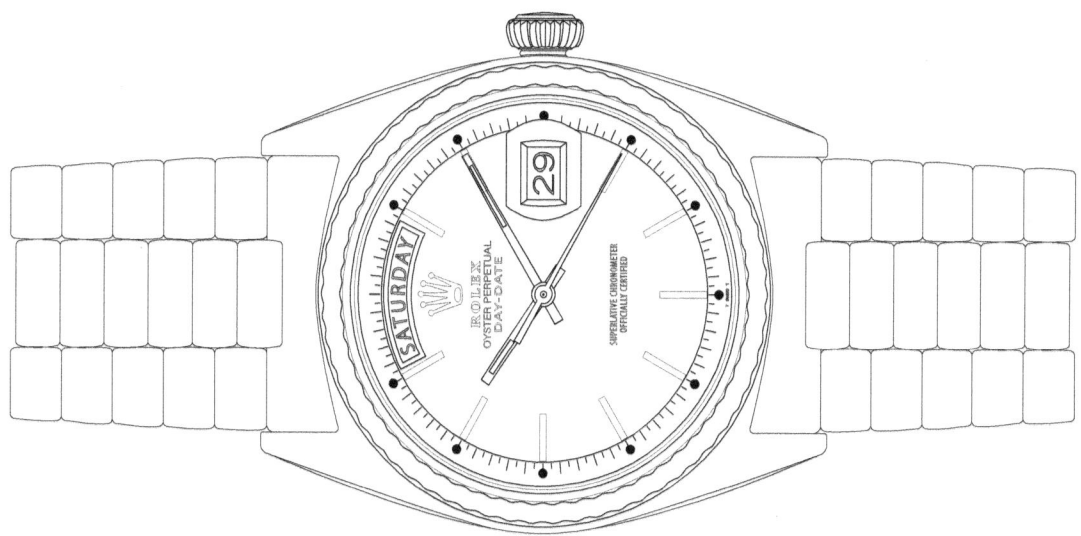

Oyster Perpetual Day-Date

The Rolex Day-Date is also known as the Day-Date President, having been worn by several heads of state and industry titans. It is a premium luxury line in precious metals only.

The Day-Date is one of several references offered with jewel-set bezels. The model comes in a variety of combinations, with some being exceptionally rare. Those described here are the most commonly encountered.

The iconic day indicator is available in the following languages - English, German, Arabic, Chinese, Danish, Spanish, Basque, Catalan, Ethiopian, Finnish, French, Greek, Hebrew, Dutch, Indonesian, Italian, Japanese, Latin, Moroccan, Norwegian, Farsi, Polish, Portuguese, Russian, Swedish and Turkish.

Rolex has offered the Day-Date with exotic finishes including bark and Morellis. These are rare and highly prized.

While the larger Day-Date II and Day-Date 40 have proven popular, the 36mm Day-Date is building a cult following among fashionable millennials. The yellow gold pairs well with jewelry and accessories, and are versatile enough to dress up or down. Stylish young collectors are breathing new interest and life into the vintage 36mm Day-Date.

6500 Series (1956 to 1959)

The Day-Date launched in 1956 with ref.6510 and ref.6511. Displaying the day of the week and the date was an industry first. Combined with a precious metal Oyster case, the formula has remained unchanged to this day.

1800 Series (1959 to 1987)

Rolex introduced an update to the 6500 series in 1959 with the Day-Date ref.1803. One of the most well-known references, it lasted into the late 1970s. Early 1800 models had cal. 1555. In the 1970s the 1800 series received a movement upgrade to cal.1556 which provided a hacking feature.

Only the ref.1804 had a factory-fitted diamond bezel, and only available in white gold with 46 brilliant cut diamonds. The ref.1805 had a combination diamond and sapphire bezel. There are no other identifying marks or hallmarks on the back of either of these bezels.

In the 1960s and 70s, Authorized Dealers could sell diamond bezels separately to anyone with a Day-Date in the 1800-1811 series. These are genuine factory Rolex parts, but to a collector, a ref. 1804 with a factory-fitted diamond bezel is more desirable than an upgraded 1803.

Combination (multi-colored) and baguette stone bezels were never sold as an upgrade and will only appear on the correct case reference. For example, only ref.1805 had a diamond and sapphire combination bezel. Only the ref.1816 had a diamond baguette cut bezel. And only ref. 1817 had an emerald, ruby, sapphire, and diamond combination bezel.

If an owner has a problem with a combination jewel bezel, Rolex will verify the correct case number before working on it. They will not work on an after market or incorrect combination jewel bezel.

In 1977, cal. 3055 arrived in the 18000 series, finally giving the Day-Date quick setting date capability. This year also saw the launch of the Day-Date Oysterquartz and the cal. 5055 quartz movement. It had a distinctive angular look that set it apart from the mechanical Day-Date.

Bezel options increased on the Crown Collection models, with sapphire, ruby, and emerald in different cuts (like a baguette) and combinations with diamonds.

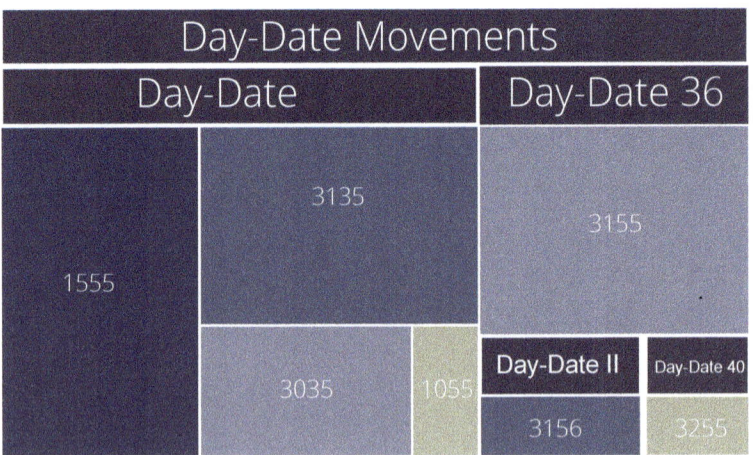

Some had 50 small baguettes, and others 24 larger baguettes.

Colored stone bezels belong exclusively to the Crown Collection. Rolex strictly controlled these combination bezels, and they were not offered for sale by ADs like the diamond-only bezels. Colored stone bezels on any other Day-Date reference are after-market.

The ref. 18000 men's diamond bezel had 44 brilliant diamonds set in yellow or white gold. Early 18000s had no other distinguishing markings. Later versions had a letter and a number stamped on the back of the bezel, but no Rolex or other hallmarks.

18200 Series (1988 to 2000)

In 1988, Rolex debuted a new Day-Date movement, the cal. 3155, and a new series of Day-Date watches with 18200 reference numbers. This updated movement introduced quick set day capability.

The 18200 series jeweled bezels were platinum, yellow or white gold to match the case. Rolex began stamping a code on the back of the bezels along with a Rolex hallmark, presumably in response to after market and counterfeit bezels.

The quality and consistency of jewel set bezels improved significantly with this series. They set the standard for classic and modern Day-Dates.

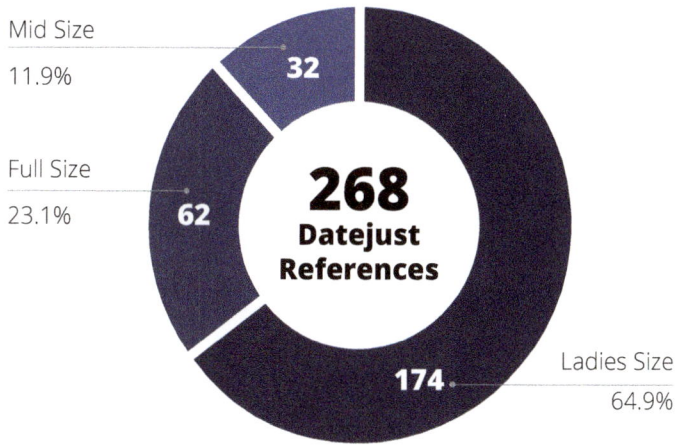

The diamonds are always VVS clarity and above E in color. If there are visible inclusions in any of the stones, it is not a Rolex bezel. All stones will be perfectly consistent in color, size, and symmetry, and they will be evenly spaced with the settings perfectly repeated.

There is a rare type of bezel called *Cartouche* that emerged in the late 1980s. Cartouches had 40 diamonds on men's Crown Collection and 36 on ladies. They have the name Rolex engraved on a plate at the six o'clock position.

Day-Date 36 Series (2000 to 2007)

Rolex introduced the Day-Date 36 in the year 2000 with the six-digit 118000 series. Improvements were limited to the bracelet and clasp, but more dial options were available.

Day-Date II Series (2008 to 2015)

The Day-Date II arrived in 2008, with a 41mm Oyster case and cal. 3156 (ref. 218238, 218239, 218235, 218206). In 2015 the reference was retired and replaced with the Day-Date 40.

Day-Date 40 Series

The Day-Date 40 Oyster case was reduced to 40mm and housed cal. 3255, which offered a longer power reserve.

Stella Dials

For a brief spell in the early 1970s, Rolex introduced some brightly colored enamel dials to the 36mm Day-Date. Named after the American artist Frank Stella and targeted at the Middle Eastern market, they were a commercial flop.

The paint used on these enamel dials was hand-mixed, so variations exist between batches of the same color. Enamel dials age better than plated and painted versions. Though prone to cracking and chipping if mistreated, their color tends to retain brightness and depth.

Today, these vintage 1970 models have become highly sought after as a unisex watch. In 2013, Rolex reintroduced some Day-Date Stella dials in blue, cherry, chocolate, rhodium, green and cognac. These are only available on leather straps; not the President bracelet like the first series.

Stella dials are a specialized domain. Brightly colored dials appearing on other references outside these date periods are most likely after market fakes. Collectors should avoid these.

Day-Date Reference Summary

Name	Ref.	Cal.
Day-Date	1800	1555
Day-Date	1802	1555
Day-Date	1803	1555
Day-Date	1804	1555
Day-Date	1805	1555
Day-Date	1806	1555
Day-Date	1807	1555
Day-Date	1810	1555
Day-Date	1811	1555
Day-Date	1816	1555
Day-Date	1817	1555
Day-Date	1820	1555
Day-Date	1823	1555
Day-Date	1824	1555
Day-Date	1829	1555
Day-Date	1830	1555
Day-Date	1833	1555
Day-Date	1834	1555
Day-Date	1836	1555
Day-Date	1837	1555
Day-Date	1838	1555
Day-Date	1839	1555
Day-Date	1894	1555
Day-Date	1895	1555
Day-Date	1901	
Day-Date	1902	
Day-Date	1903	
Day-Date	1904	
Day-Date	1905	
Day-Date	1907	
Day-Date	1914	
Day-Date	1916	
Day-Date	6511	

Name	Ref.	Cal.
Day-Date	6611	1055
Day-Date	6612	1055
Day-Date	6613	1055
Day-Date	17824	
Day-Date	18026	3035
Day-Date	18028	3035
Day-Date	18036	3035
Day-Date	18038	3035
Day-Date	18039	3035
Day-Date	18046	3035
Day-Date	18048	3035
Day-Date	18049	3035
Day-Date	18078	3035
Day-Date	18079	3035
Day-Date	18206	3135
Day-Date	18208	3135
Day-Date	18238	3135
Day-Date	18239	3135
Day-Date	18248	3135
Day-Date	18249	3135
Day-Date	18296	3135
Day-Date	18308	3135
Day-Date	18338	3135
Day-Date	18346	3135
Day-Date	18348	3135
Day-Date	18349	3135
Day-Date	18366	3135
Day-Date	18368	3135
Day-Date	18378	3135
Day-Date	18388	3135
Day-Date	18389	3135
Day-Date	18946	3135
Day-Date	18948	3135
Day-Date	18956	3135

Name	Ref.	Cal.
Day-Date 36	118205	3155
Day-Date 36	118206	3155
Day-Date 36	118208	3155
Day-Date 36	118209	3155
Day-Date 36	118235	3155
Day-Date 36	118238	3155
Day-Date 36	118239	3155
Day-Date 36	118296	3155
Day-Date 36	118338	3155
Day-Date 36	118339	3155
Day-Date 36	118346	3155
Day-Date 36	118348	3155
Day-Date 36	118366	3155
Day-Date 36	118388	3155
Day-Date 36	118389	3155
Day-Date 36	118398	3155
Day-Date II	216570	3156
Day-Date II	218206	3156
Day-Date II	218235	3156
Day-Date II	218238	3156
Day-Date II	218239	3156
Day-Date 40	228235	3255
Day-Date 40	228239	3255

Rolex Bubbleback

The Bubbleback is an unofficial category of a Rolex watch made between the mid-1930s and the mid-1950s. Numerous references fall into the Bubbleback category including several semi-bubblebacks and transitional examples.

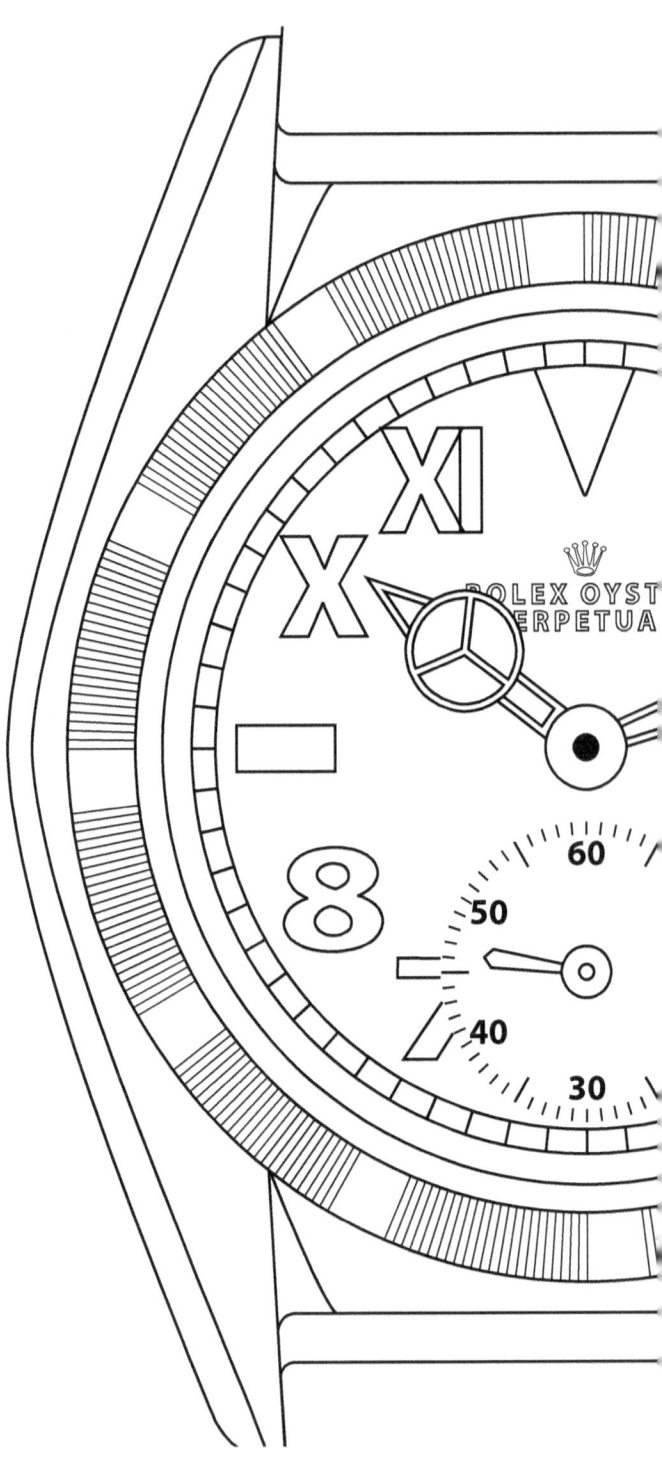

The term Bubbleback comes from a pronounced rounded and protruding case back. These watches also go by the nickname, *ovettone* which is Italian for little egg. This dome-shaped case back was necessary to accommodate the rotor of the early self-winding movements. The design choice for a convex caseback, as opposed to a thicker mid case (and flat case back), resulted in a distinctive and unusual look which proved very comfortable on the wrist.

Bubbleback case diameters are small; typically 30mm to 36mm for men's models. Combined with a domed acrylic crystal, the convex casebacks contributed to an almost egg-like profile, standing high and proud on the wrist. The look is certainly distinctive and immediately recognizable. The cases of later references are 36mm and are known as the Big Bubbleback. These are the precursors to the Datejust.

The first Bubbleback was the ref.1858, with a caliber 520 movement and a three-piece case design. In 1936 the two-piece case was introduced with refs. 3131 and 3132.

In recent decades, the Bubbleback has fallen out of fashion, as tastes now tend toward larger watch sizes. However, they represent an early and vital phase in Rolex's history and continue to be of great interest to collectors.

These self-winding movements and early Oyster cases are the precursors to the modern Oyster Perpetual. Nearly every contemporary Rolex now features the word Perpetual on its dial. In this sense, the Bubbleback is historically significant, and their role and place in the evolution of the Rolex product line cannot be understated.

BUBBLEBACK CALIFORNIA DIALS

Bubblebacks are the only models to use the California Dial. These dials consist of half Roman and half Arabic numerals. Numbers 10 to 2 are Roman, 4 to 8 are Arabic. Rolex and Panerai are the two brands most commonly associated with the California dial. The first Rolex Bubbleback to appear with such a dial was the ref. 3595.

The origins of the name are unclear, but authoritative sources such as James Dowling claim it comes from a Californian dial refinisher, Kirk Rich in the 1970s. Kirk became so well known for his high-quality restoration of these dials that clients began to call them the California dial.

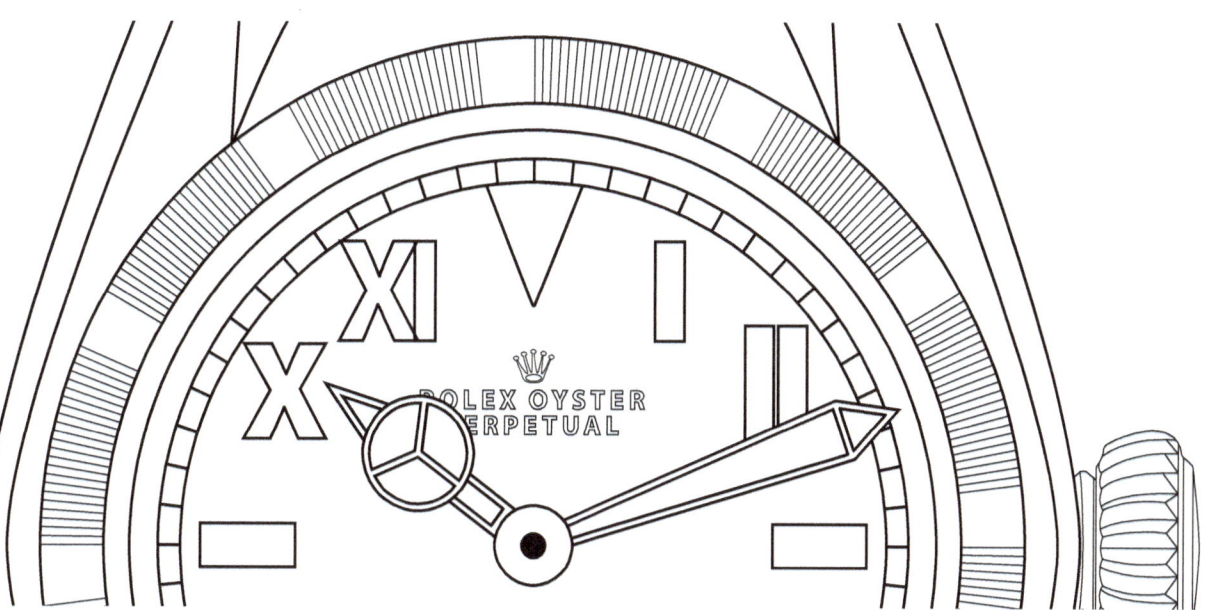

Bubbleback Reference Summary

Ref.	Cal.	Years	Bezel	Size	Case	Description
1858/0	520		Smooth (Polished)		SS	Perpetual, Chronometer, Seconds sub-dial
1858/1	520		Smooth (Polished)		YGF	Perpetual, Chronometer, SS back
1858/3	520		Smooth (Polished)		SSRG	Perpetual, Chronometer
1858/7	520		Smooth (Polished)			Perpetual, Chronometer
1858/7	520		Smooth (Polished)		RG	Perpetual, Chronometer
1858/7	520		Smooth (Polished)		YG	Perpetual, Chronometer
1858/7	520		Smooth (Polished)		RG	Perpetual, Chronometer
1858/8	520		Smooth (Polished)			Perpetual, Chronometer
1858/8	520		Smooth (Polished)		RG	Perpetual, Chronometer
1873/0	8 3/4		Smooth (Polished)		SS	Perpetual, Chronometer
1873/1	Chronometer		Smooth (Polished)		YGF	Perpetual, SS back
1873/3	Chronometer		Smooth (Polished)		SSYG	Perpetual
1873/3	Chronometer		Smooth (Polished)		In	Perpetual
1873/7	Chronometer		Smooth (Polished)			Perpetual
1873/7	Chronometer		Smooth (Polished)		RG	Perpetual
1873/7	Chronometer		Smooth (Polished)		YG	Perpetual
1873/7	Chronometer		Smooth (Polished)		RG	Perpetual
1873/8	Chronometer		Smooth (Polished)			Perpetual
1873/8	Chronometer		Smooth (Polished)		RG	Perpetual
2240/0	9 3/4		Smooth (Polished)		SS	Perpetual, Dennison case
2280/0	Manual		Smooth (Polished)		SS	Rolco
2764/0	Chronometer		Engine Turned		SS	Perpetual, Seconds sub-dial

Ref.	Cal.	Years	Bezel	Size	Case	Description
2764/1	Chronometer		Smooth (Polished)		YGF	Perpetual, SS back
2764/3	Chronometer		Smooth (Polished)			Perpetual
2764/3	Chronometer		Smooth (Polished)		SSYG	Perpetual
2764/7	Chronometer		Smooth (Polished)		YG	Perpetual
2764/7	Chronometer		Smooth (Polished)		RG	Perpetual
2764/7	Chronometer		Smooth (Polished)		YG	Perpetual
2764/7	Chronometer		Smooth (Polished)		RG	Perpetual
2764/8	Chronometer		Smooth (Polished)		YG	Perpetual
2764/8	Chronometer		Smooth (Polished)		RG	Perpetual
2765/0	Extra Prima		Smooth (Polished)			
2765/3					SSYG	
2784/0	Manual		Smooth (Polished)			Seconds sub-dial. Junior Sport
2940/0	Super Precision		Smooth (Polished)		SS	Perpetual
2940/3	Chronometer		Engine Turned		SSYG	Perpetual, Seconds sub-dial
2940/5	Chronometer		Engine Turned		YGF	Perpetual, SS back
2940/7	Chronometer		Engine Turned		RG	Perpetual
2945/0	Chronometer		Smooth (Polished)		SS	Perpetual
3042/3	Manual		Engine Turned		SSRG	
3065/0	Chronometer		Smooth (Polished)		SS	Perpetual, Hooded lugs
3065/3		1939-1950	Smooth (Polished)		SSRG	Perpetual, Hooded lugs
3065/3			Smooth (Polished)		SSRG	Perpetual, Hooded lugs
3065/7			Smooth (Polished)		YG	Perpetual, Hooded lugs
3065/7			Smooth (Polished)		1 ORG	Perpetual, Hooded lugs
3065/7			Engine Turned		YG	Perpetual, Hooded lugs
3065/7			Smooth (Polished)		RG	Perpetual, Hooded lugs
3065/8			Smooth (Polished)		RG	Perpetual, Hooded lugs

Ref.	Cal.	Years	Bezel	Size	Case	Description
3130/7	Chronometer		Smooth (polished)		YG	Perpetual, Seconds sub-dial
3130/7	Chronometer		Smooth (polished)		RG	Perpetual, Seconds sub-dial
3130/8	Chronometer		Smooth (polished)		YG	Perpetual, Seconds sub-dial
3130/8	Chronometer		Smooth (polished)		RG	Perpetual, Seconds sub-dial
3131/7	620	1936-	Engine Turned		RG	Perpetual, Chronometer
3131/7	620	1936-	Smooth (Polished)		RG	Perpetual, Chronometer
3131/7	620	1936-	Smooth (Polished)		YG	Perpetual, Chronometer
3131/8	620	1936-	Smooth (Polished)		YG	Perpetual, Chronometer
3131/8	620	1936-	Smooth (Polished)		RG	Perpetual, Chronometer
3132/0	630	1936-	Smooth (Polished)		SS	Perpetual, Chronometer
3132/3	630	1936-	Engine Turned		SSRG	Perpetual, Chronometer, Seconds sub-dial
3132/3	630	1936-	Engine Turned		SSYG	Perpetual, Chronometer, Seconds sub-dial
3132/7	630	1936-	Engine Turned			Perpetual, Chronometer, Seconds sub-dial
3132/7	630	1936-	Engine Turned		RG	Perpetual, Chronometer, Seconds sub-dial
3132/7	630	1936-	Engine Turned		YG	Perpetual, Chronometer, Seconds sub-dial
3132/7	630	1936-	Engine Turned		RG	Perpetual, Chronometer, Seconds sub-dial
3132/8	630	1936-	Engine Turned		YG	Perpetual, Chronometer, Seconds sub-dial

Ref.	Cal.	Years	Bezel	Size	Case	Description
3132/8	630	1936-	Engine Turned		18Pin	Perpetual, Chronometer, Seconds sub-dial
3133/8	Chronometer		Smooth (Polished)		YG	Perpetual
3133/0	Chronometer		Smooth (Polished)		SS	Perpetual
3133/3	Chronometer		Engine Turned		SSYG	Perpetual
3133/3	Chronometer		Smooth (Polished)		SSRG	Perpetual
3133/7	Chronometer		Smooth (Polished)			Perpetual
3133/7	Chronometer		Smooth (Polished)		RG	Perpetual
3133/7	Chronometer		Smooth (Polished)			Perpetual
3133/7	Chronometer		Smooth (Polished)			Perpetual
3133/7	Chronometer		Smooth (Polished)		YG	Perpetual
3133/7	Chronometer		Smooth (Polished)		RG	Perpetual
3133/8	Chronometer		Smooth (Polished)		RG	Perpetual
3134/0	Chronometer		Smooth (Polished)		SS	Perpetual
3134/1	Chronometer		Smooth (Polished)		YGF	Perpetual, SS back
3134/3	Chronometer		Smooth (Polished)		SSYG	Perpetual
3134/7	Chronometer		Smooth (Polished)		YG	Perpetual
3134/7	Chronometer		Smooth (Polished)		RG	Perpetual
3134/7	Chronometer		Smooth (Polished)		YG	Perpetual
3134/7	Chronometer		Smooth (Polished)		RG	Perpetual
3134/8	Chronometer		Smooth (Polished)		RG	Perpetual
3134/8	Chronometer		Smooth (Polished)		YG	Perpetual
3135/0	Chronometer		Smooth (Polished)			Perpetual
3136/0	Manual		Smooth (Polished)	Mid-Size	SS	Junior Sport
3333/3			Smooth (Polished)		SSYG	Perpetual, Hooded lugs
3348/0			Engine Turned	Mid-Size	SS	Perpetual, Seconds sub-dial
3353/0			Smooth (Polished)	Mid-Size	SS	Perpetual, Hooded lugs
3353/3			Smooth (Polished)		SSYG	Perpetual, Hooded lugs
3353/8			Smooth (Polished)		YG	Perpetual, Hooded lugs
3358/0			Fluted	Mid-Size	SS	Perpetual

Ref.	Cal.	Years	Bezel	Size	Case	Description
3372/0	630		Smooth (Polished)		SS	Perpetual, Chronometer
3372/2	630				RG	Perpetual, Chronometer
3372/3	630				SS	Perpetual, Chronometer, Hooded lugs
3372/3	630				SSRG	Perpetual, Chronometer, Seconds sub-dial
3372/7	630				YG	Perpetual, Chronometer
3372/7	630				RG	Perpetual, Chronometer
3372/8	630				YG	Perpetual, Chronometer
3372/8	630				RG	Perpetual, Chronometer
3548/0	Chronometer		Smooth (Polished)		SS	Perpetual
3548/8	Chronometer		Smooth (Polished)		YG	Perpetual
3549/0	Chronometer		Smooth (Polished)		SS	Perpetual
3595/3	Chronometer		Smooth (Polished)		SSYG	Perpetual, Seconds sub-dial, California dials
3595/3	Chronometer		Smooth (Polished)		SSRG	Perpetual, Seconds sub-dial, California dials
3598/3			Smooth (Polished)		SS	Perpetual, Seconds sub-dial
3599/0			Smooth (Polished)		SS	Perpetual, Hooded lugs
3696/3	Chronometer		Smooth (Polished)		SSRG	Perpetual
3725/3			Engine Turned		SSYG	Perpetual
3725/7			Engine Turned		RG	Perpetual, Seconds sub-dial
3725/8			Engine Turned		RG	Perpetual
3767/8	Chronometer		Smooth (Polished)	Boys-Size	RG	Perpetual

Ref.	Cal.	Years	Bezel	Size	Case	Description
3795/8			Engine Turned		RG	Perpetual, Seconds sub-dial
4392/0	Chronometer		Smooth (Polished)		SS	Perpetual
4392/7	Chronometer		Smooth (Polished)		YG	Perpetual
4392/8	Chronometer		Smooth (Polished)		RG	Perpetual
4453/0	Manual		Smooth (Polished)	Mid-Size	SS	Junior Sport
4486/8			Smooth (Polished)	Ladies	YG	Perpetual, Seconds sub-dial
4486/8			Smooth (Polished)	Ladies	RG	Perpetual, Seconds sub-dial
4777/8	Chronometer		Engine Turned		YG	Perpetual
4919/3	Chronometer		Engine Turned		SSYG	Perpetual
4939/3	Chronometer		Smooth (Polished)		SSYG	Perpetual, Seconds sub-dial
4961/0	Chronometer				SS	Perpetual, Cushion case
5001/8	Chronometer		Engine Turned		YG	Perpetual, Seconds sub-dial
5002/7			Smooth (Polished)	Ladies	YG	Perpetual, Seconds sub-dial
5002/7			Smooth (Polished)	Ladies	YG	Perpetual, Seconds sub-dial
5002/8			Engine Turned	Ladies	RG	Perpetual, Seconds sub-dial
5003/3	Super Precision		Engine Turned	Ladies	SSYG	Perpetual
5003/7			Smooth (Polished)	Ladies	YG	Perpetual
5003/8			Engine Turned	Ladies	RG	Perpetual
5003/8			Engine Turned	Ladies	YG	Perpetual
5006/3	Chronometer		Smooth (Polished)	Mid-Size	SSYG	Perpetual
5006/7	Chronometer		Smooth (Polished)	Mid-Size	YG	Perpetual
5007/3	Chronometer		Smooth (Polished)		SS 4Y	Perpetual
5010/0	Chronometer		Smooth (Polished)		SS	Perpetual
5010/3	Chronometer		Smooth (Polished)		SSYG	Perpetual
5010/3	Chronometer		Smooth (Polished)		SSRG	Perpetual
5011/3	Chronometer		Engine Turned		SSYG	Perpetual, SS back
5011/3	Super Precision		Engine Turned		SSRG	Perpetual
5011/7	Chronometer		Engine Turned		RG	Perpetual

Ref.	Cal.	Years	Bezel	Size	Case	Description
5011/8	Chronometer		Engine Turned		YG	Perpetual
5013/3	Chronometer		Engine Turned		SSYG	Perpetual, Seconds sub-dial
5015/0	Chronometer		Smooth (Polished)		SS	Perpetual
5015/3	Chronometer	1948-1952	Engine Turned		SSRG	Perpetual
5015/3	Chronometer		Engine Turned		YG	Perpetual
5015/3	Chronometer		Engine Turned		RG	Perpetual
5015/8	Chronometer		Engine Turned		YG	Perpetual
5015/8	Chronometer		Engine Turned		RG	Perpetual
5026/0			Smooth (Polished)			Perpetual, Seconds sub-dial
5045/3	Chronometer		Engine Turned		SSYG	Perpetual
5048/0	Chronometer		Smooth (Polished)		SS	Perpetual
5048/3	Chronometer		Smooth (Polished)			Perpetual
5048/8	Chronometer		Smooth (Polished)		YG	Perpetual
5050/0	Chronometer		Smooth (Polished)		SS	Perpetual
5050/7	Chronometer		Smooth (Polished)		YG	Perpetual
5050/8	Chronometer		Smooth (Polished)		YG	Perpetual
5051/7	Chronometer		Smooth (Polished)		RG	Perpetual
5055/3	Chronometer		Smooth (Polished)	Mid-Size	SSYG	Perpetual
5105/0	Chronometer		Engine Turned		SS	Perpetual
5105/1	Chronometer		Engine Turned		YGF	Perpetual, SS back
5105/3	Chronometer		Engine Turned		SSYG	Perpetual
5105/7	Chronometer		Smooth (Polished		YG	Perpetual
5105/7	Chronometer		Engine Turned		RG	Perpetual
5105/7	Chronometer		Engine Turned		YG	Perpetual
5105/7	Chronometer		Engine Turned		RG	Perpetual
5105/8	Chronometer		Engine Turned		YG	Perpetual
5105/8	Chronometer		Engine Turned		RG	Perpetual
6006/0			Smooth (Polished)	Mid-Size	SS	Perpetual, Seconds sub-dial
6006/8			Smooth (Polished)	Mid-Size	RG	Perpetual, Seconds sub-dial
6015/0	Chronometer		Engine Turned		SS	Perpetual
6048/8	Chronometer		Smooth (Polished)		RG	Perpetual

Ref.	Cal.	Years	Bezel	Size	Case	Description
6084/0	645		Smooth (Polished)	Full Size	SS	Perpetual, Chronometer
6106/0	Chronometer		Smooth (Polished)		SS	Perpetual
6428/0	Chronometer				SS	Perpetual
8056/3	Chronometer		Smooth (Polished)		SSYG	Perpetual, Hooded lugs
8056/3	Chronometer		Smooth (Polished)		SSRG	Perpetual, Hooded lugs
8056/7	Chronometer		Smooth (Polished)		YG	Perpetual, Hooded lugs
8056/7	Chronometer		Smooth (Polished)		RG	Perpetual, Hooded lugs
8056/8	Chronometer		Smooth (Polished)		YG	Perpetual, Hooded lugs
8056/8	Chronometer		Smooth (Polished)		RG	Perpetual, Hooded lugs

9 FORMAL DRESS

"Fashion is ephemeral, dangerous and unfair."
- Karl Lagerfeld

When Andre Heiniger was appointed the CEO of Rolex in 1963, he made a conscious decision to reinvent Rolex as a luxury brand and move it upmarket. This change of strategy was a marked departure from his predecessor's focus on high-specification, professional tool watches.

While it came to be known as The Doctor's Watch, it was not explicitly designed as such, and would not have been considered a dress watch by Heiniger.

The Cellini collection emerged in the late 1960s under Heiniger's guidance and was named after Benevenuto Cellini (1500-1571), an artist and adventurer.

Rolex had launched several dress watches before the arrival of the now-famous Cellini collection. The Rolex Prince Brancard of 1928 is an iconic example.

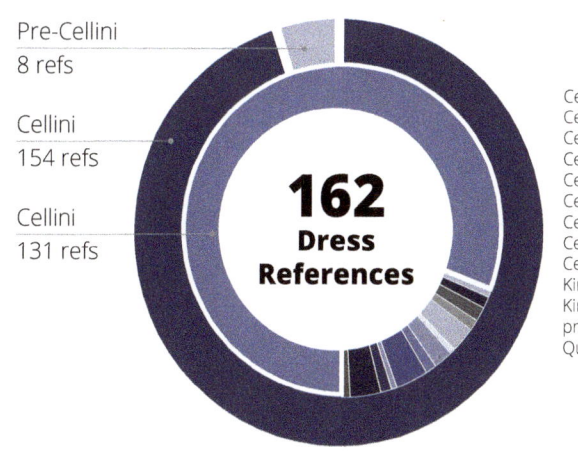

Pre-Cellini 8 refs
Cellini 154 refs
Cellini 131 refs

162 Dress References

Cellini Cellissima 1
Cellini Danaos 2
Cellini Date 2
Cellini Dual Time 2
Cellini Midas 4
Cellini Moonphase 1
Cellini Prince 3
Cellini Quartz 2
Cellini Time 5
King Midas 1
King Midas 2
pre-Cellini 5
Queen Midas 1

Benvenuto Cellini (1500 - 1571)

Cellini served as a goldsmith and sculptor to popes and royalty during the Italian Renaissance.

The Rolex Cellini collection is thought to be the first luxury watch produced in large quantities to be awarded chronometric certification.

The understated dials of vintage pieces display only time, with no second hand. Modern Cellini watches have adopted complications to make them more practical for daily wear. Cellini are described as water resistant but are not waterproof. They can withstand a rainstorm or hand washing but are not suitable for the hot tub or swimming pool.

The Cellini collection falls into the Modern Classic taxonomy, though there is disagreement over how classic any of these designs are. Like ladies vintage Rolex references in general, Cellini dress watches have a small but enthusiastic following.

Cellini Cestello (1990 to 2000)

The name Cestello was used in the 1990s to describe a series of round dress watches offered in platinum, yellow or rose gold. It appeared to be an attempt to create a product line within the Cellini Collection. The name was used in catalogs and advertising but did not appear on dials. The name and watches failed to distinguish themselves as a commercial success and were quietly retired.

Cellini Danaos (2000)

The Danaos line appeared in 2000. There is some disagreement about the origin of the name. Some sources claim it is a Latin reference to Greeks, and others claim it refers to an Egyptian king or the mythological king of Argos.

The Danaos is available in precious metals and two-tone combinations on leather straps. It is a distinctive and contemporary looking line of watches. At 39mm the pieces had more presence than the rather bland Cestello references they replaced. The Danaos references went on to have moderate commercial success, and prices on the pre-owned market are holding up well.

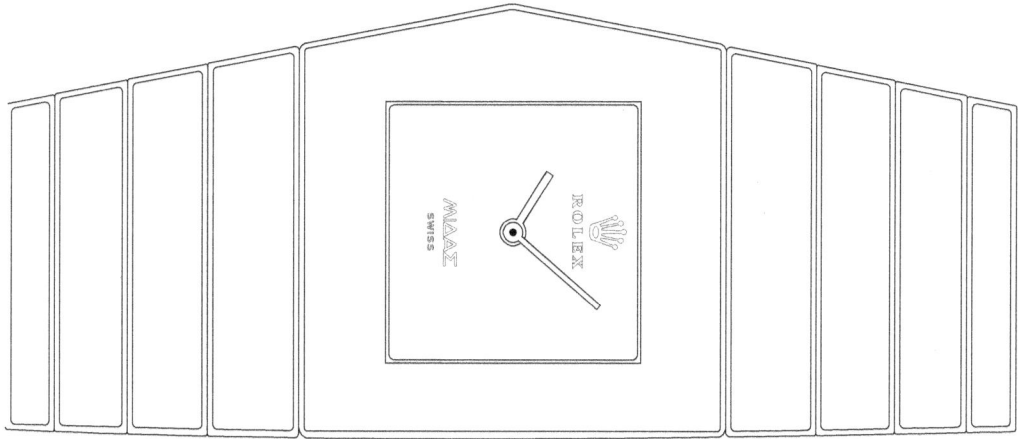

King Midas

The designer of the Rolex King Midas was Gerald Genta, the most famous watch designer in modern times. Gerald Genta was also responsible for the Audemars Piguet Royal Oak and the Patek Philippe Nautilus.

The King Midas has an asymmetric pentagonal case inspired by the Greek Pantheon. In Greek mythology, King Midas could turn anything he touched to gold.

In the late 1960s, the first King Midas ref.9630 debuted and was limited to only 1,000 numbered units. This original version pre-dated the Cellini collection, but later versions became part of the group and known as Cellini King Midas.

At launch, it was the most opulent and expensive watch Rolex offered. They are stamped from a solid block of 18K yellow gold and weigh 150 to 200 grams. The considerable weight comes from the integrated bracelet which is characteristic of many Gerald Genta watches.

The winding crown of ref.9630 does not feature a Rolex coronet like later versions but instead, shaped like a sun. It is positioned on the left side of the case; a further reference to King Midas, whose left hand had the mythical golden touch. The shape and position resemble the sun rising over the Pantheon. Engraved on either side of the left-handed crown are the words KING MIDAS, framing the rising sun.

Like most dress watches it has only an hour and minute hand. The dial features the Rolex coronet at 12 o'clock and Midas written in Greek below the centerline. These Greek letters mark the ref. 9360 as unique. Later editions from the ref. 3580 onwards feature the name Cellini instead.

Famous owners of the 9360 King Midas include Elvis Presley and John Wayne. If the King Midas appeals to you, the original and limited edition 9630 is the one to own.

Ref. 3580 arrived in 1974 as a white gold version of the original 9360. A very rare Queen Midas followed shortly after. They were also individually numbered but made in larger volume.

Above: Cellini ref. 4114 circa 1970.

Below: Cellini ref. 4127 circa 1970 with wooden dial

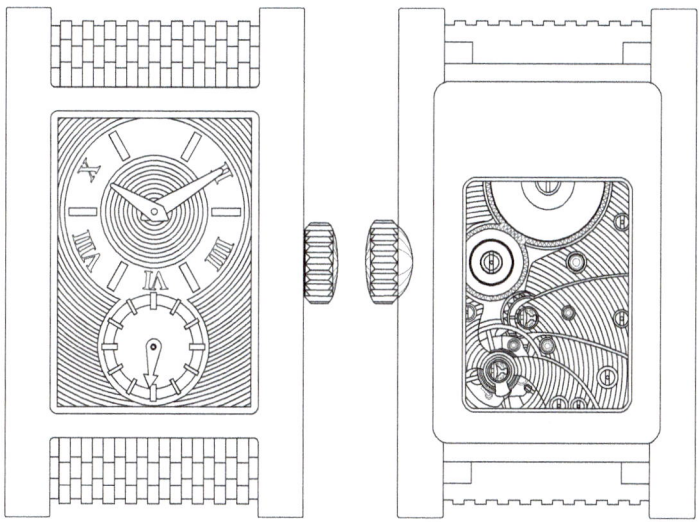

Cellini Prince

The Rolex Cellini Prince is a reinterpretation of the original Rolex Prince of 1928. The modern reinterpretation debuted in 2005 and has a distinct art deco aesthetic reminiscent of the roaring 1920s.

The original Prince had a distinctive avant-garde rectangular case. The modern version has a similar rectangular case and is equally striking.

One significant difference is the display case back to show off the highly finished, manual wind caliber 7040.

The Rolex Cellini Prince (refs. 54425, 54419 and 54439) is made only in precious metal (18K YG, WG, and Everose gold) and has five dial combinations:

- Champagne dial decorated with a clou de Paris or guilloch motif. This design is a hobnail or checkered pattern.

- Silver dial with a godron circulaire. This pattern is a radial or circular, striped ring design (illustrated).

- Diamond-pave dial with silver godron circulaire motif

- Black and silver dial with double rayon flamm de la gloire. This pattern is a radiating striped design which appears to originate from the center of the dial.

- Black and pink dial with rayon flamm de la gloire.

Dress Watch Reference Summary

Name	Ref.	Cal.	Size	Description
King Midas	3580		28mm	Pentagonal
King Midas	4015	1601	28mm	Pentagonal
King Midas	9630	650	28mm	Pentagonal. First, original King Midas
pre-Cellini	2736	Manual	Full Size	Square
Cellini	3224	Manual	Full Size	Square
Cellini	3718		Full Size	Round
Cellini	3727	1600	Full Size	Rectangular
Cellini	3729	Manual	Full Size	Oval
Cellini	3735	Manual	Full Size	Square
pre-Cellini	3737	Manual	Full Size	Square
Cellini	3759		Full Size	Round
Cellini	3804		Full Size	Round
Cellini	3811	1600	Full Size	Square
Cellini	3833	Manual	Full Size	Round
Cellini	3834	Manual	Full Size	Rectangular
Cellini	4014	1600	Full Size	Rectangular
Cellini	4016	Manual	Full Size	Rectangular
Cellini	4083		Full Size	Round
Cellini	4084		Full Size	Square
Cellini	4100		Full Size	Rectangular
Cellini	4101		Full Size	Rectangular
pre-Cellini	4102		Full Size	Rectangular
pre-Cellini	4104		Full Size	Rectangular
Cellini	4105	1601	Full Size	Other
Cellini	4109		Full Size	Round
Cellini	4112	1601	Full Size	Round
Cellini	4121	1601	Full Size	Hexagonal (6)
Cellini	4122	Manual	Full Size	Hexagonal (6)
Cellini	4126	1601	Full Size	Square
Cellini	4133	Manual	Full Size	Round
Cellini Danos	4243	Manual	Full Size	Round

Name	Ref.	Cal.	Size	Description
Cellini	4306		Full Size	Round
Cellini	4309	1601	Full Size	Round
Cellini	4310		Full Size	Rectangular
Cellini	4322	Manual	Full Size	Other
Cellini	4324	Manual	Full Size	Hexagonal (6)
Cellini	4327	Manual	Full Size	Square
Cellini	4328		Full Size	Square
Cellini Midas	4342		Full Size	Pentagonal
Cellini	4344	Manual	Full Size	Other
Cellini	4349	Manual	Full Size	Other
Cellini	4350	Manual	Full Size	Other
Cellini	4379	Manual	Full Size	Round
Cellini	4650		Full Size	Other
Cellini	4652		Full Size	Other
Cellini	5116	1602	Full Size	Round
Cellini	5156	1601	Full Size	Other
Cellini	5166		Full Size	Round
Cellini	5241	Manual	Full Size	Round
Cellini	5330	Manual	Full Size	Other
Cellini	5443	Manual	Full Size	Rectangular
Cellini Quartz	6623	6620	Full Size	Round
Cellini Time	50505	3132	Full Size	Round
Cellini Time	50509	3132	Full Size	Round
Cellini Date	50515	3135	Full Size	Round
Cellini Date	50519	3165	Full Size	Round
Cellini Dual Time	50525	3135	Full Size	Round
Cellini Dual Time	50529	3180	Full Size	Round
Cellini Moonphase	50535	3165	Full Size	Round
Cellini Time	50609	3132	Full Size	Round
Cellini Time	50705	3132	Full Size	Round
Cellini Prince	54419	7040	Full Size	Rectangular
Cellini Prince	54439	7040	Full Size	Rectangular
Cellini	2466	Manual	Ladies	Round
Queen Midas	3581		Ladies	Pentagonal

Name	Ref.	Cal.	Size	Description
Cellini	4081	Manual	Ladies	Round
Cellini	4082		Ladies	Square
Cellini	4139		Ladies	Rectangular
Cellini	4302		Ladies	Rectangular
Cellini	4304		Ladies	Round
Cellini	4321	Manual	Ladies	Rectangular
Cellini	4332	Manual	Ladies	Square
Cellini	4335	Manual	Ladies	Square
Cellini	4339	Manual	Ladies	Rectangular
Cellini	4341	Manual	Ladies	Hexagonal (6)
Cellini	4614	1601	Ladies	Oval
Cellini	4625	Manual	Ladies	Oval
Cellini	4942	Manual	Ladies	Other
Cellini	4943	Manual	Ladies	Other
Cellini	5109	1601	Ladies	Round
Cellini	5171	Manual	Ladies	Round
Cellini	5184	Manual	Ladies	Round
Cellini	5188		Ladies	Round
Cellini	5221	Manual	Ladies	Oval
Cellini	6110	A.260	Ladies	Round
Cellini Quartz	6621	1130	Ladies	Round
Cellini	6673	6620	Ladies	Round
Cellini	6692		Ladies	Other
Cellini Cellissima	6693	1215	Ladies	Other
Cellini	2704	Manual	Unisex	Square
Cellini	3612	650	Unisex	Round
Cellini	3717	1601	Unisex	Round
Cellini	3761	Manual	Unisex	Round
Cellini	3787	Manual	Unisex	Round
Cellini	3799	Manual	Unisex	Oval
Cellini	4032		Unisex	Rectangular
Cellini	4041		Unisex	Round
Cellini	4043		Unisex	Oval
Cellini	4080		Unisex	Square

Formal Dress

Name	Ref.	Cal.	Size	Description
Cellini	4087		Unisex	Square
pre-Cellini	4103		Unisex	Rectangular
Cellini	4106		Unisex	Hexagonal (6)
Cellini	4107		Unisex	Hexagonal (6)
Cellini	4108		Unisex	Rectangular
Cellini	4110		Unisex	Oval
Cellini	4111		Unisex	Oval
Cellini	4113		Unisex	Other
Cellini	4114		Unisex	Square
Cellini	4127	Manual	Unisex	Rectangular
Cellini	4129		Unisex	Round
Cellini	4131		Unisex	Rectangular
Cellini	4132		Unisex	Rectangular
Cellini	4135		Unisex	Square
Cellini	4136		Unisex	Hexagonal (6)
Cellini Midas	4294		Unisex	Pentagonal
Cellini Midas	4315		Unisex	Pentagonal
Cellini	4317		Unisex	Round
Cellini	4318		Unisex	Square
Cellini	4319		Unisex	Round
Cellini	4320		Unisex	Square
Cellini	4333	Manual	Unisex	Square
Cellini Midas	4336		Unisex	Pentagonal
Cellini	4624		Unisex	Round
Cellini	4630		Unisex	Round
Cellini	5113		Unisex	Round
Cellini	5114		Unisex	Round
Cellini Time	50709	3132	Unisex	Round
Cellini	3783			
Cellini	3790			
Cellini	3791			
Cellini	4140			
Cellini	4143			
Cellini	4211			

Name	Ref.	Cal.	Size	Description
Cellini Danos	4223			
Cellini	4305			
Cellini	4307			
Cellini	4308			
Cellini	4312			
Cellini	4329			
Cellini	4331			
Cellini	4340			
Cellini	4343			
Cellini	4347			
Cellini	4378			
Cellini	4615			
Cellini	4621			
Cellini	4622			
Cellini	4626			
Cellini	4628			
Cellini	4629			
Cellini	4631			
Cellini	4632			
Cellini	4633			
Cellini	4636			
Cellini	5167			
Cellini	5172			
Cellini	5191			
Cellini	5192			
Cellini	5222			
Cellini	6628	1135		
Cellini Prince	54425	7040		
Cellini	14233M			

10 BRACELETS

"There are two kinds of fools: one says, "This is old, therefore it is good"; the other says, "This is new, therefore it is better."
- Dean William Ralph Inge

Until the era of Modern Classics, Rolex had been using Oyster and Jubilee bracelets from the bracelet-maker Gay Freres. This company is also known for the famous Heuer beads of rice bracelet and the bracelet for the Audemars Piguet Royal Oak.

Rolex used Gay Freres exclusively until the late 1940s. From the 1950s to the mid-1970s Rolex used several suppliers to create the same bracelet but for different territories. For example, Rolex used suppliers in North America in response to US tax regulations.

C&I supplied the USA-made riveted Oyster bracelets. There are also Rolex Oyster and Jubilee bracelets marked Hecho en Mexico on the clasp, indicating production in Mexico.

Rolex acquired the Gay Freres company in 1998, bringing all their bracelet production in-house.

Rolex introduced their iconic Jubilee bracelet with the Datejust in 1945/6. The following year Rolex was awarded a patent for the Oyster bracelet (1947) which appeared in the Rolex catalog in 1948.

Throughout the 1940s, Rolex did not offer a bracelet as standard, but as an expensive upgrade. Leather straps were the most common way of wearing a watch. They were treated as consumable and disposable - particularly in hot and humid climates where they would degrade quickly.

There were a great many bracelet styles produced, but the two most commonly recognized are the Oyster and Jubilee.

Oyster Bracelet

The first generation from the 1950s was the rivet style bracelet with visible rivet studs on the outer edge of the hollow folded links. Links were fastened together with the rivets having a peaked, conical cap that became less pronounced with polishing. These bracelets were also offered in an expanding link style (refs. 6634, 6635, 6636), but this was phased out after proving less resilient and less comfortable.

The second generation (the 1960s) was the folded link style bracelet (refs. 7834, 7835, 7836, 9315). The folded link, as the name suggests is made by folding sheet metal in on itself multiple times. These Swiss rolls result in a thicker link, but the pins holding them together are hidden.

The last and current generation is the solid link bracelet. These used the same numbering convention as the second generation, but with an added zero suffix. (e.g. 93150). The solid link style has proven the most robust, with even end links evolving from folded steel to solid. These are made in either a fully-brushed or partially polished (center link) finish.

The Oyster bracelet reference number is usually found on the first or final link of the bracelet. This code indicates which generation it belongs to (four-digit or five-digit) and the appropriate end link. For example, the ref. 7206 is a riveted Oyster requiring 20mm end links, while the ref. 7205 is the very same bracelet but requires 19mm end links.

Getting a comfortable fit with an Oyster bracelet and Fliplock clasp can be challenging for some wrist shapes. Half links are available as an option.

Removing a permanent link is possible, and some independent watchmakers or jewelers may be willing to perform this procedure. While an AD won't perform this, a pair of pliers and masking tape can do the job.

The process is non-reversible, damages the permanent link during removal, and should be considered a last resort. Correcting an Oyster that has had this procedure, can be done by adding back a removable link; however not all the permanent links are the same size, so such a correction may fix the length but leave a

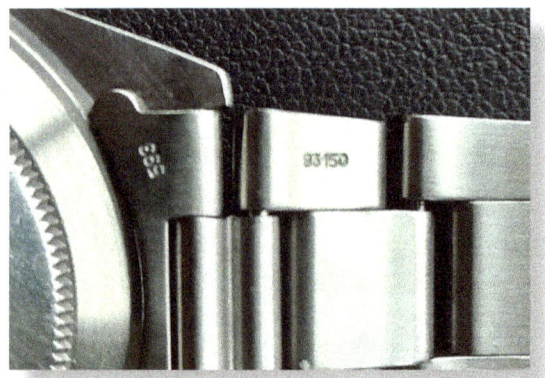

mismatched width.

JUBILEE BRACELET

The Jubilee bracelet arrived in 1945 with the new Datejust and was later offered as an option on the GMT-Master and the early Cosmograph Daytona. Today it is reserved exclusively for the Datejust and should not be confused with the flagship President bracelet.

Each link of the Jubilee is made of five-pieces, comprising three thinner inner links flanked by larger outer links. The two different link sizes are most noticeable on two-tone Rolesor versions with the inner links in yellow or Everose gold.

The Jubilee bracelet can be fitted with a concealed folding Crownclasp, which has a Rolex coronet lever to open the bracelet and reveal the folding blades. The concealment of the clasp allows the pattern of the Jubilee links to run seamlessly around the wrist.

The Jubilee bracelet is prone to wear and tear. Each of the five links are prone to friction-wear resulting in a rounding of corners and edges. The internal retaining pin is also prone to bending. This results in an overall loosening of the bracelet described as *stretching* or *sloppiness*.

Depending on the degree of wear and tear, Jubilee bracelets can be restored by replacing the pins. If the links are seriously worn, laser welding may be needed.

INTEGRATED BRACELETS

These bracelets first appeared on the Oysterquartz and have a distinct angular form which complements the case features. Like the Cellini Midas, these are claimed to be Gerald Genta designs (though in this case, the claim is controversial and unsupported).

The steel integrated Oyster bracelet, two-tone integrated Jubilee bracelet, and solid gold integrated President bracelet are close enough to their inspiration to allow them to bear the same names.

Integrated bracelets are clever and distinctive reinterpretations of the Oyster, Jubilee and President bracelets. A particularly interesting variation of the President integrated bracelet for the Oysterquartz Day-Date watches involves intricate pyramid patterns.

President Bracelet

Rolex introduced the President bracelet on the Day-Date in 1956. It is only available in precious metals and always has a concealed clasp. It is reserved exclusively for the Day-Date and available in different sizes and precious metals.

Variations include the Tridor which has center links in a mix of three shades of gold. For a brief period in the late 1970s and early 1980s, a distinctive bark finish was available as an option for the center links.

Pearlmaster Bracelet

The Ladies Pearlmaster Collection first appeared in 1992. They are lavish and opulent jewelry bracelets, and often feature jewel settings up to full diamond pave styles to match the cases. They have a rounded five-piece link construction and always have a concealed clasp. They are only available in precious metal.

Oysterflex Bracelet Strap

The Oysterflex is a thoroughly modern strap introduced in 2015 on the Everose Yacht-Master. The Rolex marketing machine insist it is a bracelet rather than a strap, due to the titanium and nickel alloy blade that runs through the middle of the rubber coating.

These bracelets (rubber straps)

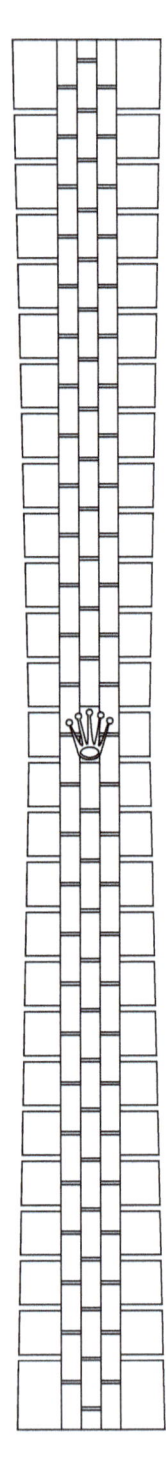

come with the Oysterlock safety clasps, which have a 5mm Easylink extension system. The Oysterflex is replacing leather options on Professional tool watches like the Daytona.

Leather Straps

Until the arrival of the Tool watches in the 1950s leather straps were the norm. Vintage leather straps are seldom worth anything and usually found in unpleasant states of decay.

Modern classics are still available on original leather straps, and in particular, dress watches from the Cellini collection.

In the early 2000s, Rolex offered an exclusive white gold Daytona as the Daytona Beach. These featured colorful dials with matching colored straps in pink, turquoise, green, and yellow leather. These Daytona Beach models are rare and quite collectible.

Classic models like the Datejust, Day-Date and the newer Sky-Dweller can be bought new with leather straps.

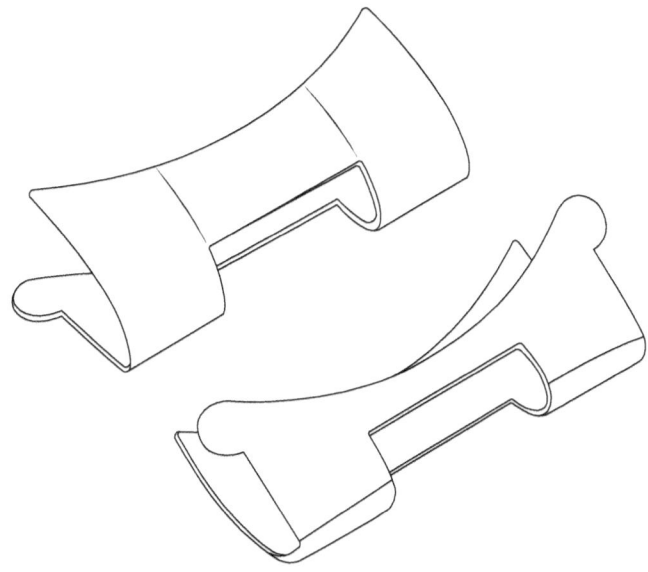

End Links & Spring Bars

Rolex introduced end links in 1952 with the launch of the GMT-Master ref. 6542. Their purpose was to reduce movement of the bracelet and pressure on the spring bars which could result in spring bar failure, and dropping or losing the watch.

In addition to improving the streamlined and integrated look of the bracelet, end links increased the durability and reliability of the bracelet. This innovation was necessary for the professional tool watches designed for, and used in harsh and demanding environments.

End links are stamped with a number and are specific to the bracelet reference and case size. They also support particular spring bar sizes (diameter).

Incorrect, twisted or poorly fitting end links will rattle on the wrist and scratch the Oyster case. Scratching and wear on the case by end links can be bad enough to obscure reference and serial numbers.

End link construction has evolved in step with the bracelets, switching from thin folded steel, to solid milled steel. The solid end link was first used on the Sea-Dweller and has become standard issue.

It is important to use the correct end links and spring bars for the bracelet and case. Ignoring this advice will accelerate wear and tear on both the bracelet and the watch case.

Incorrectly-sized spring bars will reduce the effectiveness of end links and contribute to their movement and rattle on the wrist. They can also distort the shape of the lug holes, which can be particularly bad in soft solid gold cases.

	Part Number	Length	Metal	Model	Pivot Length	Pivot Diameter
	23-9250	11 mm	0	Tudor	1,6 mm	0,9 mm
	23-9260	13 mm	0	—	1,6 mm	0,9 mm
	23-9261	13 mm	1	—	1,6 mm	0,9 mm
	23-9262	13 mm	8	—	1,6 mm	0,9 mm
	23-9263	13 mm	9	—	1,6 mm	0,9 mm
	23-9270	17 mm	0	—	1,7 mm	0,9 mm
	23-9271	17 mm	1	—	1,7 mm	0,9 mm
	23-9272	17 mm	8	—	1,7 mm	0,9 mm
	23-9273	17 mm	9	—	1,7 mm	0,9 mm
	23-9280	19 mm	0	—	1,9 mm	0,9 mm
	23-9281	19 mm	0	—	1,3 mm	0,9 mm
	23-9282	19 mm	8	—	1,9 mm	0,9 mm
	23-9283	19 mm	0	1550/5	0,8 mm	0,9 mm
	23-9290	20 mm	0	—	2,0 mm	0,9 mm
	23-9291	20 mm	0	GMT-Master Submariner	2,8 mm	1,2 mm
	23-9292	20 mm	0 x	GMT-Master	2,8 mm	1,2 mm
	23-9293	20 mm	0	Explorer-1016 Submariner	1,8 mm	1,2 mm
	23-9294	20 mm	8	GMT-Master	2,8 mm	1,2 mm
	23-9350	11 mm	0	Tudor	1,0 mm	0,9 mm
	23-9360	13 mm	0	Tudor	0,9 mm	0,9 mm
	23-9361	13 mm	8	Rolex	1,0 mm	0,9 mm
	23-9362	13 mm	9	Rolex	1,0 mm	0,9 mm
	23-9365	17 mm	8	Rolex	1,0 mm	0,9 mm
	23-9366	17 mm	9	Rolex	1,0 mm	0,9 mm
	23-9370	19 mm	0	—	1,0 mm	0,9 mm
	23-9380	20 mm	0	Day-Date**	1,0 mm	0,9 mm
	23-9381	20 mm	8	Day-Date***	1,2 mm	0,9 mm
	23-9382	20 mm	0	Day-Date***	1,2 mm	0,9 mm
	23-9383	20 mm	9	Day-Date***	1,2 mm	0,9 mm
	23-9384	20 mm	8	Day-Date**	1,0 mm	0,9 mm
	23-9385	20 mm	9	Day-Date**	1,0 mm	0,9 mm
	23-9390	22 mm	Titane	Quartz 5100	1,0 mm	0,9 mm

Professional Bracelet & End Link Fitment Table

The following table will help you know if the bracelet and end links correctly fit your watch. The correct and original combination will depend on the age of the watch, but the following combinations are known to fit.

Some collectors like to wear vintage watches with modern bracelets out of personal comfort preference (solid links and end links). There are no hard and fast rules other than to get a good fit that feels comfortable.

Model	Case Ref.	Bracelet Ref.	Endlinks	Description
Daytona	6239	7205	71	Rivet Oyster (19mm)
		7835	771, 271	Folded Oyster (19mm)
		78350	771	Solid Oyster (19mm)
		6635	71	Stretch Rivet Oyster (19mm)
		6251	74	Folded Jubilee (19mm)
Cosmograph	6240	6635	71	Stretch Rivet Oyster (19mm)
		7205	71	Rivet Oyster (19mm)
		7835	271	Folded Oyster (19mm)
Cosmograph	6241	6635	71	Stretch Rivet Oyster (20mm)
		7205	71	Rivet Oyster (19mm)
		7835	271	Folded Oyster (19mm)
Cosmograph	6262	7835	71	Folded Oyster (19mm)
Daytona	6263	7835	771, 271, 371	Folded Oyster (19mm)
		78350	771, 571	Solid Oyster (19mm)
Cosmograph	6264	7835	271	Folded Oyster (19mm)
Daytona	6265	7835	771, 271, 371	Folded Oyster (19mm)
		78350	771, 571	Solid Oyster (19mm)
Daytona	16520	78360	503	Solid Oyster (20mm)
		78390	503B	Solid PCL Oyster (20mm)
		78390A	SEL	Solid PCL Oyster (20mm)
Daytona	116520	78490	SEL	Solid PCL Oyster (20mm)
Sea-Dweller	1655	9315	285	Folded Oyster (20mm)
		93150	580, 585	Solid Oyster (20mm)
Sea-Dweller	16600	93160	592, SEL	Solid Oyster (20mm)
		93160A	SEL	Solid Oyster (20mm)
Sea-Dweller	166600	93160	592, SEL	Solid Oyster (20mm)

Model	Case Ref.	Bracelet Ref.	Endlinks	Description
GMT-Master	6542	7206	58, 80	Rivet Oyster (20mm)
		6636	58, 64	Stretch Rivet Oyster (20mm)
GMT-Master	1675	6636	58, 64	Stretch Rivet Oyster (20mm)
		7206	58, 80	Rivet Oyster (20mm)
		7836	280	Folded Oyster (20mm)
		78360	580	Solid Oyster (20mm)
		62510H	550	Solid Jubilee (20mm)
GMT-Master	16750	78360	580	Solid Oyster (20mm)
		62510H	550	Solid Jubilee (20mm)
GMT-Master	16700	78360	501B, 593	Solid Oyster (20mm)
		78790A	SEL	Solid Oyster (20mm)
		62510H	502B	Solid Jubilee (20mm)
GMT-Master II	16760	78360	501	Solid Oyster (20mm)
		78790A	SEL	Solid Oyster (20mm)
		62510H	502B	Solid Jubilee (20mm)
GMT-Master II	16710	78360	501, 501B	Solid Oyster (20mm)
		78790A	SEL	Solid Oyster (20mm)
		62510H	502B(T)	Solid Jubilee (20mm)
Submariner	5508	7206	58	Rivet Oyster (20mm)
		6636	58	Stretch Rivet Oyster (20mm)
Submariner	6536	7206	80	Rivet Oyster (20mm)
		6636	64, 65	Stretch Rivet Oyster (20mm)
Submariner	6538	6636	64, 65	Stretch Rivet Oyster (20mm)
		7206	80	Rivet Oyster (20mm)
Submariner	6200	6636	64	Stretch Rivet Oyster (20mm)
		7206	64	Rivet Oyster (20mm)
Submariner	6204	6636	64	Stretch Rivet Oyster (20mm)
		7206	80	Rivet Oyster (20mm)
Submariner	6205	6636	64	Stretch Rivet Oyster (20mm)
		7206	80	Rivet Oyster (20mm)
Submariner	5510	6636	80	Stretch Rivet Oyster (20mm)
		7206	80	Rivet Oyster (20mm)
Submariner	5512	7206	80	Rivet Oyster (20mm)

Model	Case Ref.	Bracelet Ref.	Endlinks	Description
Submariner	5513	9315	280, 380	Folded Oyster (20mm)
		93150	580	Solid Oyster (20mm)
		6306	64, 80	Stretch Rivet Oyster (20mm)
		7206	80	Rivet Oyster (20mm)
		9315	280, 380	Folded Oyster (20mm)
		93150	580	Solid Oyster (20mm)
		6636	80	Stretch Rivet Oyster (20mm)
Submariner	1680	9315	280	Folded Oyster (20mm)
		93150	580	Solid Oyster (20mm)
		7206	80	Rivet Oyster (20mm)
Submariner	16800	93150	501B	Solid Oyster (20mm)
		93250	SEL	Solid Oyster (20mm)
Submariner	168000	93150	501B	Solid Oyster (20mm)
		93250	SEL	Solid Oyster (20mm)
Submariner	14060/M	93150	501B	Solid Oyster (20mm)
Submariner	16610	93150	501B	Solid Oyster (20mm)
		93250	SEL	Solid Oyster (20mm)
Explorer	1016	7206	58	Rivet Oyster (20mm)
		7836	580	Folded Jubilee (20mm)
		78360	580	Solid Jubilee (20mm)
Explorer	14270	78790	558B	Solid Jubilee (20mm)
		78690	SEL	Solid Jubilee (20mm)
Explorer II	1655	7206	58	Rivet Oyster (20mm)
		7836	580	Folded Jubilee (20mm)
		78360	580	Solid Jubilee (20mm)
Explorer II	16550	7206	58	Rivet Oyster (20mm)
		7836	580	Folded Jubilee (20mm)
		78360	580, 593, 501B	Solid Jubilee (20mm)
		93150	501B	Solid Oyster (20mm)
Explorer II	16570	78360	501B	Solid Jubilee (20mm)
		78790	501B	Solid Jubilee (20mm)
		78790	SEL	Solid Jubilee (20mm)

Bracelet Codes & Models

Style	Ref.	Size	Metal	Gender	Links	Description
Yacht-Master	7294/8	14mm	18Y	Ladies		
Yacht-Master	7294/9	14mm	18W	Ladies		
Yacht-Master	7490/8	14mm	18Y	Ladies		
Yacht-Master	7490/8	14mm	18Y	Ladies		Center Emerald. Diamond outer row
Yacht-Master	7490/8	14mm	18Y	Ladies		Center Ruby. Diamond outer row
Yacht-Master	7490/8	14mm	18Y	Ladies		Center Sapphire. Diamond out row
Yacht-Master	7490/9	14mm	18W	Ladies		Diamonds
Yacht-Master	7494/8	14mm	18Y	Ladies		Diamond outer row
Yacht-Master	7494/9	14mm	18W	Ladies		Diamond outer row
Yacht-Master	7495/8	14mm	Tridor	Ladies		15 diamonds
Yacht-Master	7294/8	14mrn	Tridor	Ladies		
Tri-link	6490/8	13mm	18Y	Ladies		
Tri-link	2544/7	20mm	9Y	Full Size		Capture clasp
Super President Karat	8473/8	13mm	18Y	Ladies		446 diamonds
Super President	8470/6	13mm	Platinum	Ladies	36	Concealed clasp. Diamond center links
Super President	8470/8	13mm	18Y	Ladies		Concealed clasp. Diamond center links
Super President	8470/9	13mm	18W	Ladies		Concealed clasp. Diamond center links
Super President	8489/6	17mm	Platinum	Mid Size	28	340 diamonds in center links
Super President	8489/8	17mm	18Y	Mid Size	28	340 diamonds in center links
Super President	8489/9	17mm	18W	Mid Size	28	340 diamonds in center links
Super President	8485/6	20mm	Platinum	Full Size	23	288 diamonds in center links
Super President	8485/8	20mm	18Y	Full Size	23	288 diamonds in center links

Style	Ref.	Size	Metal	Gender	Links	Description
Super President	8485/9	20mm	18W	Full Size	23	288 diamonds in center links
Super Jubilee Karat	6453/8	13mm	18Y	Ladies	38	360 diamonds
Super Jubilee	6451/8	13mm	18Y	Ladies	36	344 diamonds in center links
Super Jubilee	6451/9	13mm	18W	Ladies	36	344 diamonds in center links:
Super Jubilee	6453/9	13mm	18W	Ladies	38	360 diamonds
Super Jubilee	6454/8	13mm	18Y	Ladies		89 diamonds
Super Jubilee	6454/9	13mm	18W	Ladies		89 diamonds
Super Jubilee	6451/9 Bic	13mm	Tridor	Ladies		
Super Jubilee	6411/8	17mm	18Y	Mid Size	28	263 diamonds in center links
Super Jubilee	6411/9	17mm	18W	Mid Size	28	263 diamonds in center links
Super Jubilee	6411/9 Bic	17mm	Tridor	Mid Size	28	263 diamonds in center links
Super Jubilee	8486/8	20mm	18Y	Full Size	23	218 diamonds in center links
Super Jubilee	8486/9	20mm	18W	Full Size	23	218 diamonds in center links
Super Jubilee	8486/9 Bic	20mm	Tridor	Full Size	23	218 diamonds in center links
President Karat	8472/8	13mm	18Y	Ladies		Diamond stripes
President	8153/8	13mm	18Y	Ladies	32	
President	8153/9	13mm	18W	Ladies		
President	8211/8	13mm	18Y	Ladies		Bark finish
President	8211/9	13mm	18W	Ladies		Bark finish
President	8228/8	13mm	18Y	Ladies	31	Bark finish
President	8228/9	13mm	18W	Ladies	31	Bark finish
President	8270/9	13mm	Tridor	Ladies	36	
President	8553/8	13mm	18Y	Ladies	31	Engraved
President	8570/6	13mm	Platinum	Ladies	36	Concealed clasp
President	8570/8	13mm	18Y	Ladies	36	Concealed clasp

Style	Ref.	Size	Metal	Gender	Links	Description
President	8570/8	13mm	18Y	Ladies		Concealed clasp. Baguette diamonds
President	8570/9	13mm	18W	Ladies	36	Concealed clasp
President	9235/8	13mm	18Y	Ladies	36	Concealed clasp. Bark finish
President	9235/9	13mm	18W	Ladies	36	Concealed clasp. Bark finish
President	8289/9	17mm	Tridor	Mid Size	28	Concealed clasp
President	8389/6	17mm	Platinum	Mid Size	28	Concealed clasp
President	8389/8	17mm	18Y	Mid Size	28	Concealed clasp
President	8389/9	17mm	18W	Mid Size	28	Concealed clasp
President	8390/6	17mm	Platinum	Mid Size	24	Concealed clasp
President	8390/8	17mm	18Y	Mid Size		Concealed clasp
President	8390/9	17mm	18W	Mid Size		Concealed clasp
President	7274/6	20mm	Platinum	Full Size		Concealed clasp
President	7274/8	20mm	18Y	Full Size		Concealed clasp
President	7286/8	20mm	18Y	Full Size	21	Regular clasp
President	7286/9	20mm	18W	Full Size	21	Regular clasp
President	8209/8	20mm	18Y	Full Size	21	Bark finish. Regular clasp
President	8209/9	20mm	18W	Full Size	21	Bark finish. Regular clasp
President	8285/9	20mm	Tridor	Full Size	24	Concealed clasp
President	8289/8	20mm	18Y	Full Size		Concealed clasp
President	8385/6	20mm	Platinum	Full Size	24	Concealed clasp
President	8385/8	20mm	18Y	Full Size	24	Concealed clasp
President	8385/8	20mm	18Y	Full Size	24	Concealed clasp. Baguette diamonds
President	8385/9	20mm	18W	Full Size	24	Concealed clasp
President	8385/9	20mm	18W	Full Size	24	Concealed clasp. Baguette diamonds
President	8723/8	20mm	18Y	Full Size	24	Concealed clasp. Bark finish
President	8723/9	20mm	18W	Full Size	24	Concealed clasp. Bark finish
President	1901/8		18Y	Full Size	25	Oysterquartz Day-Date Only

Style	Ref.	Size	Metal	Gender	Links	Description
President	1901/9		18W	Full Size	25	Oysterquartz Day-Date Only
President	1902/8		18Y	Full Size	25	Oysterquartz Day-Date Only
President	1914/8		18Y	Full Size	25	Oysterquartz Day-Date Only
Oysterlock	7873/3	14mm	SS/18Y	Ladies		Yacht-Master Only
Oysterlock	7873/8	14mm	18Y	Ladies		Yacht-Master Only
Oysterlock	7873/0	14mm	SS	Ladies		Yacht-Master Only
Oysterlock	7874/3	17mm	SS/18Y	Mid Size		Yacht-Master
Oysterlock	7874/8	17mm	18Y	Mid Size		Yacht-Master
Oysterlock	7875/3	17mm	SS/18Y	Mid Size		Yacht-Master
Oysterlock	7875/8	17mm	18Y	Mid Size		Yacht-Master
Oysterlock	7874/0	17mm	SS	Mid Size		Yacht-Master
Oysterlock	7875/0	17mm	SS	Mid Size		Yacht-Master
Oysterlock	7839/3	20mm	SS/18Y	Full Size		Daytona. Fliplock
Oysterlock	7839/8	20mm	18Y	Full Size		Daytona. Fliplock
Oysterlock	7879/3	20mm	SS/18Y	Full Size		Explorer
Oysterlock	7879/8	20mm	18Y	Full Size		
Oysterlock	7839/0	20mm	SS	Full Size		Daytona. Fliplock
Oysterlock	7839/3A	20mm	SS/18Y	Full Size		Daytona. Solid end links (SEL)
Oysterlock	7849/0	20mm	SS	Full Size		Daytona. Solid end links (SEL)
Oysterlock	7876/0	20mm	SS	Full Size		Yacht-Master. Fliplock
Oysterlock	7879/0	20mm	SS	Full Size		Explorer
Oysterlock	7879/OA	20mm	SS	Full Size		Daytona. Solid end links (SEL)
Oysterlock	7876/8	20mm	18Y	Full Size		Yacht-Master. Fliplock
Oyster	7204/8	11 mm		Ladies	13	Some riveted
Oyster	7834/1	11mm	YGF	Ladies	13	
Oyster	7834/3	11mm	SS/14Y	Ladies	13	
Oyster	6634/0	11mm	SS	Ladies		Riveted. Expanding
Oyster	7834/0	11mm	SS	Ladies	13	
Oyster	114	13mm	SS	Ladies		Some riveted

Style	Ref.	Size	Metal	Gender	Links	Description
Oyster	115	13mm	SS	Ladies		Expansion. Some riveted
Oyster	320	13mm	SS114Y	Ladies		
Oyster	420	13mm	14Y	Ladies		Riveted
Oyster	420	13mm	18Y	Ladies		
Oyster	515	13mm	YGF	Ladies		Tudors
Oyster	516	13mm	YGF	Ladies		Tudors
Oyster	6634	13mm	RG	Ladies		Riveted. Expanding
Oyster	6634/7	13mm	9Y	Ladies		Riveted. Expanding
Oyster	6634/8	13mm	18Y	Ladies		Riveted. Expanding
Oyster	7204/7	13mm	14Y	Ladies	13	
Oyster	7204/8	13mm	18Y	Ladies	13	Some riveted
Oyster	7204/9	13mm	18W	Ladies	13	
Oyster	7805/3	13mm	SS/18Y	Ladies		
Oyster	7824/3	13mm	SS/18Y	Ladies		
Oyster	7834/1	13mm	YGF	Ladies	13	
Oyster	7834/3	13mm	SS/14Pink	Ladies	13	
Oyster	7834/3	13mm	SS/14Y	Ladies	13	
Oyster	7834/3	13mm	SS/18Y	Ladies	13	
Oyster	8363/8	13mm	18Y	Ladies		Moire finish
Oyster	8606/8	13mm	18Y	Ladies		
Oyster	6634/0	13mm	SS	Ladies		Riveted. Expanding
Oyster	7805/0	13mm	SS	Ladies		
Oyster	7824/0	13mm	SS	Ladies		
Oyster	7834/0	13mm	SS	Ladies	13	
Oyster	6490/8	14mm	18Y	Ladies		100 pink sapphires
Oyster	6490/8	14mm	18Y	Ladies		
Oyster	6490/9	14mm	18W	Ladies		Riveted. Expanding
Oyster	6490/9	14mm	18W	Ladies		100 pink sapphires
Oyster	7295/9	14mm	18W	Ladies		
Oyster	7497/8	14mm	18Y	Ladies		270 diamonds
Oyster	7497/9	14mm	18W	Ladies		270 diamonds
Oyster	7498/8	14mm	18Y	Ladies		286 diamonds
Oyster	7498/9	14mm	18W	Ladies		286 diamonds

Style	Ref.	Size	Metal	Gender	Links	Description
Oyster	7295/8 Bic	14mm	Tridor	Ladies		
Oyster	7205/7	15mm		Ladies	13	Some riveted
Oyster	6635/0	15mm	SS	Ladies		Riveted. Expanding
Oyster	202	17mm	SS	Mid Size		Expansion
Oyster	204	17mm	SS	Mid Size		Straight ends. Expansion
Oyster	206	17mm	SS	Mid Size		Same as 202, but not expansion
Oyster	211	17mm	SS	Mid Size		Expansion
Oyster	216	17mm	SS	Mid Size		Same as 211, but non-expansion
Oyster	302	17mm	SS/14Y	Mid Size		Some riveted. Some expansion
Oyster	306	17mm	SS/14Y	Mid Size		
Oyster	311	17mm	SS/14Y	Mid Size		
Oyster	402	17mm	14Y	Mid Size		Some expansion
Oyster	406	17mm	14Y	Mid Size		Same as 402, but non-expansion
Oyster	411	17mm	14Y	Mid Size		Polished center links
Oyster	7205/7	17mm	14Y	Mid Size	13	Cosmograph & Oyster Perpetual Date
Oyster	7205/8	17mm	18Y	Mid Size	13	Cosmograph & Oyster Perpetual Date
Oyster	7205/9	17mm	18W	Mid Size	13	Some riveted
Oyster	7805/3	17mm	SS/18Y	Mid Size		
Oyster	7835/3	17mm	SS/14Y	Mid Size	13	
Oyster	7835/3	17mm	SS/18Y	Mid Size	13	
Oyster	6635/0	17mm	SS	Mid Size		Riveted. Expanding
Oyster	7805/0	17mm	SS	Mid Size		
Oyster	7835/0	17mm	SS	Mid Size	13	
Oyster	201	19mm	SS	Full Size		Straight ends. Expansion
Oyster	202	19mm	SS			Some riveted. Some expansion
Oyster	206	19mm	SS			Same as 202, but not expansion

Style	Ref.	Size	Metal	Gender	Links	Description
Oyster	219	19mm	SS			
Oyster	301	19mm	SS/14Y			Straight ends: Expansion
Oyster	302	19mm	SS/14Y			Some riveted. Some expansion
Oyster	306	19mm	SS/14Y			Oyster Perpetual Date
Oyster	314	19mm	SS/14Y			Oyster Perpetual Date
Oyster	401	19mm	14Pink			
Oyster	401	19mm	14Y			Some expansion
Oyster	402	19mm	14Y			Some riveted. Some expansion
Oyster	405	19mm	14Y			
Oyster	406	19mm	14Y			
Oyster	411	19mm	14Y			
Oyster	501	19mm	10YGF			Straight ends. Expansion
Oyster	502	19mm	10YGF			Some riveted. Some expansion
Oyster	506	19mm	10YGF			
Oyster	514	19mm	10YGF			Some riveted
Oyster	7205/7	19mm	14Y		13	Some riveted
Oyster	7205/8	19mm	18Y		13	Cosmograph
Oyster	7205/9	19mm	18W		13	Some riveted
Oyster	7215/5	19mm	YGF			
Oyster	7835/1	19mm	YGF		13	
Oyster	7835/3	19mm	SS/14Pink		13	
Oyster	7835/3	19mm	SS/14Y		13	
Oyster	7835/3	19mm	SS/18Y		13	Oyster Perpetual
Oyster	6635/0	19mm	SS			Riveted. Expanding
Oyster	7835/0	19mm	SS		13	Cosmograph, Air King & Oyster Perpetual
Oyster	203	20mm	SS	Full Size		Explorer. Expansion. Some riveted
Oyster	207	20mm	SS	Full Size		Explorer, Milgauss, GMT
Oyster	308	20mm	SS/14Y	Full Size		
Oyster	6635	20mm	RG	Full Size		Riveted. Expanding

Style	Ref.	Size	Metal	Gender	Links	Description
Oyster	6635/7	20mm	9Y	Full Size		Riveted. Expanding
Oyster	7205/8	20mm	18Y	Full Size	13	Some riveted
Oyster	7205/9	20mm	18W	Full Size	13	Some riveted
Oyster	7206/7	20mm	14 Y	Full Size	13	Datejust & GMT II
Oyster	7206/8	20mm	18Y	Full Size		
Oyster	7385/5	20mm	18R	Full Size		President concealed clasp
Oyster	7385/8	20mm	18Y	Full Size		President concealed clasp
Oyster	7836/1	20mm	YGF	Full Size	13	Datejust
Oyster	7836/3	20mm	SS/14Y	Full Size	13	GMT & Datejust
Oyster	7836/3	20mm	SS/18Y	Full Size	13	GMT & Datejust
Oyster	7866/8	20mm	18Y	Full Size	13	Daytona
Oyster	7879/3	20mm	SS/18Y	Full Size		GMT II
Oyster	7879/8	20mm	18Y	Full Size		GMT II
Oyster	9290/8	20mm	18Y	Full Size	12	GMT & Submariner. Fliplock
Oyster	9315/3	20mm	SS/18Y	Full Size	12	Submariner. Fliplock
Oyster	9325/3	20mm	SS/18Y	Full Size		Submariner. Fliplock
Oyster	6635/0	20mm	SS	Full Size		Riveted. Expanding
Oyster	6636/0	20mm	SS	Full Size		Riveted. Expanding
Oyster	7836/0	20mm	SS	Full Size	13	Milgauss, Datejust GMT, Explorer
Oyster	7879/0	20mm	SS	Full Size		Explorer II, GMT & GMT II
Oyster	9315/0	20mm	SS	Full Size	12	GMT & Submariner. Fliplock
Oyster	9316/0	20mm	SS	Full Size	14	Sea-Dweller. Fliplock
Oyster	9316A/0	20mm	SS	Full Size	14	Sea-Dweller. Fliplock
Oyster	9325/0	20mm	SS	Full Size		Explorer & Submariner. Fliplock
Oyster	9351/0	20mm	SS	Full Size		Submariner. Fliplock
Oyster	1700/0		SS	Full Size		Oysterquartz Only
Mesh	8606/8	13m	18Y	Ladies		Loose mesh
Mesh	71770	13mm	14Y	Ladies		Chameleon
Mesh	71779	13mm	14W	Ladies		Chameleon

Style	Ref.	Size	Metal	Gender	Links	Description
Mesh	8363/7	13mm	14Y	Ladies		Brushed mesh for Datejust
Mesh	8363/8	13mm	18Y	Ladies		
Mesh	8363/8	13mm	18Y	Ladies		
Mesh	8363/7	17mm	14Y	Mid Size		
Mesh	8363/7	17mm	18Y	Mid Size		
Mesh	R24	17mm	14Y	Mid Size		
Mesh	716	19mm	18Y			
Mesh	725	19mm	14Y			
Mesh	8363/7	19mm	14 Y			
Mesh	102/8	19mm	18Y			Moire finish
Mesh	8607/8	20mm	18Y	Full Size		Loose mesh
Mesh	715	20mm	18Y	Full Size		
Mesh	704		14Y	Ladies		
Mesh	732		14Y	Ladies		
Mesh	7491		18W	Mens		
Mesh	7491		18Y	Mens		
Mesh	7435/8		18Y			Flush-fit for Non-oyster models
Mesh	7435/9		1W			Flush-fit for Non-oyster models
Mesh	7491/8		18W			Fits only case ref# 9578 dress watch
Mesh	7491/9		18W			Fits only case ref# 9578 dress watch
Matte weave	2558/7	20mm	9Y	Full Size		Capture clasp
Ladies	114	13mm	SS	Ladies		
Ladies	101/8	13mm	18Y	Ladies		
Ladies	102/8	13mm	18W	Ladies		
Ladies	102/9	13mm	18W	Ladies		
Jubilee	6251/3	13mm	SS/14K	Ladies		
Jubilee	6251/3	13mm	SS/14Pink	Ladies		
Jubilee	6251/3	13mm	SS/18K	Ladies		
Jubilee	6252/3	13mm	SS/14Pink	Ladies		
Jubilee	6251/0	13mm	SS	Ladies		

Style	Ref.	Size	Metal	Gender	Links	Description
Jubilee	6251/3	19mm	SS/14K			
Jubilee	6251/3	19mm	SS/18K			
Jubilee	6251/3	20mm	SS/14K	Full Size		
Jubilee	6251/3	20mm	SS/14Pink	Full Size		
Jubilee	6251/3	20mm	SS/18K	Full Size		
Jubilee	201	13mm	SS	Ladies		Folded links
Jubilee	210	13mm	SS	Ladies		
Jubilee	310	13mm	14Y	Ladies		
Jubilee	310	13mm	SS/14Y	Ladies		
Jubilee	410	13mm	14 Y	Ladies		
Jubilee	410	13mm	14W	Ladies		
Jubilee	6251/7	13mm	14Y	Ladies	21	
Jubilee	6251/8	13mm	18Y	Ladies	21	
Jubilee	6251/9	13mm	18W	Ladies	21	
Jubilee	6252/3	13mm	SS/14K	Ladies		
Jubilee	6252/3	13mm	SS/18K	Ladies		
Jubilee	8211/7	13mm	14Y	Ladies	21	Bark finish
Jubilee	8211/8	13mm	18Y	Ladies		Bark finish
Jubilee	8211/9	13mm	18W	Ladies		Bark finish
Jubilee	8554/8	13mm	18Y	Ladies	21	Moire finish
Jubilee	8554/9	13mm	18W	Ladies		Engraved
Jubilee	8571/8	13mm	18Y	Ladies	36	Concealed clasp
Jubilee	219	17mm	SS	Mid Size		
Jubilee	314	17mm	SS/14Y	Mid Size		
Jubilee	405	17mm	14Y	Mid Size		Oyster Perpetual Date
Jubilee	6252/3	17mm	SS/18K	Mid Size		
Jubilee	6311/3	17mm	SS/18Y	Mid Size		
Jubilee	6311/8	17mm	18Y	Mid Size	26	
Jubilee	6311/9	17mm	18W	Mid Size		
Jubilee	8391/8	17mm	18Y	Mid Size	28	Concealed clasp
Jubilee	6251/0	17mm	SS	Mid Size	20	
Jubilee	6311/0	17mm	SS	Mid Size		
Jubilee	209	19mm	SS			
Jubilee	304	19mm	SS/14Y			

Style	Ref.	Size	Metal	Gender	Links	Description
Jubilee	314	19mm	SS/14Y	Ladies		
Jubilee	403	19mm	14Y	Ladies		
Jubilee	405	19mm	14Y	Ladies		
Jubilee	6252/3	19mm	SS/14K	Ladies		
Jubilee	6252/3	19mm	SS/18K	Ladies		
Jubilee	6311/8	19mm	18Y	Mid Size		
Jubilee	6251/0	19mm	SS	Mid Size		
Jubilee	109	20mm	18YGF	Full Size		
Jubilee	200	20mm	SS	Full Size		Folded links
Jubilee	200	20mm	SS/YG	Full Size		Folded links
Jubilee	208	20mm	SS	Full Size		Datejust
Jubilee	218	20mm	SS	Full Size		Datejust
Jubilee	303	20mm	SS/14Y	Full Size		Datejust & Thunderbird
Jubilee	308	20mm	SS/14Y	Full Size		Datejust & GMT
Jubilee	313	20mm	SS/14Y	Full Size		Datejust & GMT
Jubilee	6252/3	20mm	SS/14Pink	Full Size		
Jubilee	6252/3	20mm	SS/14Y	Full Size		GMT
Jubilee	6252/3	20mm	SS/18Y	Full Size		GMT & Datejust
Jubilee	6311/3	20mm	SS/18Y	Full Size		
Jubilee	6311/7	20mm	14Y	Full Size		
Jubilee	6311/8	20mm	18Y	Full Size	21	GMT, Oyster Perpetual, Datejust & Submariner
Jubilee	6311/9	20mm	18Y	Full Size		Datejust
Jubilee	8210/7	20mm	14Y	Full Size	21	Engraved
Jubilee	8210/8	20mm	18Y	Full Size	21	Bark finish
Jubilee	8386/7	20mm	14Y	Full Size		Concealed clasp
Jubilee	8386/8	20mm	18Y	Full Size	24	Concealed clasp. Datejust
Jubilee	8387/8	20mm	18Y	Full Size		Concealed clasp. GMT & Submariner
Jubilee	8552/8	20mm	18Y	Full Size		Bark finish
Jubilee	6251/0	20mm	SS	Full Size	22	GMT & Datejust
Jubilee	6311/0	20mm	SS	Full Size	23	
Jubilee	1701/3		SS/18Y	Full Size	13	Oysterquartz Only
Jubilee	9667/3		SS/14Y	Full Size	13	Oysterquartz Only
Jubilee	1701/0		SS	Full Size	13	Oysterquartz Only
Jubilee	6251/3	17mm	SS/14K	Mid Size		
Jubilee	6251/3	19mm	SS/14Pink			
Flat Squares	2557/7	20mm	9Y	Full Size		Capture clasp
Five-link	2563/7	20mm	9Y	Full Size		Capture clasp
Chameleon	705		14W	Ladies		Chameleon

Style	Ref.	Size	Metal	Gender	Links	Description
Chameleon	706		14Y	Ladies		
Brick	705		14Y	Ladies		
Brick	706		14W	Ladies		
Basle Fair	704		14Y	Ladies		
Bark	100/8	13mm	18Y	Ladies		
Bark	100/9	13mm	18W	Ladies		
	101/8	17mm	18Y	Mid Size		
	101/9	17mm	18W	Mid Size	22	Oyster Perpetual Date, Datejust & Thunderbird
	102/8	17mm	18Y	Mid Size		

Bracelet Clasp Codes

From 1976 to 2010, the folding clasp was stamped on the inner blade indicating the year of production.

Not all vintage bracelets were made in Switzerland, and subcontractors produced them for specific regions. This practice was for tax purposes and has resulted in a wide variety of code stamps and hallmarks.

Bracelets were not necessarily made the same year as the case. Inventory is known to have languished at both the factory and the dealer, so it is acceptable for date stamps to mismatch by a year or two. The following codes span four decades, covering late vintage and modern classic watches.

The rules governing which bracelets could be sold with which watches became stricter in the 1970s. Before this, dealers had considerably more discretion and would routinely swap bracelets and even dials to make a sale.

When buying you should check,

- The date code on the clasp is consistent with, and within a year or two of the serial number of the watch

- The bracelet model was originally available for sale with that reference.

While these two factors *might* indicate the bracelet is original to the watch, it is quite acceptable to wear a new bracelet on an older watch.

As long as you know they are mismatched, you can make appropriate price and value adjustments.

Prospective buyers should note that an S was used to denote a service replacement clasp and that a clasp can be replaced independently of the bracelet links.

This is a service replacement clasp denoted by the S. The AB3 code suggests production in the third quarter of year 2000. The 93150 indicates a Oysterlock clasp for a Submariner and should be paired with a matching Oyster bracelet marked 93150.

Not all bracelets and clasps were made in Switzerland.

Year	Code	Year	Code
1976	A or VA	1997	Z or U
1977	B or VB	1998	Z or W
1978	C or VC	1999	X
1979	D or VD	2000	AB
1980	E or VE	2001	DE
1981	F or VF	2002	DT
1982	G	2003	AD
1983	H	2004	CL
1984	I	2005	MA
1985	J	2006	OP
1986	K	2007	EO
1987	L	2008	PJ
1988	M	2009	LT
1989	N	2010	RS
1990	O		
1991	P		
1992	Q		
1993	R		
1994	S		
1995	T or W		
1996	V or U		

11 MOVEMENTS

"A body in motion can maintain this motion only if it remains in contact with a mover".
- Aristotle

Most collectors don't know or care much about the movement in their beautiful vintage heirloom. Provided it keeps good time, there's little need to worry. However, unscrupulous practices can rob an owner or buyer of significant value, and it helps to have some sense of what should be in the watch and how to identify it.

Experienced collectors insist that before buying a vintage watch, it is essential to inspect what lies beneath the caseback visually; or at the very least, to see high-quality photos of the watches inner workings. It is common practice to ask for (and get) high-quality movement photos during purchase negotiations, and even during service. Any refusal should be considered suspicious.

Dealers will often claim that opening the watch will break the integrity of the waterproof seal, or that they don't have the tool to open it. While this may be true, it is also a warning they may be trying to conceal something. In these instances, confirm their return policy in writing, and make it clear you plan to have the piece opened and inspected as soon as you receive it.

There is some risk in allowing an independent watchmaker to work on your vintage watch. It is not difficult or uncommon to substitute generic, after market, or even fake components for rare and valuable vintage parts. Watchmakers who have built a career and reputation for working on vintage Rolex should be sought out by engaging the collector community and asking for recommendations and referrals.

Don't send your precious Rolex heirloom to just any old watchmaker who says they can work on a Rolex. Whether they are just inspecting, or servicing the watch, they will need to be equipped with specialized tools, vintage Rolex service manuals, and have access to tightly restricted parts.

Ideally, your watchmaker should be known to the collector community, professionally certified or accredited, and willing to communicate openly and often throughout the service process. This communication typically includes progress photos of your watch in various states of disassembly

A trusted and recognized vintage Rolex watchmaker nearly always has a backlog of work and impatient clients. The technical work typically takes a few days, and they will have several concurrent projects on their bench in various states of assembly. Progress can halt if they are waiting on parts, and it can take several months to turn your watch around. Some movements are more challenging and can take longer than others. Particularly those with complications, like chronographs.

Each movement is uniquely numbered (like cases), but it is not currently possible to match a movement number with a case serial number. Rolex has never released this data, so it is impossible to say whether a movement left the factory in the watch case it currently inhabits. However, an experienced vintage Rolex watchmaker will be able to determine if the movement number falls within the range expected for the case number.

For antique movements with no movement number, a watchmaker should be able to assess the finish of the movement and say if it's consistent for the manufacturer, the reference and the era. This determination is subjective, technical, and requires a lot of experience. Like any opinion, it is open to controversy and debate.

Availability of antique and vintage movement parts is a growing challenge. Collectors and watchmakers often hoard new genuine (NOS) vintage parts as well as donor movements. Donor movements and parts will occasionally show up on EBay, and this is not an uncommon source of parts for a watchmaker. So, offering to help your watchmaker locate parts can reduce the turnaround time of your watch, allowing them to focus on the work rather than EBay. Sending along a donor watch or parts can help, too.

Contemporary modern classics have better production records, and an RSC can check if a movement number matches the case number. Unless the movement is entirely Franken or fake, they are likely to replace any after market parts and bring it up to their required quality standards.

A watchmaker can order new parts from Rolex if they have access to a coveted Parts Account (or a fellow watchmaker with said access). Rolex have increasingly strict rules governing who can buy parts, and independent watchmakers can struggle to get what your watch needs. Before sending your vintage watch for service, ask the watchmaker how they source their parts.

Rolex relied on parts from numerous subcontractors and suppliers over the years - up to 23 distinct entities at one point. Movements came predominantly from Aegler except for chronograph movements supplied by Valjoux and later Zenith. These are *ebauche*, or generic base movements, intended to be customized and finished by the watchmakers.

Today, Rolex makes everything at only three factories - Bienne for the movements, Plan-Les-Ouates for cases and bracelets, and Les Acacias for final assembly and testing. This fully-integrated supply chain is a modern phenomenon and has only been in existence since 2004.

Rolex has been buying movements from its close partner Aegler since Rolex's inception in 1908. Rolex finally acquired the Aegler company in 2004. It wasn't until this merger with their most influential supply chain partner, that Rolex was able to produce genuinely in-house movements. So for vintage and antique Rolex watches, we're looking at third-party movements (mostly Aegler) with parts branded and finished by, or for, Rolex.

Aegler was not an exclusive supplier to Rolex, and there were periods (pre-1950) in which they could not meet demand. Rolex had to source movements and parts from other manufacturers like Beguelin. Just because an antique Rolex has a non-Aegler movement does not mean it is fake or Franken.

Rolex deployed Aegler movements in a wide variety of references spanning half a century (antique, vintage, and modern classic era). While it makes for a convoluted family tree, it adds interest and variety to a challenging combination of possible configurations.

Lubricants

Movements are powered by the unwinding of a tightly-coiled flat spring that drives a train of gears. Unless they are left to run down, the parts are under constant pressure and in continuous motion. Several types of lubricant are used to reduce wear and maximize the longevity of the movement. The specific type, quantity, and the location of the oils are specified in the watchmaker's lubrication schedule, and these old service manuals are becoming as sought after as the watches themselves.

A movement service of a caliber 3035 and 3135 calls for up to six different lubricants (!), ranging from light oil to grease.

Lubricants will break down over time, irrespective of whether the movement is running. Modern synthetic oils last longer but experience the same gradual degradation. With the passing of time and an inactive movement, lubricants can move and pool (thanks to gravity), so it's considered a good practice to wind a vintage movement every few weeks.

Desiccated lubricants can be difficult to clean from small parts, with remaining traces causing unwanted friction and final calibration problems. Watchmakers go to great lengths with sophisticated cleaning machines and harsh cleaning agents to remove old lubricants. This often tricky task is one of the arguments in favor of regular servicing. Current advice says you should service your watch every 5-10 years, depending on the era of the movement.

Even if correctly oiled and diligently but sparingly wound, parts will eventually wear out. Critical components were designed to be consumable and replaced during service intervals. These include barrel springs and pivot jewels. It is common and accepted by all but the most obsessed collectors, to use after market non-Rolex consumables in antique and vintage movements.

Finishing

Antique and vintage Rolex are not generally known for refined movement finishing. The practice is usually associated with Haute Horlogerie, which embodies the ideal pursuit of design excellence and watchmaking as high art.

Rolex have always finished their movements, but to a lesser degree than other Swiss watchmakers. Their aim seemed to be to stamp their visual identity on ebauche and visually distinguish their pieces from those made by other watch companies, rather than show off their finishing prowess. Except for Cellini, Rolex has never used see-through casebacks to display their movement finishing.

Movement finishing includes a variety of techniques applied to individual components once they've been stamped or milled out of base metal. All signs of machining or tool marks, such as burred edges, are removed by polishing. Components are then painstakingly decorated by hand.

Some types of finishing can have a practical application, but it is mostly for aesthetics. For example, electroplating can help prevent corrosion, and Geneva Stripes are sometimes said to trap dust away from moving parts. Heat treating steel screws turns them a deep royal blue color, but will also harden them. While there may be some minor engineering advantages, these techniques are just signs of the incredible care and attention watchmakers have given to the tiniest details.

Geneva Stripe is a traditional type of

decoration consisting of regular parallel wave-like patterns applied to plates, bridges, and rotors. The stripes can be straight or circular but are always aligned perfectly across different parts. These most often appear on Rolex dress watches.

Anglage refers to beveling or chamfering and found on antique and vintage Rolex movements. It involves beveling edges of parts (in general to 45 degrees) like bridges and plates. The beveled edge can be meticulously polished, emphasizing the shape of the component and should be regular and consistent across all parts.

Perlage is a finish seen on antique and vintage Rolex. It is also known as circular-graining or stippling and consists of covering a surface with a pattern of overlapping small circles using a rotating peg. This technique is seen on Rolex casebacks, but also movement base plates.

Sinks are a concave chamfer around screw holes or seats for jewels. These chamfered rims of the drilled holes are often hand-polished.

Not all Rolex movements had the same degree of finish or type of finish, but all had some. It takes considerable experience to recognize Rolex finishing and know what is correct for a specific movement and period.

ANTIQUE MOVEMENTS

In 1905, Hans Wilsdorf placed the largest order for movements that Aegler had ever received. These were for Rebberg movements in two grades - 15 and 7 Jewel, all machine-finished. This order established a business partnership that would last a century and end in a business merger.

The movements Aegler supplied to Rolex in the early days (the antique period) fall into one of two categories - the Rebberg and the Hunter.

The name Rebberg was registered as a trademark in 1902 and was an homage to the Rebberg part of Bienne, home of the Aegler factory. Rebberg-class movements were used first and were available with both lever and cylinder escapements. The lever escapement is considered the more refined and collectible movement.

Later, the Hunter movement replaced the aging Rebberg. Production and use of the Hunter would run almost twice as long as the Rebberg. Introduced in 1923 in 9 1/2 ligne and 10 1/2 ligne sizes, they had a polished rhodium finish.

The first Hunter was a 15-jewel movement made in three grades: Prima, Extra Prima, and Ultra Prima. Later iterations with 16, 17 and 18 jewels were the first capable of achieving chronometer precision, and these watches bore the Chronometer designation on the dials.

Caliber 1035 with butterfly-style winding rotor. The aged appearance of the movement is consistent with the worn and pitted case.

Caliber 1215 manual wind. Note the service parts and a large movement spacer ring to fit a larger 36mm case.

VINTAGE MOVEMENTS

In 1935, Rolex was awarded patent # 188,077 for the Superbalance.

This patent leads to the three Prima grades being retired. Aegler manufactured the Superbalance Hunter movement in partnership with Rolex in 15 and 17 jewel configurations until 1969.

The differences between Superbalance movements were all in the quality of the jewels and pivots. The various movement grades had adjustment points, small screws that can be tightened to alter the performance characteristics of moving parts. These adjustment screws are located on the main plate and can be seen easily if the caseback is removed. The simplest movements had two adjustment screws, while higher grade movements could have up to seven adjustments.

The automatic, self-winding Oyster Perpetual movement first appeared in 1931.

It was created by fitting a semi-circular winding rotor to the Hunter 9 3/4 ligne. In 1944, the Oyster Perpetual mechanism was applied to the 10 1/2 ligne Hunter and renamed the Rolex cal.720 which ran until 1950.

CALIBER 1030 (1950 - 1957)

In 1950, the cal. 720 and Hunter series was retired and replaced by the entirely new base cal. 1030.

There was a base cal. 1000, but few details are available, and it didn't survive long. The cal. 1030 was a 25 jewel affair and represented a significant engineering leap forward.

This movement featured Rolex Perpetual on the bi-directional butterfly-style rotor. This movement was adjustable to 5 positions and was able to reach COSC levels of performance before the existence of the COSC testing authority. A date complication was added around 1952 and became cal. 1035.

The cal 1030 (and 1035) are identifiable by this uniquely styled rotor. It has two angled cuts which end in circles resembling a butterfly.

The two cuts were designed to eliminate rotor shake, which occurred during excessive movement and causing the rotor to twist, stressing the axel and making contact with the case. The cuts allowed the rotor to flex and absorb the motion. The 1030 series was very successful and provided the platform for the 1530 base caliber that replaced it in 1957.

Caliber 1200 (1954 - 1984)

The 1200 series were manual-winding movements based on the Hunter A720. Their reputation for being lesser movements of lower quality than the ref. 1030 is unfounded. They were merely different, less advanced designs. Seasoned watchmakers will attest to the accuracy these robust movements can attain - often within COSC standards (-4 /+6 secs per day) and even achieving Rolex's standards of -1/+5 secs per day.

The 1200 series received the Precision designation similar to the A720 Hunter Prima designations. The top 10% most precise movements received the Super Precision designation. The remaining 90% are Extra Precision and Precision grades.

The 1200 series of movements were mechanically simple and very robust. They eventually received an upgrade in 1967 before being finally withdrawn in 1984.

Rolex continued to sell these manual wound Precision movements alongside their COSC certified automatic, Perpetual chronometers like the ref.1035.

- Cal.1210 18,000bps 1954 - 1964
- Cal.1215 18,000 bps (Date) 1954 - 1964
- Cal.1225 26,600 bps (Date) 1967 - 1984

Aegler made these for Rolex in enormous numbers for use in 32mm and 34mm Oyster Precision and Oysterdate models. These relatively simple watches are inexpensive and very popular among collectors.

Caliber 1530 (1957 - 1963)

The cal.1530 had a higher beat rate and better accuracy and power reserve than the cal.1030 and 1035 that it replaced. It featured numerous incremental technical improvements. The series also received a date complication with the cal.1535. A day of the week complication was later added to become the ref.1555 (1959 to 1967) and used in the Day-Date President models. It later received an upgrade to cal.1556 (1965 to 1978) along with 25 and 26 jewel versions.

The ref. 1530 has a flat semi-circular rotor with ring-shaped cuts and two red click wheels, making it easy to identify. It went through several upgrades before being retired in 1965.

The 1530 series including the 1550 derivative, was hugely successful and ran for 20 years before being phased out across all models by 1977

Caliber 1520 (1963 - 1977)

Curiously, the ref. 1520 came after the ref.1530 in 1963. It appeared to be an attempt to simplify and reduce the production costs of the ref. 1530. Despite being a high performer, it was never submitted for COSC certification but instead used in watches marked Precision.

It later received a date function with the cal. 1525, and the two powered all of the non-chronometer watches until 1980. By then, all but the Air-King had gained COSC certification, and the 3000 series had arrived. The cal. 3000 was to become the standard issue for Rolex for many years.

Caliber 1560 (1959 - 1965)

The ref. 1560 has come to be known as the start of the second generation of the 1500 series (the first generation being cal. 1530, 1520 from 1963 to 1977). Its appearance and use overlapped with its predecessor, the ref. 1520.

It is a 26 jewel self-winding automatic movement with a date function added in the cal. 1565. A 24-hour hand was later added to make it the 1560GMT. Although there was no quick set mechanism, the system was able to create an instantaneous date change at midnight.

The first, no-date cal.1560 movement was used in the Oyster Perpetual series beginning with ref. 1002 in the late 1950s. The movement's modest size (5.75mm height, 28.5mm diameter, 12.5 ligne) allowed it to fit comfortably in the 34mm Mid-Size and 36mm Full-Size cases of the era.

The Explorer ref. 1016 (1963 to 1989) initially launched with the cal. 1530, but was upgraded to the more accurate and chronometer-certified 1560. The Submariner 5512 followed a similar path.

Caliber 1570 (1965 - 1974)

Cal. 1570 marked the third generation of the 1500 series and introduced a hacking feature. It was now possible to stop the sweeping second hand by pulling out the crown and activating a hacking lever that interrupted the balance wheel. This innovation allowed for accurate setting of the time and synchronizing with other timing instruments.

The ref. 1570 has become one of the most highly regarded Rolex movements and is a feature of some of the most desirable vintage references. A date function and GMT-hand was added and deployed in the Explorer II, Sea-Dweller 1665 and GMT-Master.

Modern Classic Movements

Caliber 3000 (1990 - 2001)

Cal. 3000 first appeared around 1977 and began replacing the 1500 series. It was a long-running process with both movements overlapping well into the 1990s. The cal. 3000 features in the Air-King 14000 series, the Submariner 14060, and Explorer no-date models. The COSC version, cal. 3130 became the upgrade path for models like the Submariner 14060M and Explorers 14000, 14010, 14060, 14270.

Caliber 3035 & 3135 (1977 - Present)

The 3035 was the first to be fitted with a quick set date wheel, making its debut in a Datejust.

The cal. 3135 arrived in 1988 as a modest

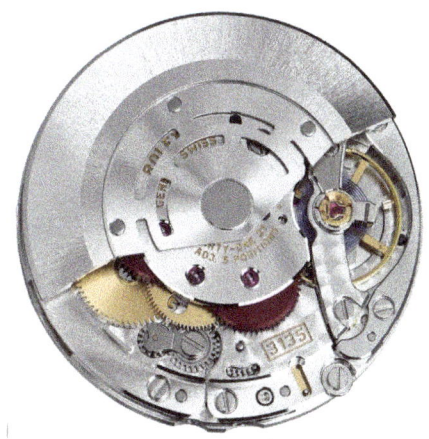

Modern caliber 3135

engineering evolution of the 3035. Modern classic watches with sapphire crystals used the caliber 3035 and 3135 throughout the 1990s.

The cal. 3135 has been used more broadly in more references than any other movement. It is highly finished compared to its predecessors and quite large at 28.5mm diameter and 6mm height. It also has a high beat rate (28.8 Hz) and jewel count (31), making it consistently accurate.

Industry observers and commentators consider cal. 3135 one of the most commercially successful and highest-performing calibers produced by Rolex.

Approximate Movement Timeline

Rolex has never published the production history for their movements. However, collectors, enthusiasts, and watchmakers have been able to compile an approximate timeline using case serial numbers and records from other watch manufacturers that used similar ebauche. These are approximations of the year of introduction and should be used as a rough guide only.

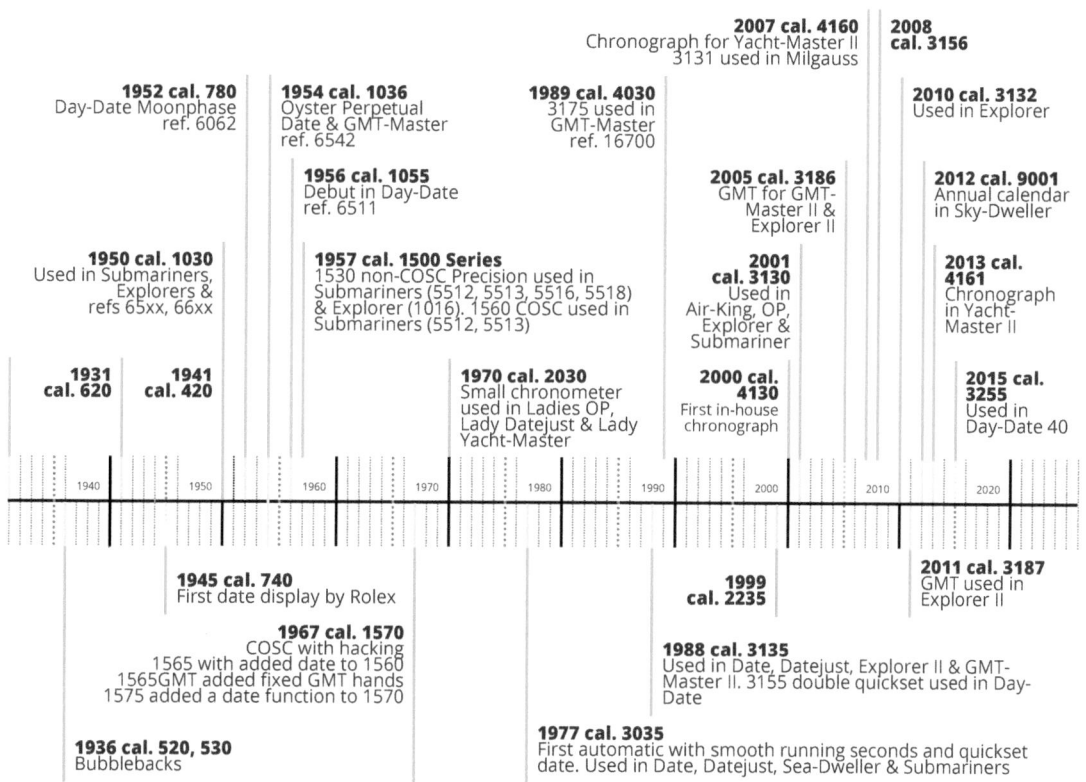

Movement Reference Summary

Cal	Origin	Jwls	Rate (Hz)	Shape	Type	Engraving	Years	Desc.
23	22	17	18	Rnd	Manual Chronograph		1960 - 1960	Valjoux twin register chronograph
59		17	18	Rnd	Manual		-	Fontmelon used in Oyster Watch Co. and Canadian Junior Sport
72	Base Cal.	17	18	Rnd	Manual			
72A	Base Cal.	17	18	Rnd	Manual Chronograph	Balance Wheel	1964 - 1964	Shock Protecting
72B	72A	17	18	Rnd	Manual Chronograph	Balance Wheel	1968 - 1968	Shock Protecting
72C	72A	17	18	Rnd	Manual Chronograph	Balance Wheel	1962 - 1962	Shock Protecting
90	Base Cal.	17	18	Rect	Manual		1961 - 1961	
100	Base Cal.	17	18	Rect	Manual		1945 - 1945	Super Balance
150	100	17	18		Manual		1950 - 1950	
160	100	17	18	Rect	Manual		1947 - 1947	Super Balance
161	100	17	18	Rect	Manual	Plate	1950 - 1950	Super Balance
170	Base Cal.	17	18	Rect	Manual		1952 - 1952	Princess
180	Base Cal.	17	18	Oval	Manual		1950 - 1950	Super Balance
190	160	17	18	Rect	Manual	Balance Wheel	1952 - 1952	
191	160	17	21	Rect	Manual	Balance Wheel	1953 - 1953	
192	160	17	21.6	Rect	Manual	Balance Wheel	1956 - 1956	
193	160	17	21.6	Rect	Manual		1961 - 1961	

Cal	Origin	Jwls	Rate (Hz)	Shape	Type	Engraving	Years	Desc.
200	Base Cal.	17		Oval	Manual		1938 - 1938	Extra Prima
210	210	17		Oval	Manual		1945 - 1945	Prima
250	Base Cal.	15		Oval	Manual		1945 - 1945	Extra Prima
270	Base Cal.	17	18		Manual		1950 - 1950	
280	270	17	21.6		Manual	Balance Wheel	1954 - 1954	
281	270	17	21.6		Manual	Balance Wheel	1958 - 1958	
282	270	17	21.6		Manual	Balance Wheel	1963 - 1963	Shock Protecting
300	Base Cal.	18		Rect	Manual Chronometer		1938 - 1938	
310	300	18		Rect	Manual Chronometer		1938 - 1938	
350	300	18	18	Rect	Manual	Balance Wheel	1938 - 1938	Extra Prima
360	Base Cal.	18	18	Rect	Manual Chronometer	Balance Wheel	1953 - 1953	Super Balance
400	Base Cal.	17			Manual		1953 - 1953	Super Balance
420	400	18			Auto		1952 - 1952	
510	500	17			Manual		1953 - 1953	Super Balance, Precision
520	500	18			Auto		1948 - 1948	
530	500	17			Auto		1948 - 1948	
600	Base Cal.	17			Manual		1951 - 1951	Precision
620	600	18			Auto Chronometer		1951 - 1951	Super Balance
630	600	18			Auto		1951 - 1951	
635	600	18			Auto		1954 - 1954	Shock Protecting
640	635	18			Auto		1954 - 1954	Moonphase

Cal	Origin	Jwls	Rate (Hz)	Shape	Type	Engraving	Years	Desc.
645	635	18			Auto		1954 - 1954	
650	Base Cal.	17	18	Ultra-slim	Manual	Train Wheel Bridge	1977 - 1977	
651	650	18	21.6	Ultra-slim	Manual	Train Wheel Bridge	1992 - 1992	
700	Base Cal.	18			Manual Chronometer		1951 - 1951	Super Balance
710	700	17			Manual		1951 - 1951	Super Balance, Precision
720	Base Cal.	18			Auto Chronometer		1952 - 1952	Super Balance
722	72A		18	Rnd			1968 - 1968	Shock Protecting
727	72A	17	21.6	Rnd	Manual Chronograph		1984 - 1984	Shock Protecting
740	720	18		Rnd	Auto Chronometer		1955 - 1955	Date
730	720	18	21.6	Rnd	Auto Chronometer		1952 - 1952	
745	720			Rnd	Auto		1955 - 1955	Date
750	Base Cal.	20	21	Rnd	Manual	Barrel Bridge	1992 - 1992	Pocket Watch
760	700			Rnd	Manual		1956 - 1956	Date
765	720	18		Rnd	Manual		1955 - 1955	Date
775	720	18		Rnd	Manual		1955 - 1955	
780				Rnd	Manual			Moonphase
722-1	72A	17		Rnd	Manual Chronograph		1969 - 1969	Shock Protecting
800	Base Cal.	17		Rnd	Manual Chronometer		1960 - 1960	Ultra Prima, Pocket Watch, Shock Protecting
850	800	17		Rnd	Manual Chronometer		1960 - 1960	Pocket Watch, Shock Protecting
1000	1030	18	18	Rnd	Manual	Balance Wheel	1955 - 1955	Shock Protecting
1016			18	Rnd	Auto	Self-winding Bridge	1985 - 1985	

Cal	Origin	Jwls	Rate (Hz)	Shape	Type	Engraving	Years	Desc.
1030	Base Cal.	17	18	Rnd	Auto	Self-winding Bridge	1957 - 1957	Shock Protecting
1030	1030	25	18	Rnd	Auto	Self-winding Bridge	1957 - 1957	Shock Protecting
1035	1030	25	18	Rnd	Auto	Self-winding Bridge	1957 - 1957	Date, Shock Protecting
1036	1030	25	18	Rnd	Auto	Self-winding Bridge	1957 - 1957	Date, Shock Protecting
1040	1030	26	18	Rnd	Auto	Self-winding Bridge	1957 - 1957	Shock Protecting
1040	1030	25	18	Rnd	Auto	Self-winding Bridge	1957 - 1957	Shock Protecting
1051	1030	25	18	Rnd	Auto	Self-winding Bridge	1956 - 1956	
1055	1030	25	18	Rnd	Auto	Self-winding Bridge	1956 - 1956	Day-Date, Shock Protecting
1065	1030	25	18	Rnd	Auto	Self-winding Bridge	1959 - 1959	Date, Shock Protecting
1066	1030	25	18	Rnd	Auto	Self-winding Bridge	1957 - 1957	Date, Shock Protecting
1080	1030	25	18	Rnd	Auto	Self-winding Bridge	1956 - 1956	Anti-magnetic, Shock Protecting
1036 GMT	1030	25	18	Rnd	Auto	Self-winding Bridge	1957 - 1957	Date, Shock Protecting
1055B	1030	25	18	Rnd	Auto	Self-winding Bridge	1956 - 1956	Day-Date, Shock Protecting
1065 GMT	1030	25	18	Rnd	Auto	Self-winding Bridge	1957 - 1957	Date, Shock Protecting
1065M	1030	25	18	Rnd	Auto	Self-winding Bridge	1959 - 1959	Shock Protecting
1066 GMT	1030	25	18	Rnd	Auto	Self-winding Bridge	1957 - 1957	Date, Shock Protecting
1066M	1030	25	18	Rnd	Auto	Self-winding Bridge	1957 - 1957	Anti-magnetic, Shock Protecting
1100	1120	17	19.8	Rnd	Manual	Balance Wheel	1957 - 1957	Shock Protecting
1120	Base Cal.	27	19.8	Rnd	Auto	Self-winding Bridge	1956 - 1956	Shock Protecting
1130	1120	26	19.8	Rnd	Auto	Self-winding Bridge	1967 - 1967	Shock Protecting
1135	1120	26	19.8	Rnd	Auto	Self-winding Bridge	1967 - 1967	Date, Shock Protecting

Cal	Origin	Jwls	Rate (Hz)	Shape	Type	Engraving	Years	Desc.
1160	1120	26	19.8	Rnd	Auto	Self-winding Bridge	1968 - 1968	Shock Protecting
1161	1120	26	19.8	Rnd	Auto	Self-winding Bridge	1970 - 1970	Shock Protecting
1165	1120	26	19.8	Rnd	Auto	Self-winding Bridge	1968 - 1968	Shock Protecting
1166	1120	26	19.8	Rnd	Auto	Self-winding Bridge	1970 - 1970	Shock Protecting
1170	Base Cal.	21	18	Rnd	Manual	Balance Wheel		Shock Resisting
1173	1170	17	18	Rnd	Manual	Balance Wheel		Shock Resisting
1200	1210	17	18	Rnd	Manual	Balance Wheel	1964 - 1964	Shock Protecting
1210	Base Cal.	17	18	Rnd	Manual	Balance Wheel	1967 - 1967	Shock Protecting
1215	1210	17	18	Rnd	Manual	Balance Wheel	1967 - 1967	Shock Protecting
1216	1210	17	18	Rnd	Manual	Balance Wheel	1967 - 1967	Oysterdate, Shock Protecting
1220	1210	17	21.6	Rnd	Manual	Balance Wheel	1984 - 1984	Shock Protecting
1225	1210	17	21.6	Rnd	Manual	Balance Wheel	1984 - 1984	Oysterdate, Shock Protecting
1300	Base Cal.	17	18	Rect	Manual	Balance Wheel	1967 - 1967	Shock Protecting
1240	1200				Manual			Shock Protecting
1310	1300	18	18	Rect	Manual	Balance Wheel	1967 - 1967	Shock Protecting
1315	1300	17	18	Rect	Manual	Balance Wheel	1967 - 1967	Date, Shock Protecting
1400	Base Cal.	18	21.6		Manual	Balance Wheel	1984 - 1984	Shock Protecting
1401	1400	18	21.6		Auto	Balance Wheel	1966 - 1966	Shock Protecting
1525	1530	26	19.8		Auto	Self-winding Bridge	1984 - 1984	Date, Shock Protecting
1530	Base Cal.	17	18		Auto	Self-winding Bridge	1964 - 1964	Shock Protecting (US Version)
1530	Base Cal.	25	18		Auto	Self-winding Bridge	1964 - 1964	Shock Protecting (EU Version)

Cal	Origin	Jwls	Rate (Hz)	Shape	Type	Engraving	Years	Desc.
1535	1530	26	18		Auto	Self-winding Bridge	1967 - 1967	Date, Shock Protecting
1536	1530	26			Auto		1977 - 1977	
1555	1530	26	18		Auto	Self-winding Bridge	1967 - 1967	Day-Date, Shock Protecting
1556	1530	26	19.8		Auto	Self-winding Bridge	1978 - 1978	Day-Date, Shock Protecting
1560	1530	26	18		Auto	Self-winding Bridge	1967 - 1967	Shock Protecting
1565	1530	26	18		Auto	Self-winding Bridge	1967 - 1967	Date, Shock Protecting
1566	Base Cal.	17	18		Auto	Plate	1967 - 1967	Shock Resisting
1566	1530	25	18		Auto	Hub sinking	1967 - 1967	Shock Resisting
1570	1530	26	19.8		Auto Chronometer	Self-winding Bridge	1979 - 1979	Shock Protecting
1575	1530	26	19.8		Auto	Self-winding Bridge	1979 - 1979	Date, Shock Protecting
1580	1530	26	19.8		Auto	Self-winding Bridge	1979 - 1979	Shock Protecting
1565 GMT	1530	25	18	Rnd	Auto	Self-winding Bridge	1967 - 1967	Date, Shock Protecting
1575 GMT	1530	26	19.8	Rnd	Auto	Self-winding Bridge	1979 - 1979	Date, Shock Protecting
1600	1600	19	19.8		Manual	Balance Wheel	1984 - 1984	Shock Protecting
1601	1600	20	19.8		Manual	Balance Wheel	1979 - 1979	Shock Protecting
1602	1600	20	21.6		Manual	Train Wheel Bridge	2006 - 2006	Shock Protecting
1800	Base Cal.	17	21.6		Manual	Balance Wheel	1974 - 1974	Shock Protecting
1895	Base Cal.	21	21.6		Auto	Balance Wheel	1977 - 1977	Day-Date, Shock Resisting
2030	Base Cal.	28	28.8		Auto	Self-winding Bridge	1979 - 1979	Shock Protecting
2035	2030	28	28.8		Auto	Self-winding Bridge	1979 - 1979	Shock Protecting
2130	Base Cal.	29	28.8		Auto	Self-winding Bridge	1992 - 1992	Shock Protecting

Cal	Origin	Jwls	Rate (Hz)	Shape	Type	Engraving	Years	Desc.
2135	2130	29	28.8		Auto	Self-winding Bridge	1992 - 1992	Date, Shock Protecting
3000		27		Rnd	Auto		1992 - 1992	OP, Air King, Explorer, Submariner
3035	Base Cal.	27	28.8	Rnd	Auto	Self-winding Bridge	1990 - 1990	Date, Shock Protecting
3055	3035	27	28.8	Rnd	Auto	Self-winding Bridge	1990 - 1990	Day-Date, Shock Protecting
3075	3035	27	28.8	Rnd	Auto	Self-winding Bridge	1992 - 1992	Date, 12/24 Hr hand
3085	3035	27	28.8	Rnd	Auto	Self-winding Bridge	2004 - 2004	Date, 12/24 Hr hand
3130		31	28.8	Rnd	Auto			OP, Air King, Explorer, Submariner
3135	Base Cal.	31	28.8	Rnd	Auto	Self-winding Bridge	2001 - 2001	Quickset Date, Datejust, Submariner Date, Sea Dweller, Yacht Master
3155	3135	31	28.8	Rnd	Auto	Self-winding Bridge	2001 - 2001	Day-Date
3175		31	28.8	Rnd	Auto		1992 - 1992	Quickset Date, GMT
3185	3135	31	28.8	Rnd	Auto	Self-winding Bridge	1992 - 1992	Quickset Date, GMT II
4030	Base Cal.	31	28.8		Auto	Chrono Bridge	1992 - 1992	Daytona, Shock Protecting, Zenith El Primero
4130	4030	44	28.8		Auto			
5035	Base Cal.	11	32.3		Quartz	Bridge	1992 - 1992	Quickset Date, Datejust
5055	5035	11	32.3		Quartz	Bridge	1992 - 1992	Quickset Day-Date
6620	Base Cal.	8			Quartz	Bridge	1992 - 1992	Ultra-slim
2766							1977 - 1977	
2230	Base Cal.	31	28.8		Auto			

12 ACCESSORIES

"Two things are infinite: the universe and human stupidity; and I'm not sure about the universe."
- Albert Einstein

The term *full-set* describes the accessories that accompany a new watch when first sold. These include all the original packaging, booklets, sales receipts, hang tags, and warranty papers. These artifacts add value to the implied provenance and history of the watch, and some collectors will obsess over these items as much as the watches themselves.

Counterfeit accessories are as common as the watches they accompany. A counterfeiter may add genuine accessories to throw a buyer off the scent of a fake watch. Or a seller may cobble together accessories to goose the price of a sub-par, authentic watch.

As a general rule, the older the watch, the less likely it is to have the original accessories. Antique watches are unlikely to have their original boxes and warranty papers at all. These older watches are lucky to have survived a century of wear (and war), and offers of original documents and packaging are improbable at best.

Vintage era watches may have surviving accessories from the 1950s. Collectors prize these for their nostalgia rather than any intrinsic value. Any price premium varies with the popularity of the watch model, and condition of both the watch and accessories. For example, old Submariner boxes and papers are more attractive than Datejust equivalents.

Modern Classics are quite likely to include their accessories. Many loose items are circulating on eBay, which can quickly be cobbled together to make a set. The unwary buyer may miss the cues of an incorrect and hurriedly assembled collection of mismatched accessories.

There is a vibrant market for accessories and collectors enjoy the challenge of assembling them correctly. Verifying a set of accessories are period correct, authentic and original to the watch, can be a challenging and technical task. Some love this challenge. Others choose to ignore accessories all together.

The specific type and combination of accessories vary with the era and model of watch. All had inner and outer boxes, warranty papers and booklets of various sorts. COSC watches had hang-tags, and dive watches had other unusual items like anchors and bracelet tools.

Buyers are discouraged from placing too much emphasis on accessories. After all, they can't be worn and will likely spend their time in the darkness of a drawer or safe. However, they are worth acquiring if you plan to resell the watch. If you plan to own the watch long term, any price premium is entirely personal and subjective.

Boxes

There are a wide variety of boxes used over the years. All were made to look and feel luxurious with velvet and faux leather. Service boxes, pouches, and booklets also exist but are more functional and less luxurious. These too, varied by region and era.

During the vintage era, Boxes were made by subcontractors and paired with the watch at the point of sale by the jeweler or dealer. So it is not unusual to see inconsistencies, particularly between different territories. Generally, men's watches were sold in green boxes and ladies in red. Special boxes were used for the top of the line, jeweled models.

Box packaging should include both a luxurious inner box and an outer cardboard box, printed in various different styles. The style of box is collection specific, and print markings and identification codes changed over the years. All inner boxes feature a product number on their base. To date, there is no consensus amongst collectors on what they indicate.

Distressed or corroded boxes can be restored and refinished. Several craftsmen (and women) offer their services through social media. The quality of their work is high, and they can return a box to almost-new condition. Restoration includes replacing faux leather exterior coverings and reupholstering interior cushions, padding, and linings.

Counterfeit boxes are common and can be easily purchased online. They can be difficult to identify and distinguish from authentic ones unless you have handled lots of genuine examples. The best way to guard against them is to know exactly what style is period correct for the reference you're pursuing.

Booklets

There are generally three booklets included with a watch when sold new - a model specific brochure, an Oyster Bracelet brochure and a generic translation of the guarantee and warranty commitment.

The model brochures have a date of printing on the penultimate page. This should be within one or two years of the production date of the watch to be considered correct. Booklets are easy to counterfeit, so look for appropriate aging and fading and be sure you know exactly what style is period correct for the watch it accompanies.

Anchors

Around 1969, Rolex redesigned their packaging and began including an anchor trinket with their dive watches. This item is a small, keyring-like, miniature anchor bearing the depth rating of the watch with meters on one side and feet on the other. They were included with Submariners and Sea-Dwellers until around F-serials, in 2005.

Although no longer produced, anchors have become coveted despite not having any particular purpose. Anchors typically appear in silver, steel color but a gold color version accompanied the solid gold Submariner.

Fake anchors are known to exist, presumably made to accompany fake Submariners and Sea-Dwellers.

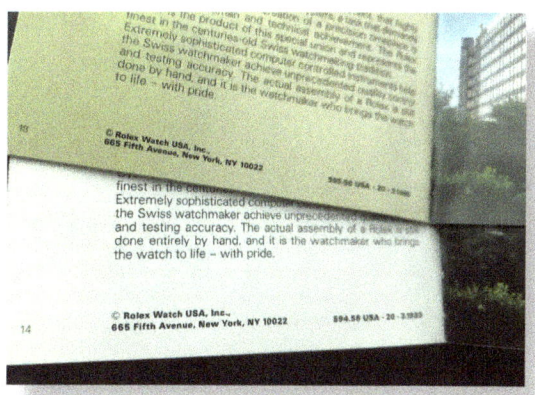

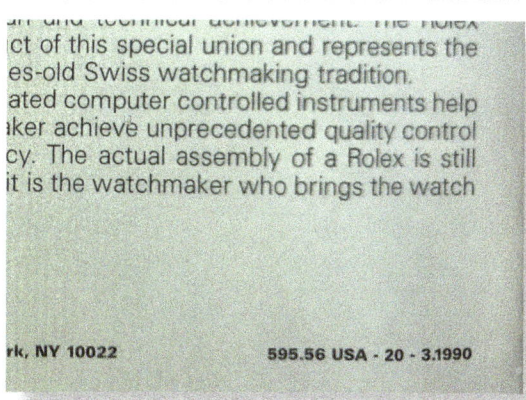

Hang Tags

There are two types of hang tags a buyer can expect to encounter - a chronometer tag and a green Swimproof Oyster tag.

The chronometer tag first appeared in the mid-1940s, as a small, dark, red disk, resembling a wax seal attached to a decorative string.

The tag indicates the watch movement has passed COSC certification and performs to chronometer standards. These tags replaced the paper COSC testing certificates that were phased out.

The red COSC tag went through several iterations. The first version was an all-red disc with a swirling marbled appearance. The text was embossed, and the decorative string (or twine) was burgundy and gold. This style lasted into the early 1960s.

The second version had the same embossed text but over-printed in gold. The dark maroon colored plastic had a less obvious marble-effect, and the string was green and gold. Around 1967, the string color changed again, back to the red and gold of the first version. This second variant lasted until about 1970.

In the 1970s, the coronet changed to the distinctive frog-foot style, and the embossed word Geneve became Geneva-Bienne.

In the 1980s the coronet style changed again to a wide-style. In 1989, around the R-serial range, the red tag acquired a hologram depicting a single coronet. In 2000, this hologram changed to include multiple coronets. This multi-crown hologram persisted through the transition to the green chronometer tag in 2015.

In July 2015 the chronometer tag became green, marking the change of the Rolex warranty from two years to five.

All modern models will have a green chronometer tag and a multi-crown hologram. The green tags can have a hologram with either large or small multi-crowns.

Above: Red COSC hang tags from the 1980s, with multi-crown hologram and a green Swimpruf Oyster tag.

Below: Early COSC tag, pre-1960s.

Warranty Papers

There is a misconception that Rolex warranty or guarantee papers ensure (with absolute certainty) the authenticity of a vintage watch. This assumption is not valid and old warranty papers, sales and service receipts are not guarantees of a watches authenticity. However, they contain useful data that can help validate the watch and reduce the degree of uncertainty.

Warranty and guarantee documents usually bear the details of the jeweler, many of which have long ceased to exist. It would not be unreasonable to try and contact the jeweler to see if they have any record of having sold the watch. The antique period pre-dates the official Rolex dealer network, and this may not be practical. So while the documents are interesting, they're of little value for determining authenticity.

Vintage warranty papers appear in several styles, languages, and sizes. Most have visible watermarks embedded in the document. The watermark should be visible if the certificate is held up to a window or bright light.

It's not uncommon for old papers to have the watch details handwritten with a ballpoint pen. These are easily *washed*.

Soaking the paper in acetone (nail polish remover), will remove the ink and the solvent will dry without warping or marking the paper. Washed documents can be found on eBay and used for all manner of shady purposes. Typewriter ink is much harder but not impossible to remove. As a result, collectors prefer punched-style papers over handwritten.

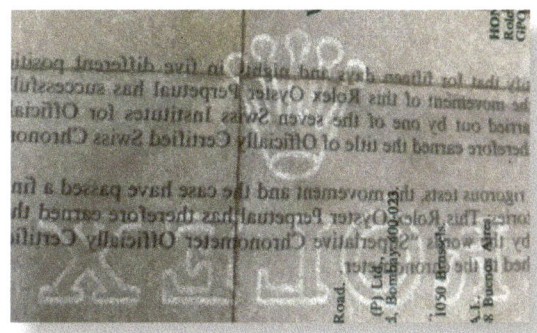

Warranty paper watermark

Warranty paper punched numbers are 4 x 6 holes. Counterfeit papers are sometimes punched with 5 x 7 or 5 x 9 holes.

Vintage Rolex warranty paper punch issued to Authorized Dealers.

However, vintage certificate punching machines are still in circulation from long defunct dealers, and these can be used to punch serial numbers onto washed or forged papers.

Original documents are desirable and helpful, but the absence of any papers is preferable to suspicious, mismatched or fake papers. You should be aware that it is possible to convincingly engrave a counterfeit Oyster case with serial and reference numbers that match a genuine warranty paper. This unsavory practice has been observed at the high end of the vintage market with top-dollar, highly desirable early Daytonas.

Watches sold in the USA had warranty papers featuring some codes that are unique to the US market. Papers printed prior to 2000, had a five digit code on the back printed in red.

These digits indicate the date Rolex USA shipped the watch to the dealer. So a code like "C OWCE" would be "9 2694", which translates to September 26 '94.

Letter	Key
R	1
O	2
L	3
E	4
X	5
W	6
A	7
T	8
C	9
H	0

On the front of the paper is a 14 digit Style No. This is typically printed (or typed) above the Serial No.

e.g. R16520A50B7839

This Style No. can be parsed into six fields

(L) NNNNN(N) X NX (L XXNN)

(L) : BRAND

- R = Rolex
- T = Tudor

NNNNN(N): WATCH REF.

- Five or six digits, e.g. 16528, 116520 etc.

X : CASE MATERIAL

- A = Stainless steel (French, *acier*)
- 3 = Gold and steel
- 4 = Stainless steel and white gold
- 8 = Yellow gold
- 9 = White gold

NX : DIAL STYLE:

- 0U = Black Mother of Pearl with diamonds
- 0W = Black Mother of Pearl Roman
- 10 = Silver
- 18 = Silver Tapestry
- 20 = Champagne
- 28 = Champagne Tapestry

- 30 = Black
- 3H = Onyx Arabic with 2 diamonds
- 50 = White
- 51 = White Roman
- 52 = Ivory Pyramid Roman
- 57 = White Arabic
- 83 = Rose Roman
- 8X = Onyx Serti
- 9K = White Mother Pearl Arabic
- 9R = Mother Pearl Roman

L : BRACELET

- B = Bracelet
- S = Strap

For integrated bracelet (like Oysterquartz) this code is missing.

XXNN : BRACELET TYPE

- Four digits or two characters and two digits. e.g. 7839, 7876, 9315, etc.

In the example this would translate to:

1. (R) Rolex

2. (16520) Ref. for a Zenith Daytona

3. (A) Stainless steel

4. (50) White dial

5. (B) Bracelet

6. (7839) Bracelet ref. 78390

13 EPIGRAPH

"Obsessed is a word the lay use to describe the dedicated"
- Anonymous

And so you have it - As much data as any reasonable Rolex enthusiast can digest in one sitting.

You should now have a sense for the variety of watches circulating in the wild, and the many pitfalls in the path between you and them. Along the way, you will encounter crooks and conmen, spivs and posers, all seeking to take your money and your pride. Fakes, replicas, counterfeits are increasingly common in the antique, vintage pre-owned markets.

- 15-30% of internet searches on watches involve people looking for replicas (Source: Forbes 2013). Increasingly people are seeking the faux vintage aesthetic.

- In 2017 Switzerland exported 25 million watches. China exported 663 million. While there are some well known Chinese brands in this number, none have the demand or cache of Rolex.

- The Swiss Customs Service claims there are some 30 to 40 million counterfeit watches entering circulation each year (2005).

- Swiss Customs estimates that 40% of fake watches come from China (2006). Irrespective of the accuracy of this estimate, large numbers of replica watches are being made or assembled elsewhere, including the US and EU.

- According to a 2012 Federation of Swiss Watches estimate, counterfeit Swiss watch sales generated over a $1 billion in sales per year.

There are a lot of people buying fake watches and no shortage of supply. Counterfeiters are willing to risk jail and financial penalties to profit from this demand. Their replica watches are illegal to buy and sell and typically crap. They can be found in fake districts of every major city around the world and increasingly online.

In the pre-owned market, the phenomena of the Super Fake continues to grow. Fakes are not a harmless imitation or homage but a product of organized crime.

If you are even remotely inclined to buy a fake vintage Rolex, then this book and these watches are not for you. Don't feel bad that you're missing the gene or the disposable income. You're just not ready for vintage Rolex. Instead, spend your money on a genuine, more affordable, vintage Longines, Seiko, Zenith or numerous other increasingly collectible brands. You'll be much happier.

If you wear a fake Rolex, you will eventually be called out. You can either admit you're a jerk and acknowledge it's crap. Or you can prove you're a jerk and insist it's legit. Either way, you'll be outed and shamed as an embarrassed jerk. Don't do it.

Fortune favors the brave, and your life is only getting shorter. So, find a genuine vintage Rolex you like, make sure you can afford it, and then wear the heck out of it. Admire it; show it off; enjoy it; share it. And love it's well worn and unoriginal peculiarities.

If you have got this far through this guide, I'd like to thank you for buying it and taking the time to read it.

I hope it's helpful in your journey. If you use it to buy a watch, I would love to hear from you. If you have feedback, corrections, or even more data, please get in touch. Also be sure to check out the updated and revised Chevalier Edition, now in hard cover with additional and expanded content.

www.vrfm.io

You can find me on Instagram

@morning_tundra

And old fashioned email

morningtundra@gmail.com

Bonne Chance!

www.ingramcontent.com/pod-product-compliance
Lightning Source LLC
Chambersburg PA
CBHW061752290426
44108CB00029B/2975